Just Business

Business Ethics in Action

Second Edition

ELAINE STERNBERG

OXFORD

UNIVERSITY PRESS

OXFORD
UNIVERSITY PRESS

Great Clarendon Street, Oxford OX2 6DP

Oxford University Press is a department of the University of Oxford
It furthers the University's objective of excellence in research, scholarship,
and education by publishing worldwide in

Oxford New York

Athens Auckland Bangkok Bogotá Buenos Aires Calcutta
Cape Town Chennai Dar es Salaam Delhi Florence Hong Kong Istanbul
Karachi Kuala Lumpur Madrid Melbourne Mexico City Mumbai
Nairobi Paris São Paulo Singapore Taipei Tokyo Toronto Warsaw

with associated companies in Berlin Ibadan

Oxford is a registered trade mark of Oxford University Press
in the UK and in certain other countries

Published in the United States
by Oxford University Press Inc., New York

Second edition first published in Great Britain in 2000
by the Oxford University Press

First edition first published in Great Britain in 1994
by Little, Brown and Company

British Library Cataloguing in Publication Data

Data available

Library of Congress Cataloging in Publication Data

Data available

ISBN 0-19-829662-2 (Hbk.)
ISBN 0-19-829663-0 (Pbk.)

3 5 7 9 10 8 6 4 2

Printed in Great Britain
on acid-free paper by
Biddles Ltd.,
Guildford & King's Lynn

Preface to the Second Edition

One of the great advantages of eternal verities, is that they never change. Because the analysis developed in the first edition of *Just Business: Business Ethics in Action* was based on eternal verities, there is little to alter in this second edition. The only amendments have been those that help to make the original argument clearer.

As I argued in the first edition, the fundamental values of business ethics are

> . . . not limited in application to any one legal jurisdiction, geographical region, industrial sector or temporal period. Rather, they hold good across all economic, cultural and religious divides.[1]

The reason that they are so widely applicable, is because they are a function of the equally unchanging nature of business, that which differentiates business from all other human activities.

Unfortunately, there are many reasons why people doubt that business has an unchanging nature. Most commonly, they confuse business itself, which is the activity of maximising long-term owner value by selling goods or services, with other things that indeed do vary. As the first edition of *Just Business* acknowledged, the degree to which the pure activity of business is diluted or disguised in multi-purpose organisations is clearly not the same everywhere. Another variable is the ability of enterprises to pursue the activity of business as such free from religious or regulatory restrictions. But despite such variations in the extent to which business is actually pursued, the essential nature of business itself is always the same. Claiming otherwise, is like claiming that salt does not have a constant or essential nature, because it is used in different amounts with different ingredients to enhance the different flavours of many diverse foods.

Another variable that sometimes prompts people to doubt the unchanging nature of business, is motivation: the variety

Acknowledgements

The ideas expressed in this book were initially developed in 1986–1988, in the course of attempting to work out what was wrong with the way particular financial services businesses were being run. I am grateful to Elizabeth Vallance for prompting me to turn those ideas into a book, and would like to thank Stephen Gale and Daniel Moylan, whose unfailing willingness to argue fundamentals did much to make that book better. I am also indebted to Robert Laird, Daniel Moylan again, David Weisberg and David Weissman, who struggled with awkward printouts to provide constructive criticism of the text.

of motives that prompt people to engage in business, leads some people to doubt that business can be properly characterised as simply 'maximising long-term owner value by selling goods or services'. But again, they are wrong.

A motive is that which induces someone to act. It typically refers to the personal, usually emotional, satisfactions that a person may seek in pursuing the objectives that define activities; a motive can also characterise the way in which the definitive objective is pursued. Though some motives (benevolence) are conventionally associated with particular activities (medicine), motives are independent of the activities they inspire. The same motive (benevolence) can lead to different activities (medicine, making charitable donations, excusing mistakes). Conversely, the same activity (medicine) can be prompted by different motives (benevolence, avarice, ambition). Unlike objectives, motives therefore cannot serve to identify activities. Equally, the undoubted variety of human motivation is no obstacle to activities, including business, having a single, essential purpose. As the first edition of *Just Business* argued, the essential nature of business is independent of the diverse motivations that lead people to engage in business, whether as entrepreneurs, investors or employees.

Because the nature of business is constant, so are the conditions that must be satisfied if conduct in and by business is to be ethical. The first edition of *Just Business: Business Ethics in Action* argued that in order to be ethical, business had to be directed at maximising long-term owner value, subject only to respecting (classical) distributive justice, and what I called 'ordinary decency': honesty, fairness, avoiding physical violence and coercion, and a presumption in favour of legality. Had I realised then how easily the labels 'distributive justice' and 'ordinary decency' would permit confusion with other concepts—despite my careful and frequently repeated definitions—I might have devised more distinctive names. But the names are all I would have changed.

Equally, I might have called the realist model embodying those values something that sounded less generic than the 'Ethical Decision Model': perhaps 'Realist Ethical Decision Model', to reflect its realistic attitude towards business, and

its foundations in realist philosophy. Again, however, all that
would have changed would have been the label. The actual
Model has proved itself sound against the wide variety of
actual business problems brought to me by consultancy
clients, and the hypothetical ones proposed by academic
commentators. The experience of the last few years has thus
provided additional evidence for the claim made in the first
edition, that the Ethical Decision Model can resolve business
ethics problems "in all their current variety, and as they arise
in new and unanticipated forms"[2]. The reason why the Model
works, and that the claim is valid, is because it is based on the
constant nature of business. It is partly to emphasise the
enduring nature of the Model and its foundations that most
of the supporting endnotes have been left unchanged even
when later sources have been available.

One thing that has changed since *Just Business: Business
Ethics in Action* was first published, is the attention paid to
business ethics. Business ethics has become more generally
accepted as an academic subject, and more widely recognised
as one that businesses can ill afford to ignore. Partly as a
result, a great many books have been published about business ethics. Virtue ethics, with its emphasis on the character
traits that are essential for the good life, has become more
important, and has served as a useful reminder that there is
more to ethics than the conventional dichotomy of utilitarianism and deontology. But unfortunately, even the emer-
gence of virtue ethics has done little to increase the realism of
academic approaches to business ethics. Business ethics
books still typically exhibit a remarkable lack of interest in or
understanding of what business is, and thus fail to illuminate
what it takes for business to be ethical.

There is, consequently, still a need to combat what can
most appropriately be called the 'oxymoronic approach' to
business ethics. In the early 1990s, this view was commonly
associated with social responsibility; now it is more often
described in terms of stakeholding. In whatever form it is
expressed, however, the oxymoronic view holds that being
ethical in business means replacing the pursuit of owner
value with the pursuit of some other end—social welfare,

Dedicated to the memory of
Professor Michael J. Oakeshott

"... [one] should ... make a return to those with whom one has studied philosophy; for their worth cannot be measured against money, and they can get no honour which will balance their services...."

Aristotle, Nicomachean Ethics, 1164b3–5.

environmental protection or stakeholder interests, for example. Since, however, the essence of business is maximising owner value by selling goods or services, this view of business ethics is literally absurd: it makes refraining from business the condition of being ethical in business. *Just Business: Business Ethics in Action* discloses this central contradiction, identifies business ethics as what it takes to conduct business ethically, and provides a powerful theoretical Model that can be used to resolve practical business ethics problems as they occur in all their actual novelty, complexity and variety. *Just Business* is therefore as distinctive now as it was when the book was first published.

The shifting focus of public concern has brought about not just a greater interest in business ethics, but also a change in the main issues attracting popular attention. Derivatives are currently considered more troublesome than the junk bonds that were problematic when the first edition was being written; mis-selling, whether of pensions, mortgages or savings products, has become a greater worry than insider trading. Privacy is another issue that has increased in importance. Surveillance by closed-circuit television was not considered much of a business problem in the early 1990s. Similarly, the extent to which employers could monitor their employees' email did not often arise, when few people had even heard of the internet, and fewer still had ever encountered it. Fortunately, even though showing it will have to wait until *Just Business Volume II* is written (if indeed it is), all these issues can be dealt with quite straightforwardly by applying the Ethical Decision Model.

The analytical framework of *Just Business: Business Ethics in Action* can also handle the many issues associated with globalisation that have become more prominent since the early 1990s. The same framework that was used in the first edition to determine the ethical response to bribery, can be used to identify the ethical infrastructure of business, and to help resolve the problems that arise when attempting to do business without it, in disorderly jurisdictions. That framework can also help to clarify the differences between businesses, markets and economic systems, and to explain why economics can no more answer questions of business ethics than physics can. Once again, however, showing how in detail will have to wait for *Just Business Volume II.*

A major change in the world that has required more immediate treatment, is the substantially increased attention paid to corporate governance. Issues of corporate governance were just beginning to attract public notice in the early 1990s. Now, they are of such public concern (and such general confusion), that I have had to devote a whole book *(Corporate Governance: Accountability in the Marketplace,* Institute of Economic Affairs, 1998[3]) to addressing them.

What about criticisms of *Just Business: Business Ethics in Action?* One sort that has recurred, has come from those who mistakenly associate all claims to ethical truth—including truths about business and business ethics—with dangerous forms of absolutism. Because, sadly, some believers in ethical truth have felt justified in forcibly imposing their absolutist beliefs, and particularly their religious beliefs, on others, some prominent advocates of the free society have attacked the notion of absolute truth. But though the objective of opposing authoritarian restrictions of liberty is laudable, that strategy is misguided: protecting liberty requires limiting the use of coercive force, not denying the possibility of truth. That liberty is a value is itself an ethical truth. Moreover, simply denying that a truth is true is not sufficient: arguments must be provided. But no satisfactory ones have been supplied.

There have been very few other criticisms of *Just Business.* Most reviewers seem to have been so surprised or offended by its challenging of received wisdom, that they have not dealt with the text that was published. Even relatively lengthy examinations, by academics and others, have been directed instead at views that their authors have simply attributed to me—independent of, and often contrary to, what was published in the text. Reference to the actual text can answer all their criticisms.

London,
January 2000

Contents

Section II: Resolving Ethical Perplexities

Section III: Ethical Direction

Introduction:
What Makes This Book Distinctive

'True arguments seem, then, most useful, not only with a view to knowledge, but with a view to life also.'

Aristotle[1]

'I have not been disposed to acquiesce in acknowledged evils, either from the mere superstitious reverence for ancient usages, or from the dread of labour or responsibility in the application of a remedy.'

Sir Robert Peel[2]

ITS AIM AND METHOD

The aim of *Just Business: Business Ethics in Action* is to provide substantive solutions to real problems. *Just Business* answers specific questions of business ethics, and provides a powerful explanatory framework—the Ethical Decision Model—that unifies and justifies those answers. It supplies the basis for resolving business ethics questions whenever and wherever they arise, in all their actual variety and complexity and novelty.

By introducing conceptual clarity to business ethics, *Just Business* provides solid arguments for rebutting trendy, but unethical, demands for 'social responsibility' in business. Combining business realism with philosophical rigour, and employing a global perspective, the book demonstrates that business's correct ethical concern is *Just Business*—nothing but business, but business that is just.

Unlike most books on business ethics, this book does not apply incoherent philosophical doctrines to misunderstood business practice. It is neither a potted history of moral philosophy, nor an uncritical compendium of conflicting views. Nor is it a collection of anecdotal examples or a set of *ad hoc* responses to isolated questions. Rather, *Just Business* is a systematic, reasoned argument about what constitutes ethical conduct for business.

Although the book includes incidental observations on psychology and law, the subject of *Just Business* is not what people like or what is likely to change their attitudes: its sole concern is what is ethically correct. Nevertheless, the emphasis of *Just Business* is not moral fervour but clear thinking. As they are commonly posed by the media and vocal pressure groups, many business ethics questions resemble the classic 'When did you stop beating your wife?' This book unpacks the questions and offers substantive answers. Though its argument is rigorous, *Just Business* presupposes no philosophical knowledge on the part of the reader; it is intended for, and should be professionally valuable to, active businessmen as well as academic philosophers. Its arguments should indeed be accessible and useful to all who have dealings with business, whether as employees or customers or lenders, shareholders or formulators of public policy.

ITS APPRECIATION OF BUSINESS

What understanding business ethics requires first, is understanding business. Unlike most books on business ethics, *Just Business: Business Ethics in Action* takes business seriously. It appreciates that business is a distinctive activity, with its own objectives and guiding principles. And it appreciates that it is wrong to judge business conduct by the standards of fields whose objectives are altogether different. Nevertheless, it does not propound a separate 'business ethic': doing so would do violence to ethics without doing justice to business.

The understanding of business expressed in *Just Business* derives from direct, practical experience of doing business in the 'real world'. The arguments of this book are informed by years spent as an investment banker in Britain, the United States and Europe, by the experience of founding and running profitable businesses in the City of London, and by experience as the founder and proprietor of an independent consulting firm. Initially derived in the course of analysing the problems of particular financial services businesses, the Ethical Decision Model presented in this book has been successfully tested on the problems of both large and small businesses, and against the needs of manufacturers, retailers and resource extraction firms as well as providers of professional and other services.

Thanks to its understanding of business, *Just Business* can supply the theoretical underpinning for key management practices, showing how they are correct and why they work. For example, it can illuminate the ethical basis of such strategies as Total Quality Management and business process re-engineering, 'management by objectives' and performance-related pay. Such policies necessarily involve focusing on business's essential purpose. *Just Business* identifies that purpose, and demonstrates its connection to ethical conduct.

ITS REALISTIC PHILOSOPHY

In addition to a direct understanding of business, *Just Business: Business Ethics in Action* benefits from an exceptionally solid philosophical base. Most commentaries on business ethics either have no theoretical foundation, or else rely on inadequate, often incoherent, philosophical doctrines[3]: theories that cannot accommodate human action have little hope of making sense of ethics or of business.[4] In contrast, *Just Business* calls upon a comprehensive, naturalistic, philosophical framework[5] that makes the world of action more, not less, intelligible.

The teleological approach

One of the most distinctive features of this approach is that it identifies and explains human activities by reference to their ends/aims/goals/objectives/purposes. Accordingly, the approach is often characterised as 'teleological', from 'telos', the Greek word for 'end'. It recognises that the same physical acts can be undertaken for very different purposes, and that their proper interpretation requires knowing what the purpose is. When a youth knocks an old man down in the street, it matters to assessing the youth and his action whether his objective is mugging the old man or shielding him from a mugger.

Purposes are essential for evaluating goodness. Because of their very different purposes, the criteria of a good pillow are necessarily different from the criteria of a good knife. And what counts as a good car depends crucially on whether the objective is inexpensive motoring or setting speed records. Just as a good object is identified by reference to the object's purpose, what counts as the proper conduct of an activity depends on the activity's purpose. If the purpose of writing is to inform, then what counts as good writing will be different than if the purpose is to amuse or to confuse. What counts as morally right action also depends on objectives. Cutting someone's throat is normally wrong, but it can be the right thing to do—ethically as well as medically—in the course of a lifesaving tracheotomy. It is a central theme of *Just Business* that what constitutes ethical conduct in business depends critically on business's definitive purpose.

Given the significance of ends in defining and judging, it is important to get the ends right. It is therefore useful to have a label for the serious phenomenon of getting the ends wrong: 'teleopathy'[6], from the Greek 'telos' and the root 'pathy', referring to suffering or disease. Choosing the wrong end, and misunderstanding the end in question, and pursuing the right end in the wrong way are all examples of teleopathy. It is another key theme of this book that many business wrongs are actually examples of teleopathy, of misunderstanding the purpose of business, or of substituting some other end for the proper business aim.

Eternal verities

Because it is based on sound theoretical foundations, the argument of *Just Business* supports strong conclusions. Unlike less well-grounded theories, which are forced to reduce justice to mere utility or procedure, *Just Business*'s concept of justice fully incorporates the notions of merit and desert that are commonly and rightly associated with the term. Equally, *Just Business* can accommodate the fact that context is relevant to moral judgements, without reducing ethics to relativism[7] or consequentialism[8]. Its firm theoretical basis also protects *Just Business* against the false dichotomies that undermine too many discussions of business ethics; this book is not forced to choose between facts and values[9], between virtue[10] and prudence, between ethics and business.

Finally, because it deals with fundamental truths, the book's analyses are not limited in application to any one legal jurisdiction, geographical region, industrial sector or temporal period. Rather, they hold good across all economic, cultural and religious divides. The Ethical Decision Model can resolve business ethics problems in all their current variety, and as they arise in new and unanticipated forms.

In summary, then, *Just Business* provides reasoned answers to key questions of business ethics. Starting with a realistic analysis of business and ethics, it offers a sustained argument to demonstrate that business can be true to its definitive objective of maximising long-term owner value and still be fully ethical. Contrary to popular belief, it is not necessary either to emasculate or to adulterate business for business to be moral.

THE ARGUMENT IN OUTLINE

The argument of *Just Business: Business Ethics in Action* falls into three main sections. The first section, Chapters 1–3, introduces The Conceptual Framework, and analyses the key concepts of business and ethics.

Chapter 1, The Importance of Business Ethics, argues that business ethics is necessary not because it is fashionable, but because ethical concerns unavoidably permeate all business activity. Ethical issues are not just raised by environmental disasters or major frauds, but by the way the business conducts itself in its ordinary, everyday, routine activities: the challenge is to make essential ethical decision making explicit so as to make it better. Confronting the fact that business ethics, like sex education, typically encounters resistance, the chapter identifies the ways in which business ethics is, and is not, the same as common sense. It then reviews the specific benefits of business ethics, and the reasons why it is particularly relevant now.

Chapter 2, The Nature of Business, provides a teleological analysis of business. It argues that business is a very specific, limited activity, whose defining purpose is maximising owner value over the long term by selling goods or services. Accordingly, business is not an association to promote social welfare, spiritual fulfilment or full employment; such organisations are legitimate, but they are not businesses. Equally, a business is not a family, a club or a hobby. Nor is business the same as government, despite the popular stakeholder theory that mistakenly confounds the two. *Contra* Milton Friedman, the chapter argues that business organisations that seek anything but long-term owner value are guilty not of socialism, but of theft.

Chapter 2 then goes on to clarify the components of the business definition. It explains the meaning of 'value', differentiating financial from moral value, and contrasting owner value with profits, 'added value' and share price. It explains why the value sought is that of owners rather than of stakeholders generally or of customers, employees or managers. And it explores the meaning of 'long term' and explains the importance of maximising. It then argues that to maximise long-term owner value, it is necessary to take into account behaviour by, and to, all stakeholders; that which alienates stakeholders or discourages repeat business is unlikely to maximise long-term owner value. The chapter concludes by refuting suggestions that business is intrinsically immoral.

Chapter 3, The Business of Ethics, starts by eliminating a variety of dispensations that are normally claimed to justify unethical conduct in business. Business is not a game or a war or a machine; professional codes of conduct do not constitute a separate 'business ethic'. It then differentiates ethics from compliance with law and contracts, from religion, from suffering, sacrifice and struggle, and from prudence and altruism. Finally, it argues against ethical relativism; the rightness of ethical principles is prior to their business application and their effect on owner value.

The key principles of business ethics are identified as those enjoining the values without which maximising long-term owner value would be impossible: distributive justice and ordinary decency. Distributive justice exists when organisational rewards are distributed on the basis of contributions made to organisational goals. Ordinary decency is not 'niceness', but the conditions of trust necessary both for taking a long-term view and for surviving over the long term; it consists of honesty, fairness, the absence of physical violence and coercion, and the presumption of legality. The chapter explores the meaning of these key concepts, and illustrates them with reference to product safety and advertising. It then goes on to argue that since being ethical in business consists of maximising long-term owner value subject only to distributive justice and ordinary decency, it is entirely plausible that 'good ethics is good business', even internationally.

The second section of *Just Business*, Chapters 4–7, addresses and resolves particular Ethical Perplexities.

Chapter 4, Ethical Implications, applies the analysis to resolving some general problems of business ethics. Considering the fundamental question 'If it's good for the business, can it really be ethical', it answers with a resounding Yes. It then goes on to investigate the ethical implications of fiduciary responsibility, and explains why not all disappointing outcomes constitute violations of it. The chapter argues that conflicts of interest should be managed, not banned; the worst conflicts of interest are those that arise from moral hazards, when the business's own rules create a positive incentive to do the wrong thing. The chapter then argues that bribery is always unethical, that pandering to stakeholder prejudices can be unethical, but that even aggressive competitive techniques normally are not unethical.

Chapter 5, The Ethical Enterprise, provides a general framework for resolving questions of business ethics: the Ethical Decision Model. The Ethical Decision Model has four main steps. Step 1 clarifies the question. Step 2 determines whether and how the question is relevant to a particular *business*. Step 3 identifies the circumstantial constraints on responses. Step 4 assesses possible responses against the business purpose of maximising long-term owner value and the requirements of distributive justice and ordinary decency. The right course of action prescribed by the Model is that which is directed at maximising long-term owner value while satisfying distributive justice and ordinary decency. Using the Model to clarify business's environmental responsibilities, the chapter demonstrates how the Ethical Decision Model enables many supposedly difficult problems of business ethics to be resolved quite straightforwardly.

Chapter 6, Personnel, resolves key ethical questions that arise in connection with the personnel function. It starts by differentiating questions of business ethics from those of law and psychology, and considering the role of motivation. It argues that, as typically conducted, consultation is neither productive nor ethical; what is morally required is not 'employee involvement' but heeding the best information, including information supplied by employees. The chapter then dismisses the notion that employees as employees have any special 'rights' beyond those specifically conferred on them by law or contract.

With respect to recruitment, business's defining purpose makes the correct principle of selection very clear: the business should hire that candidate who will contribute most to maximising long-term owner value. The chapter differentiates valuable discrimination from teleopathic prejudice, identifies the proper and improper uses of 'old boy networks', and highlights the dangers of rejecting candidates because they are overqualified or the wrong age. The chapter also explains the ethical pitfalls of relying on credentials and testing to identify who should be hired. Finally, it explores the conditions of equality of opportunity.

In considering remuneration, the chapter argues against the claims of need, effort and ability, seniority and loyalty, inflation, the 'going rate' and differentials, rejecting them all in favour of performance-related pay. It attributes performance-related pay's frequent failure to improve productivity, to the fact that pay is typically related to the wrong performance. It demonstrates that perks such as 'golden handshakes' and 'golden handcuffs' can be entirely ethical, and shows that the extent to which intrusive perks are appropriate depends crucially on the reactions of the recipients.

Finally, the chapter argues that firing can be perfectly ethical, whether it is 'at will', 'for cause' or in the course of business restructuring. Even mass redundancies are entirely ethical when the right people are fired for the right reasons and in the right way.

Chapter 7, Finance, starts by investigating why finance seems subject to so many ethical problems, and argues that it is largely because finance is so very pervasive. It maintains that the most serious ethical challenge for finance is making sure that internal financial reporting is honest and reliable. It then considers takeovers, and argues that there is nothing intrinsically immoral about them: they need not involve any breach of trust, misallocation of resources or unethical 'short-termism'. Even hostile takeovers and 'shark repellents' can be wholly ethical, if they have shareholder approval. Similarly, though buyouts often involve conflicts of interest, they can be moral if conducted in ways that maximise long-term owner value while respecting distributive justice and ordinary decency.

The chapter then investigates junk bonds, arguing that their ethical status, like that of any instrument, depends on how they are used. The chapter concludes with an analysis of insider trading. Rejecting common criticisms that the practice is a violation of equality of opportunity, it identifies the genuine wrong of insider trading to be teleopathy and misappropriation. Insider trading is emphatically not a victimless crime; it can nonetheless be ethical if it is explicitly approved by shareholders.

The third section of *Just Business: Business Ethics in Action*, Chapters 8–10, deals with Ethical Direction.

Chapter 8, Corporate Governance, identifies the specifically ethical task of corporate governance as being that of holding corporate agents to their proper corporate purposes. It argues that shareholders have no moral duty to be active or long term investors, and no obligation as shareholders to anything but the corporate purpose; it shows that 'short-termism' is a very different problem from that commonly supposed. The chapter then analyses whistle-blowing, and shows it to be a corporate governance tool fully compatible with corporate loyalty. Finally, it considers the problems of executive remuneration and dividend payouts, and resolves them by considering specific corporate circumstances in relation to the purpose of business.

Chapter 9, Ethical Accountability, examines the way in which systems, particularly those dealing with incentives and critical information, can be structured to enhance business accountability. It considers the proper role of directors, and suggests ways of making them more independent of management and more accountable to shareholders. It then considers the role of owners and governance committees, and the ethical implications of corporate wrongdoing. Finally, it explores the contributions that ethical audits, codes of conduct, ethical training and business ethics consultants can make to the indispensable task of keeping business accountable.

Chapter 10, Morals and Markets, considers the limits of business ethics. The chapter argues that the worth of business compared with other human activities, and the extent to which business objectives should be subordinated to non-business goals, are issues that necessarily go beyond business and business ethics; they raise questions about the most fundamental human values. The chapter maintains that the way for individuals to convey their views on such subjects to business, is to act conscientiously in their private capacities in deciding whether and when to engage with business.

When they do so, then their moral values will both influence business's actual activities and determine business's importance relative to other institutions. The chapter recognises such conscientious individual action as the proper meaning of 'social responsibility'.

The chapter then proceeds to consider the value of business, and the extent to which the values and methods of business can be usefully applied elsewhere, particularly in those public institutions that are increasingly being enjoined to be more 'businesslike'. The chapter argues that business methods will only be productive outside of business if the notions of efficiency and accountability, competition and markets are clearly distinguished from the business objective.

I

THE CONCEPTUAL
FRAMEWORK

1

The Importance
of Business Ethics

'Will not knowledge of [the good], then, have a great influence
on life? Shall we not, like archers who have a mark to aim at, be
more likely to hit upon what is right?'

Aristotle[1]

'. . . the glue which holds a company together is its beliefs and values, rather than its structures and systems.'

Sir Adrian Cadbury[2]

'. . . any closely held value, no matter how well concealed (even
from yourself), inevitably prompts action that is consistent with
it, because all your people are boss watchers, boss students, boss
anthropologists of the first order.'

Tom Peters and Nancy Austin[3]

WHY BUSINESS ETHICS IS NECESSARY

Business ethics is essential for business. Business ethics is vital
not because it is fashionable—though business can ill afford
to ignore anything, however silly, that seriously influences
the markets in which it operates. Rather, business ethics is
necessary because ethical choices are unavoidable. The business ethics challenge is to make that inevitable ethical decision-making explicit so as to make it better. Far from being
anti-business, business ethics actually provides essential support for maximising long-term owner value.

The pervasiveness of ethical considerations

Business ethics is commonly associated in the media with environmental disasters and financial scandals, with bribery and sexual harassment and competitive 'dirty tricks'. But though such transgressions demand attention, they nevertheless do not constitute the whole or even the main part of business ethics. Contrary to popular belief, ethical issues can arise in respect of any and all business activities. As a result, the need to consider business ethics is not an optional extra, but a central, inescapable fact of business life.

Ethical concerns permeate every aspect of business activity, because ethical concerns permeate all human activity. Ethical issues obviously arise in connection with core ethical values: when there are questions of, for example, honesty or justice. They are also potentially at issue whenever actions or decisions affect other people, either by helping or by harming them. But ethical issues can even arise when other people's rights and interests are not directly at stake. Whenever there is a choice to be made between values, or a better and a worse way of doing something, or a thing is deemed to be a good one of its kind, an ethical judgement is involved. In this broad sense, most judgements and choices and decisions about goals, standards, quality and priorities are ethical.

Describing something as 'ethical' in this way does not mean that it is ethically correct.[4] Nor does it mean that it is nothing but ethical. Recognising the ethical aspect of a judgement does not rob it of its other characteristics; judgements can be both ethical and factual. All that describing a judgement or a decision as 'ethical' in this way means is that it is 'related to ethics'.

Accordingly, most business actions and choices, decisions and judgements have ethical aspects: they involve specifically ethical values, or help or harm people, or indicate character, or all of the above. Hiring and firing, choosing suppliers, setting prices; establishing objectives, allocating resources, determining dividends; disciplining workers, planning schedules, awarding contracts . . . all involve ethical choices. Even the most trivial decisions, and ones that appear to be made on purely technical or economic grounds, typically have ethical aspects. It is not just in the fringe areas of 'do gooding' that ethical issues occur, but throughout all of business: ethics is inescapable, in business as in life. In order, therefore, to know which ethical issues should concern business as business, and to resolve ethical problems in ways that are appropriate for business, a clear understanding of business ethics is essential.

Everyday ethics

The key business ethics concern is the way that the business conducts itself in its ordinary, everyday, routine activities. The way the firm deals with its staff and its customers, the way it designs and supports its products, the way it awards contracts and apportions blame . . . these are the key determinants of whether a business is ethical, and are as important as the way it deals with crises.

Ironically, the events that attract most attention—major frauds, for example—may not represent ethical dilemmas for business: in such cases business people often agree on what is right. The problems that such events pose are real ones, but often concern practical difficulties: how to implement agreed moral standards, how to deal with the villains who sadly exist in business as elsewhere.

The really thorny business ethics issues, in contrast, are those where there is genuine disagreement about what is right. Views may diverge because of unfamiliarity with the issues, or from lack of analysis: few business people have had occasion to reflect deeply on the meaning of bribery or the implications of whistle-blowing. Even more frequently, however, serious ethical perplexities arise because business people are faced with apparently incompatible objectives. When, for example, employees are exhorted to improve quality, but are rewarded politically and financially for sacrificing quality to cheapness, they can face a genuine moral dilemma. Similarly, they can suffer acute ethical anxiety when they are obliged to defend the indefensible. Such dilemmas are, unfortunately, all too common, and give rise to a variety of traditional business problems; loss of productivity is a regular result. Though seldom recognised as such, both the sources and the solutions of many standard business difficulties are in fact ethical in nature.

Business ethics as a corporate governance tool

Since ethical concerns are both widespread and inescapable, business ethics is not a dispensable option: the choice facing business is not *whether* to confront ethical concerns, but *how*. A business can rely on instinct and inertia and unexamined assumptions. It can let itself be dominated by vocal pressure groups and prevailing prejudices. Or businesses can understand what is genuinely involved in business ethics, and take control.

In helping the business to make informed decisions, business ethics is rather like management accounting. Of course, businesses can and do operate without management accounts. Small businesses often dispense with formal accounting systems altogether, and even large firms can survive in favourable circumstances ignorant of exactly where their costs arise, or which of their activities are profitable. That it is possible to operate blindly, however, does not mean that it is sensible to do so. A business without management accounts suffers from a serious handicap: it lacks a fundamental management tool, as basic to directing business as a map is to navigation. Operating without such aids may be more adventurous, but is unlikely to be as effective: it is easier to hit a target whose location and identity are known.

A proper understanding of business ethics illuminates the business target. Like management accounting, business ethics provides greater awareness of what is important in business activities, and can therefore improve business performance. It can do so, because the principles of business ethics[5] clarify the proper goals of business and the conditions of achieving them. And perhaps as importantly, business ethics helps to identify what the goals of business are not. Business ethics can therefore save the business from wasting its resources on objectives, notably those called 'social responsibilities', that are by their very nature *wrong* for business.[6] Properly understood, business ethics is therefore not an extraneous anti-business option, but a rigorous, analytical business tool. Essential for good governance, business ethics is of value to all businesses everywhere, be they large or small, domestic or international, corporate or not; it is equally necessary for manufacturers and retailers and providers of services.

The costs of being unethical

One measure of the value of business ethics to business is the damage that a lack of it can cause. And the lack of business ethics can cost dear. Failure to recognise and address ethical problems can lead to very substantial charges, both legal and financial; being unethical can cost a business its very life. Many of the most dramatic business failures and the most significant business losses of the last decade have been the result of unethical conduct.[7] In almost all cases, 'bad ethics is bad business': the short-term gains that may be won by unethical conduct seldom pay in the end.

A business that ignores the demands of business ethics, or gets them wrong, is unlikely to maximise long-term owner value. The business that characteristically lies or cheats or steals, or breaks its promises, is difficult and unrewarding to deal with. The business that treats its customers contemptuously, or its staff unjustly, or its suppliers dishonestly, will often find them hard to retain. In a free market, the most productive staff, the finest suppliers and the cheapest and most flexible sources of finance can do better than to stay with a business that cheats or treats them unfairly. And discerning customers are unlikely to be loyal to a business that offers dangerous or unreliable products or grudging, unhelpful service. In the long run, unethical business is less likely to succeed.

Even in the short run, businesses whose conduct is unethical, or who do not understand the requirements of business ethics, can operate at a distinct disadvantage. Many standard business problems have unsuspected ethical elements, that businesses without a proper moral framework typically fail to recognise. High fault levels, high 'shrinkage', high turnover of staff and suppliers, employee illness, anxiety and absenteeism, low productivity and low repeat business are among the many business difficulties that typically result from unethical business conduct; unsatisfactory behaviour by stakeholders often results from unethical treatment of them. When the underlying ethical questions are ignored, it is usually not the problems, but the business that goes away.

And when the principles of business ethics are not properly understood, even attempts to be ethical can be bad for the business. Business is constantly entreated to support all sorts of charitable causes, and to foster social welfare in all its many guises. Business help is sought to save the whale and house the homeless, to fund medical research and promote the arts. But though such demands are frequently made in the name of business ethics, they parade under false pretences. Unless the business is able to distinguish the genuinely ethical from the counterfeit, it is likely to find its ethical impulses perverted, and its resources hijacked to unsuitable ends. If a business's attempts to do good are not to be self-defeating, a proper understanding of business ethics is essential.

RESISTANCE REBUTTED

Despite the fundamental importance of business ethics, and its usefulness for business, the mention of business ethics often evokes resistance from businessmen. Some are defensive about business's supposedly inferior ethical conduct. Others deny that there either can be or should be any such thing as business ethics. A great many businessmen are contemptuous of the subject, rejecting conventional applications of ethical standards to business as irrelevant or anti-business.

And all too often, business's dismissive attitude towards business ethics is wholly justified. If 'business ethics' is taken to denote a separate business ethic, a set of ethical rules that apply exclusively in business and nowhere else, then there is indeed no such thing. And most of the sanctimonious criticisms of business that pass as business ethics deserve to be dismissed.[8] But that is because much of what masquerades as business ethics is nothing of the sort, having little to do with either business or with ethics. Most demands that business promote 'social responsibility' fall squarely into this category. So, too, do applications of confused academic philosophies to misinterpreted business practice. Such travesties are rightly disparaged by both businessmen and philosophers; they undermine the reputation of business ethics and hinder attempts to improve business.

Unfortunately, obeying a variant of Gresham's Law, bad expositions of business ethics tend to drive good ones out of circulation; the resistance that is justified in respect of counterfeits of business ethics often extends inappropriately to the real thing. Some of this resistance comes from the belief, common amongst businessmen, that values are separate from, and less important than, other aspects of business. But ethical considerations are not an optional extra, to be bolted on to business in response to faddish concerns. Genuine ethical issues are intrinsically embedded in all business activity, and must be faced as part of ordinary business life.

Business ethics and sex education

Another kind of unjustified resistance to business ethics resembles that which is associated with sex education. In both subjects, formal instruction is often deemed unnecessary and inappropriate for those who have been properly brought up: people are supposed to do the right things naturally, without any need for outside help. When facing something new, however, even the most carefully reared individual can normally benefit from instruction or moral support. But guidance in business ethics is rarely available informally or vicariously: whereas tales of love and lust are commonplace, ethical issues in business are seldom portrayed in art or the media. Explicit training in business ethics can therefore be of value.

Resistance to business ethics can also stem from the difficulties of recognising, admitting and discussing ethical problems. As in sex, the lack of an acceptable vocabulary is typically a major source of embarrassment and silence; when people don't know what words to use, it is hard for them even to identify, far less to describe or to discuss a problem. The 'moral muteness'[9] of managers is renowned, and explains much of their reluctance to raise ethical concerns.

Fear is also a great inhibitor, in business ethics as in sex. Fears of disturbing an ostensibly harmonious status quo often deter businessmen from airing their ethical concerns. So do fears of disloyalty, fears of being thought insufficiently tough and fears of being unbusinesslike. The forces of conformity within organisations can be extremely powerful, and the wish to avoid ostracism correspondingly strong—especially when businessmen have little confidence in their ethical judgement. The sense that 'it's more than my job's worth', and that good employees 'don't rock the boat', is common, especially when there are few precedents for ethical discussion, and fewer still for their being welcomed. The way to deal with such fears is, however, not to suppress them, but to confront them. The solution is to eliminate such fears by equipping business with a vocabulary and an Ethical Decision Model that enables it to address ethical concerns routinely, explicitly and productively.

Business ethics and common sense

Resistance to business ethics also comes from those who believe that business ethics is nothing but common sense. If what is right or wrong for business is simply common sense, no special effort should be needed to implement or to understand it; claims to business ethics expertise would be unjustifiable.

In some ways, of course, business ethics is very like common sense. The principles of business ethics are certainly sensible: grounded in the nature of business, they make sense of business and for business. And at least potentially, the principles of business ethics are commonplace. Being fundamentally simple, and not tied to any particular cultural or religious heritage, they are capable of being widely understood and generally applied; they are, indeed, likely to strike a familiar chord with anyone who understands business. Like the dictates of common sense, therefore, the principles of business ethics are readily accessible.

Nonetheless, business ethics is not just a matter of common sense.[10] Understanding what constitutes ethical conduct for business, and what makes such conduct ethical, normally requires both time and systematic analysis. The need for careful analysis is particularly strong because, though businesses are made up of people, businesses are not themselves people. They are organisations, not organisms, and have very limited purposes.[11] As a result, what is ethical for an individual can be unethical for a business, and vice versa.[12]

Furthermore, given the complexity and scope of modern business, business decisions often involve issues seldom encountered elsewhere; most private lives provide little experience of assessing insider trading or ordering mass redundancies. Personal ethical habits and unreflective common sense are therefore unreliable as guides to ethical conduct for business. Important though they are, they need to be supplemented with an explicit framework for dealing with business ethics issues.

Fortunately, despite widespread suspicions otherwise, such a framework is perfectly possible: the principles of business ethics are readily susceptible to rational analysis and straightforward application. Business ethics is neither self-defeating nor bad for business nor rendered impossible by relativism. Commercial enterprises cannot, of course, ignore the cultural, geographical and religious differences that affect their markets. But those differences have no bearing on what is morally correct, in business[13] or otherwise.[14]

THE VALUE OF AN ETHICAL DECISION MODEL

So business ethics is possible. But how does it positively help a firm? It is useful here to recognise that 'business ethics' can refer to several different things. Most commonly, it refers to ethical conduct in and by business. In this sense, its benefits to business have already been outlined: doing the right things typically promotes achievement of business purposes, while doing the wrong things hinders the successful pursuit of those goals. To recognise which things are the right things, however, it is helpful to understand the principles that underlie ethical conduct in business. Accordingly, business ethics as the knowledge and study of such principles can also be of value to business. For business purposes, such principles are most usefully presented in the form of an ethical decision model.[15]

An ethical decision model that clearly sets out the principles of business ethics can help business both to identify and actually to resolve business ethics problems. A model is the functional equivalent of a map: it can help guide a business through the ethical issues that it inevitably must handle. A model is not, however, a panacea. Just as a map does not physically smooth out the terrain, or furnish bridges where none exist, a moral model will not eliminate ethical problems or the complexity of real situations[16]. Having a model cannot eliminate the need to make difficult choices or supply backbone or provide a guarantee that all will be well.

What an ethical decision model can do is nevertheless extremely valuable. Most fundamentally, it can help to eliminate conceptual confusions. By providing tools for analysing complicated issues, an ethical decision model can help a business avoid wasting its resources on spurious problems and unwarranted guilt. And by clarifying the meanings of ethical terms and their relevance to business, an ethical decision model can indicate when and how ethical discussion is appropriate in a business context. When all within the business share a common vocabulary for ethical matters, they can articulate moral standards and moral questions more easily. By reducing 'moral muteness', and promoting the early detection and resolution of ethical issues, an ethical decision model therefore enables the business to benefit from the vigilance of its staff.

Accordingly, an ethical decision model can do much to reduce the costs and adverse consequences of ethical problems. By illuminating what is at stake in any situation, and what the alternative courses of action might be, an ethical decision model can indicate what information is relevant, and what can be ignored. By making explicit the principles on which a business's ethical decisions are taken, an ethical decision model can make it more likely that decisions will be consistent over time and place and individual decision maker, and more likely that the business will be able to deal with ethical problems as they arise in new and unfamiliar forms. When ethical issues are not handled in a vacuum, and the wheel need not be re-invented each time, ethical issues are less likely to provoke business crises, and a firm is more likely to learn from its experience.

In addition, employing an ethical decision model reduces the need for staff to second-guess management. When a business lacks an explicit moral framework, employees are often unsure about what is expected of them. Business time and effort are wasted in agonising over what is right, and in scrutinising executive entrails in search of clues. A framework that clearly sets out the principles of business ethics makes such diversions unnecessary. When the grounds for ethical decisions are explicit and consistent rather than mysterious and unpredictable, ethical decisions are easier both to understand and to implement.

WHY BUSINESS ETHICS IS PARTICULARLY RELEVANT NOW

Although business ethics is universal in its scope and application, there are particular political, social and demographic reasons why business needs to pay exceptional heed to business ethics just now. Businesses are affected not just by economic circumstances, but by social, political and technological changes, and the shifting attitudes and outlooks of their stakeholders. Even when the purpose of business is conceived narrowly, as nothing but the maximisation of long-term owner value, business must still take into account everything that affects achievement of that limited goal.

Many of the most prominent trends of the last decades

have focused attention on business ethics, and made it something that businesses ignore at their peril. Consumerism, 'social responsibility', stakeholding, demographic changes, privatisations, investigative journalism, global markets, economic cycles, environmentalism, management theories . . . all have raised public awareness of business conduct and the need for business to respect business ethics.

Whether as a reaction to the 1980s yuppie culture, or a reflection of the 'caring, sharing'[17] 1990s, business ethics has become fashionable. Unlike hoola hoops or Rubik cubes, however, business ethics is not just a passing fad. Business ethics is more like the fashion for keeping fit. It may currently be trendy, and some contemporary methods for achieving it may be peculiar and self-defeating, but the underlying objective is both sound and of ancient lineage.[18] In like fashion, though much of what is recommended in the name of business ethics is absurd and counterproductive, business ethics is and always will be fundamental to business health. Its importance has nonetheless been made even more prominent by changing circumstances.

The actions of governments, for example, have brought business ethics issues into sharp relief. Privatisation programmes have required previously government-owned enterprises to conduct themselves more as businesses. In response, they have undertaken large scale redundancies and awarded their executives sharply increased remuneration. Questions have arisen as to the ethics of such actions, and indeed as to the proper objective of the enterprises themselves: is it to serve the public welfare or the interest of their shareholders?

With governments attempting to withdraw from sectors they have dominated for decades, questions have arisen more generally as to the extent to which business should fill in the gaps. Hopes that business might support the arts or sponsor invention or further education are of course not new. What is relatively new, however, is the transformation of hopes into expectations, and stronger still, into demands: what was once voluntary beneficence is ever more frequently regarded as 'social responsibility'. Also new is the extent to which business is being called upon to cure all the ills of society: not just to make safer products or improve employment conditions, but to save endangered species and alter fundamental social attitudes[19]. The prevalence of such demands makes it essential to investigate their ethical status: the mere fact that demands are widely made does not mean that they are in any way justified.

Questions of business ethics have also been prompted indirectly by the actions of government, through their effect on the economy. Whereas the boom years of the 1980s raised questions about business profligacy, and the role and legitimacy of takeovers, subsequent recessions have forced businesses to make hard choices about cutbacks and layoffs and paying their suppliers. With their very survival at stake in the face of global competition, businesses have had seriously to consider unfamiliar patterns of conduct that have proved notably successful overseas.

Awareness of business ethics questions has also been raised by the growing media attention paid to business. As business has increasingly come to be front page news, so has business misconduct. The efforts of investigative journalists have done much to disclose the deeds and misdeeds of business. So have a variety of semi-official reports and investigations. Concern about business probity has led to, and been heightened by, the creation of the Serious Fraud Office. Though affecting only a tiny percentage of businesses, and sometimes highly technical in nature, the length and prominence of very large criminal trials[20] have brought business ethics into the spotlight. And changes in law have increased the practical value of paying attention to business ethics: firms that can demonstrate possession of an effective ethics programme may reduce the penalties to which they are liable for corporate offences such as bribery and fraud.[21]

The actions of stakeholder groups have also made business ethics more important. Increasingly, the best employees are attracted not just by pay and perks, but by job satisfaction, potential for growth, and the ethical character of their employers.[22] With the number of candidates from the traditionally favoured groups expected to decline, a firm's ethical stance may therefore be a key determinant of its ability to attract and retain preferred staff. And whereas past consumer movements concentrated on the qualities of the product, the new trend is to 'vigilante consumerism', in which consumption choices take into account the character of the producing firm. So the firm that wants to attract increasingly critical customers must have a care for business ethics.

Shareholders are also attending to the ethics of the companies they own. In 'ethical investment'—'social investment' as it is more appropriately known in America—investment decisions are based on companies' attitudes and behaviour, rather than on solely financial criteria. In both the US and the UK, institutional investors have started to rebel against bad business practice. No longer content to express their dissatisfaction by selling their shares, or limited in their ability to do so by the very size of their holdings, shareholders have started to take an active interest in the way their firms are run, vetoing management proposals and voting out managements. Such shareholder activism is spreading world-wide: American investors in overseas companies are exporting their concerns along with their capital. So firms everywhere are increasingly liable to be assessed on the basis of the quality of both their business ethics and their corporate governance.

An increased focus on business ethics has also been provoked by the changing nature of business itself. Business has become more international, complex and fast-moving than once it was. New issues have arisen, and the easy certainties of the local club have been replaced by a multinational, multicultural context in which standards seem constantly in flux. As a result, even old familiar issues are harder to resolve: businesses need to consider explicitly matters that once could have been taken for granted.

Paying heed to business ethics has also been made more essential by changing corporate strategies and structures. Total quality management, organisational process re-engineering and benchmarking have all led to traditional practices being overthrown. Layers of management have been stripped away and hierarchies flattened. As a result, authority has been devolved more widely throughout businesses: key decisions are being made at ever lower levels and by greater numbers of employees. It is therefore essential for everyone in the business, not just the top management, to have a thorough understanding of business ethics; all need to be aware of the organisation's key values and aims, and how they are meant to be reflected in the business's conduct. For business ethics to be disseminated throughout the organisation, however, it must first be understood. Understanding is especially important, because the new structures also lead to new complexities—of information management and team assembly and organisation—for which there may be no traditional precedent. For 'empowerment' to be successful, a proper understanding of business ethics is vital.

So business ethics is necessary for business. It is vital because it is a valuable business tool, essential for identifying and resolving questions of business conduct. And it is topical because recent developments have increased public awareness of business ethics. Trends in government, economics and social attitudes and in business itself have created a climate in which key business stakeholders are increasingly making their business choices on the basis of businesses' ethical characters.

The first step in coming to terms with business ethics is to clarify what business and ethics are. The next two chapters will therefore address those subjects in some detail, examining first the nature of business and then the nature of ethics.

2

The Nature of Business

'. . . every word must be intelligible and indicate something, and
not many things but only one; and if it signifies more than one
thing, it must be made plain to which of these the word is being
applied.'

Aristotle[1]

'In . . . [a free] economy, there is one and only one social responsibility of business—to use its resources and engage in activities
designed to increase its profits so long as it stays within the rules
of the game, which is to say, engages in open and free competition, without deception or fraud.'   Milton Friedman[2]

In order to understand what is ethical for business, it is first
necessary to recognise how business differs from all other
activities and associations. This chapter will clarify both what
business is, and what it is not. Taking business to be the distinctive activity of maximising long-term owner value by selling goods or services, this chapter will explore the
implications of defining business strictly. It will show how
business's objective is related to rational self-interest, and
explain why there is no justification for supposing that business is intrinsically immoral.

THE DEFINITIVE APPROACH

A fundamental prerequisite for understanding business
ethics is understanding exactly what business is. Unless business's distinctive purpose is clearly understood, business is
likely to be confounded with other activities and associations,

and evaluated by inappropriate standards. Defining business precisely is far from an academic trick; precise definition is a technique often required in business. Technical specifications rely on exact definitions and descriptions; so do most kinds of contracts. Financial statements depend on strict definition: to draw them up or to use them, it is necessary to understand what differentiates 'current assets' from 'non-current assets' and 'net operating profit' from 'net profit'. In tackling business ethics, it is business itself that needs to be defined.

Isn't it obvious what business is? Surely businesses are easy to pick out and identify? Some certainly are: it is generally accepted that Marks and Spencer and IBM are businesses, while St. Paul's and Cambridge are not. But is the village fête? What about the German industrial/financial complexes, and the Japanese *keiretsu*? And is the (UK) Post Office a business? Is the National Health Service? Merely dealing with vast sums of money does not automatically make an organisation a business. And at the other end of the scale, a business must be distinguished from a profitable hobby. In order to identify the very subject matter of business ethics, it is necessary to understand precisely what business is. Unless business is clearly differentiated from organisations and activities which it may closely resemble, it will be impossible to determine what is good in or for *business.*

The first step in understanding business, is to recognise that business is something very specific and limited. Despite widespread belief to the contrary, business is not even the whole of economic life, far less the whole of life. Business is neither the same as, nor a substitute for, other associations or activities; it is but one small part of human existence, albeit an extremely important one. In highlighting the fact that business has boundaries, and that it specifies something particular and distinctive, the classic business pronouncement that 'Business is business' expresses a fundamental truth. But though 'Business is business' is both true and significant, and basic to any proper understanding of business and business ethics, it does not specify what makes business different from all other undertakings and organisations. What does that is business's characteristic objective.

THE DEFINITIVE GOAL OF BUSINESS

The defining purpose of business is maximising owner value over the long term by selling[3] *goods or services.*[4] This simple statement is the key to understanding business, and consequently one of the foundations of understanding business ethics. Elucidating its meaning, and setting out its implications, will take up the rest of this chapter and, *inter alia*, much of the book.

To some, defining business in this way may seem obvious, even trivial. Until quite recently, after all, an even narrower definition of business—in terms of owner profits—was taken for granted by most business people and commentators. Even now such key business studies as corporate finance still take financial gains for owners to be the evident and undisputed end of business.

Increasingly, however, such a narrow definition of business has come to seem controversial. The trend has been to see business not as something that exists solely for the financial benefit of its owners, but as something with a myriad of other objectives, social and psychological, political and economic. As the objectives have multiplied, so have the groups to which business is assumed to be accountable. It has become almost commonplace for owners to be reduced to just one of the many 'stakeholders' whose interests must be served. Since these proliferating objectives and interested parties are of growing importance, they cannot be ignored. But nor can they serve to define business.

It is important to explain just why and in what ways they cannot. One of the key reasons can be illustrated by an ancient comedy routine. In it, the head of a household confides that he is responsible for dealing with the family's 'big issues': he decides on how to bring about world peace, he determines how to eliminate inflation, he chooses the next prime minister. His wife, meanwhile (this is a very old joke), handles the less significant matters: all that she decides is how they budget their income, where the children go to school, whether they move house. The irony is obvious. His 'big issues' are so big that he cannot affect them; the issues that really matter to the family are the ones that he disparagingly relegates to his wife. Those who treat business as more inclusive than it is make the husband's mistake. By substituting a comprehensive, pretentious notion of business for the narrow, prosaic one, they sharply reduce their chances of achieving either objective. The broad objectives they are seeking are beyond the range of business, while the goal that should be their focus is ignored.

Maximising long-term owner value[5] may well be a less noble objective than curing the ills of the world[6]—but if it is, then so is business. To reject maximising long-term owner value as the defining purpose of business because it is too paltry and too insignificant, or because business is too important to be restricted to a narrow commercial end, is to mistake the function of definition: the purpose of defining a term is not glorification, but clarification. Accepting a definition is not the same as approving of what is defined; precise definition is equally a precondition for criticising and rejecting a subject. To incorporate extraneous elements into the definition of business simply because they are perceived to be good, or important, is to distort the truth. It is to confuse the desirable with the essential, rather as one might do by including electric windows and a sunroof in defining 'motorcar': a car without those accessories might possibly not be worth having, but it is nonetheless a car.

The need to define business narrowly is not an ideological requirement, but a logical one: business that is everything to everyone is not anything at all in itself. A concept that excludes nothing is useless; since it refers equally to everything it cannot distinguish one thing from another.[7] A category that is too broad is correspondingly uninformative. To investigate business ethics, it is therefore not enough to focus on 'human activity' or even 'socially beneficial commercial activity'; a concept of business that cannot distinguish it from a charity or a hobby will not do. A definition that incorporates all social goals into the purpose of business, risks making business meaningless.

It may be protested that defining business narrowly is unrealistic. Actual business organisations pursue all sorts of objectives, and do so as a matter of course. Actual businesses sponsor the arts and give to charity and constitute social communities. Indeed, businesses are obliged by law to do things other than maximise long-term owner value: in many jurisdictions they are required to act as tax collectors in respect of VAT and income taxes. That actual organisations undeniably do pursue such varied ends, however, does not count against the strict definition of business: it simply means that such organisations are not exclusively businesses.[8]

It is precisely because most large commercial organisations pursue a variety of objectives that defining business strictly is so important. For unless the specifically *business* activity can be clearly identified, and distinguished from all the other things that such organisations do, the role that business should play within the multi-purpose organisation cannot even be discussed. In order to rank or reconcile or evaluate an organisation's possibly incompatible aims, one must first know what they are, and how they differ.

Although business is inseparably intertwined with other activities and objectives in practice, it can nevertheless be distinguished from them conceptually. Differentiating for analytical purposes that which is inseparable in fact is a technique often used in business. 'Lines of business' and geographical contributions are routinely separated out to give a better understanding of what is going on, even when they are not actually free-standing. And financial modelling depends heavily on the technique: in estimating business's future performance, variables are often isolated in order to sensitise projections. Strict definition of business is an attempt to isolate business itself.

In effect, strict definition is an attempt to provide a 'pure play' on business. Businesses sometimes restructure or create separate classes of equity to allow investors a purer play on some sub-set of their complex activities.[9] In like fashion, a clear definition of business permits examination of business itself, free of extraneous considerations. When the specifically business aspects of a multi-purpose organisation are clearly identified, their ethical status can more realistically be assessed. And when business is not just one obscure end hidden amongst the many—often unconsidered and ill-assorted—objectives that characterise most actual firms, the core business goal is more likely to be achieved.

Focus on the business purpose is, in fact, what underlies the effectiveness of business process re-engineering and its variants. Such strategies recognise that within actual firms, different groups have often, for bureaucratic, social and functional reasons, acquired their own discrete and fixed objectives. Although understandable historically, those objectives—be they filling out particular forms, or performing particular manufacturing tasks—may well be incompatible both with each other and with achieving the business's central aim. Business process re-engineering eliminates artificial and unnecessary divisions in the activity flow, and replaces them with purpose-built, unfragmented processes. Its success comes from identifying the business aim clearly, and radically redesigning the activities and structures of the firm specifically to achieve it. Equally, the effectiveness of total quality management comes from recognising that quality consists of excellence in achieving the business goal, and from insisting on its attainment.

WHAT BUSINESS IS NOT

In order to be useful for specifying or evaluating business, the definition of business must identify that which characterises business alone. What differentiates business from everything else is its purpose: maximising long-term owner value by selling goods or services. Only this definitive goal is essential to business. All other goals are at best incidental to business, and are justified for business only insofar as they contribute to achievement of the definitive goal. Many of the commonest characterisations of business are therefore radically incorrect.

The purpose of business is not to promote the public good.[10] Business is a prime contributor to the public good, but that role does not distinguish it from the other activities—medicine and education, for example—that also are; promoting the public good therefore cannot be the definitive purpose of business. Similarly, business does not exist to foster employees' physical or psychological well being; still less is its goal their ultimate fulfilment. Nor is it the aim of business to provide full employment for the nation's labour force or even jobs for local workers. Business's purpose is not to serve the interests of customers or of managers or of the community. Such positive benefits routinely result from business, but they do not constitute its defining aim.

Equally, business's definitive purpose is not to produce goods or services, or to add value. Producing goods or supplying services and adding value are, of course, indispensable elements of doing business: unless it produces goods or supplies services, business will have nothing to sell, and no way of maximising long-term owner value. But producing goods and services and adding value are not exclusive to business, and therefore cannot serve as business's defining goal. The army, the courts and housewives supply services, and children's carpentry classes produce goods, but they are not businesses. Similarly, though cooking a meal, tidying a garden and telling a joke all add value, they do not normally constitute businesses.

To focus on business's function as a producer, supplier or adder of value is to misconstrue business's purpose. If the nature of the goods or services, or the way they are produced, takes priority over maximising long-term owner value, then the activity involved is not business. An organisation whose guiding principle is producing the absolutely best widgets (e.g., engines, books, healthcare) or the very cheapest ones— *independent of the consequences for long-term owner value*—is not operating as a business . . . even if, incidentally, it sells the widgets profitably.

Business is also not a charity or a church, a school or a club; it is not, except incidentally, an agency of government or of social policy. Since, however, business is so often confused with such organisations and activities, it is worth examining in some detail how they differ from business. Failure to differentiate them clearly is responsible for some of the seemingly most fundamental and intractable problems of business ethics.

Family

All too frequently, managers boast that they treat their employees like 'one big happy family'. The ethical difficulty is not (just) that they may be hypocritical in making that claim, but even worse, that they might not be. The more literally managers consider their staff to be an extended family, the more likely it is that basic moral issues will be confused, and that the ends of both business and of family will be subverted.

Different things count as correct conduct for families and businesses, because families and businesses have different functions. Families exist for the mutual care and support of family members, particularly those, like children and the very old, who are less capable of looking after themselves. A family takes care of its members simply because they are family, without any particular regard for reciprocity or merit; family members are kept and cared for, come what may. Business, in contrast, only exists to maximise long-term owner value. As a result, those who undermine achievement of that end are rightly penalised or dismissed. It is as 'dysfunctional' for a business always to excuse errant action as it is for a family never to.

What is appropriate conduct also differs with respect to financial support. Given the family's caring function, family resources are typically allocated on the basis of current need: those who cannot contribute are supported by those who can. Within a business, in contrast, all must contribute, and resources are allocated in proportion to contributions made to the business goal. A firm that stresses its 'family' character, and tolerates or indulges non-performance, is unlikely to achieve its business ends. But in going out of business, it does not thereby become a family. Far from it, it makes achievement of real family goals—the goals of actual families—less rather than more feasible.

Club

Just as a business is not a family, nor is it a club. A club is typically defined by its members' shared interests, amusements or values. The defining objective need be nothing more than the members' wish to associate with people who are in some way like themselves, and to exclude all others: consider small boys who club together precisely to exclude even smaller boys. What differentiates a club from other associations is that, subject only to the law and its articles (if any), the criteria determining a club's membership and activities are simply whatever the club's members please.

As a result, clubs and businesses have very different approaches to recruitment. For a club, the sole criterion of a suitable new member is acceptability to the existing members. Business, in contrast, has a definitive purpose to accomplish, and selects candidates for their ability to contribute to it: recruits qualify because of their ability to maximise long-term owner value, not their congeniality.

Hobby, game

Just as business as an association differs from a social club, business as an activity differs from a hobby. A hobby is something done in one's spare time to pass the time agreeably. As pleasurable pastimes, hobbies by their nature are subordinate to most other activities: when duties or even other pastimes call, hobbies are typically forsaken. Business, in contrast, has a serious purpose; its commitment to maximising long-term owner value means it cannot be abandoned just because it ceases to be fun or convenient. Business commitments affect people's lives and livelihoods, and should not be undertaken lightly; when business creates expectations, it has a responsibility to correct or to fulfil them.

Like hobbies, games are conducted primarily for amusement, and even more than clubs, games are defined by their rules. The notion that business might be a game is therefore implausible. It has, however, arisen frequently in connection with the (mistaken) view that separate and less stringent moral standards apply to business. It will therefore be considered and refuted below, in the Chapter 3 discussion of the principles of ethical business.

Government

Businesses are also definitively different from governments. Actual institutions, of course, are often complex mixtures. Governments are deeply involved in business, in regulating and in owning vast commercial organisations; conversely, businesses are often required by law to act as agents of the state. Businesses also require effective corporate governance.[11] Nevertheless the definitive functions of business and government are radically different, and can and must be distinguished if they are properly to be understood. When they are, it will be seen that businesses are not unethical for lacking stakeholder representation and employee 'rights'.

The purpose of business is to maximise long-term owner value by selling goods or services. The essential function of government, in contrast, is to provide the framework within which business and all other purposes can peaceably be pursued.[12] To achieve this equally limited but fundamental end, government and its officially designated agents—mainly the armed services and the police—normally have a monopoly on the legitimate use of physical violence[13].

This definitive power of government has several important consequences. Crucially, it makes consent an essential condition of legitimate government. Since government has the power forcibly to deprive the governed of their lives[14], liberty and property, it is vital that those subject to its power have a say in how that power is used. Because those from whom consent is required, and to whom the government is legitimately accountable, are too numerous to do the job in person, representatives are frequently employed.

Comparable representation is inappropriate in business

for anyone except shareholders. First, it is not justified. Unlike government, business cannot legally use force to compel anyone to do anything; it cannot even enforce its own contracts without recourse to the courts. Since business has no coercive power, participants in a business have no need for a vote in the business in order to ensure their freedom from that power. Those who do not wish to comply with a decision or a policy can simply leave[15]; in business, unlike in government[16], participants can vote with their feet. The choice to become, or to stay, a participant in a particular business is a matter of voluntary contractual agreement.

Moreover, unlike citizens who are all[17] equal under the law, participants in a business are not all equal, or equally entitled to a vote. Within the business, the owners and their interests are paramount, and are so by the very nature of business. This does not mean that employees and other stakeholders do not count, or that they cannot influence the outcomes of businesses. But their concerns are important to the business only insofar as they influence the maximising of long-term owner value. Far from business's being accountable to its employees, it is the employees who are properly accountable to the business: employees and managers are agents of the business, not vice versa. Those who seek 'industrial democracy' are as much mistaken as those who endorse 'corporate government'[18].

The notions of freedom of speech and other political rights also do not apply within business. Such rights exist[19] as a means of limiting coercive powers. Since business has no coercive power, specific rights to protect against abuse of it do not make sense. Business must, of course, respect the civil and natural rights of all members of society; business should never be above the law. But in their capacity as participants in a business, stakeholders have no rights other than those explicitly conferred on them by law and contract.

FRIEDMAN DEFENDED AND EXTENDED

In reviewing the differences between business and government, it is instructive to re-examine the quotation from Milton Friedman that heads this chapter. In opposition to stakeholder theorists and others who advocate a more 'socially responsible' role for business, Professor Friedman has steadfastly maintained that "The Social Responsibility of Business is to Increase its Profits"[20]. For business to pursue any goals other than maximising profits, he maintains, is to pursue ends different from, and contrary to, the ones approved by the business's owners. Most of the 'social responsibilities' that commentators would have business take on are just such extraneous goals.

As a political economist, Professor Friedman naturally castigates use of the firm's resources for nonprofitable moral purposes as 'socialism' and unauthorised 'taxation'. Far from being too harsh, that characterisation is in fact too polite. Using business resources for non-business purposes is tantamount to *theft*: an unjustified appropriation of the owners' property. Managers who employ business funds for anything other than the legitimate business objective are simply embezzling: in using other people's money for their own purposes, they are depriving owners of their property as surely as if they had dipped their hands into the till.

That the diverted resources are applied to ends that are commonly regarded as laudable, or as 'social responsibilities', does not make the act of diverting them any less larcenous. However worthy the charity being helped, if the employee uses company time and telephones to solicit contributions rather than business, he is cheating the business's owners. Despite what might be called the 'Robin Hood Syndrome', stealing from the rich to give to the poor is still stealing; so is all embezzling from business owners to give to others. Wrongdoing is not annulled by worthy motives[21] or by applying the ill-gotten gains to popular ends. Had the proceeds of the Great Train Robbery been donated to charity, the monies used would still have been stolen, and the robbers would still have been thieves.

Business managers who use business funds for non-business purposes are guilty not just of the legal crime of theft, but of the logical offence of teleopathy: in diverting funds from strictly business objectives to other purposes, they are pursuing the wrong ends.[22] And teleopathy is a serious offence, the generic form of prostitution. Just as prostitution occurs when sex is proffered for money rather than love, so it exists when business pursues love—or 'social responsibility'—rather than money. Business managers who eschew maximising long-term owner value, and direct their firms to any other goal, are as much prostitutes as artists or sportsmen who sell out for financial gain. In each case, the activity is perverted, and the 'right, true end' is neglected in favour of some other, extraneous objective.

'MAXIMISING LONG-TERM OWNER VALUE' EXPLAINED

It should now be clear that much depends on properly identifying the purpose of business. It is therefore important to dispel any misunderstandings that might arise concerning the business definition and its components.

The first point that needs clarification is the relationship that the elements of the business definition bear to one other. 'By selling goods or services' indicates how long-term owner value is to be maximised. Business is not about maximising long-term owner value through theft, or alchemy, or increasing or preserving personal assets. Adding a loft extension to one's house, polishing the family silver, and getting interest on one's savings can all enhance the value of what one owns, but they are not the same as doing business. Business is only conducted when long-term owner value is maximised by selling goods or services.

Conversely, 'selling goods or services' only constitutes business when it is conducted so as to 'maximise long-term owner value'. Business activities and decisions—about what sort of widgets to sell, and how to price them, and whether widget components should be produced or bought in—are characterised by their reference to expected effects on maximising long-term owner value. If selling striped widgets contributes more to long-term owner value than selling spotted ones, then a business will concentrate on stripes.

'Maximising long-term owner value' qualifies not only 'selling goods or services', but everything that the business does. To maximise long-term owner value by selling goods or services a business has to perform ancillary activities: it must produce or acquire those goods or services; it must also distribute them. Consequently, a business normally must, among other things, own assets and arrange finance and employ staff; simply by existing, it automatically plays a part in a community, and may even constitute a community of its own. The extent to which ancillary purposes and incidental activities should be pursued by business, and the way in which they should be pursued, are governed by the definitive need to maximise long-term owner value.

'Maximising long-term owner value' normally operates as a criterion within a business, rather than in the choice of which business to pursue initially. When starting a business, the choice of what goods or services to sell will reflect the founders' interests, opportunities and available capital as well as the comparative gains to be made from different lines of activity. If maximisation were necessary for choosing which business to start, most coeval businesses would pursue the same market niche. Once a business is underway, however, and capital has been committed on the understanding that a particular line of business is being pursued, all deviations from that line must be justified on the grounds of maximising long-term owner value.

What exactly does 'maximising long-term owner value' mean?

The meaning of 'owner value'

Financial vs. Moral Value
'Value' is what philosophers call 'systematically ambiguous': it can mean different things in different contexts. In its economic usages, as in 'owner value', 'value' is a monetary

measure, free of all ethical connotation. In its ethical occur-
rences, in contrast, 'value' is explicitly a measure of moral
worth. Which usage is intended should normally be clear
from the context.

In the definition of business, 'value' is simply financial
value. Contributions to financial value may not always be
immediately obvious: they may well be indirect, qualitative
and only evident over the long term. But in the end, activities
must contribute to financial value to be appropriate for business.

That business is devoted exclusively to financial value does
not, of course, deny the validity or importance of other values, be they ethical or spiritual or artistic. Indeed, financial
value, though an end in itself for business, is both a product
of, and a precondition for, the myriad other values held by
individuals. In stressing the primacy of financial value within
business, nothing is being asserted about the relative rank-
ings of values; the definition does not imply that financial
value is more important than other values, for owners or anyone.

It is also important to recognise that in defining business
by reference to maximising financial value, nothing at all is
being suggested about motivation.[23] No view is being taken
about the reasons why people either do go or should go into
business, or about the value of financial versus other incentives for affecting their performance within business. People
are in fact motivated by all sorts of different things. That they
are, however, is not an argument against business's essence
being maximising long-term owner value; business's connection to financial value is logical, not psychological.

What if owners want something other than maximum
financial value from their enterprises? Examples are not
hard to find. 'Ethical investment' is becoming more prominent, and firms have increasingly been stressing their
explicitly non-financial aims. Moreover, the Anglo-Saxon
emphasis on owner value is not equalled in other major commercial centres. Japanese *keiretsu* have traditionally been
more concerned with achieving market share to save jobs,
while the German industrial complexes have focused on con-

solidating power. Owners are perfectly entitled to devote their organisations to all sorts of ends. To the extent that they pursue something other than maximum long-term owner value, however, they are simply not engaging in business.

Owner Value vs. Wealth, Assets, Revenues
But why specify the defining purpose of business in terms of maximising owner *value*? Why not wealth, or assets or revenues? The defining purpose of business could well be specified in terms of maximising wealth. The main reason for preferring the term 'value', is that it carries no suggestion of opulence. A very small business, which generates only meagre sums for its owners, can nevertheless be as much of a business as one that produces great riches: in this, as in so much else, size is not important.

'Value' is preferable to 'assets' and 'revenues' for a more significant reason: not all assets are worth having. An unused building may incur property taxes while generating no income, and constitute a financial liability. The purpose of business is not simply to amass things, but to maximise the financial worth of the owners over the long-term. For the same reason, it is not the purpose of business to maximise revenues or turnover or unit sales, all of which may generate losses. What is important about business activity is not its level, but its outcome: volume without value is seldom worth pursuing.

Owner Value vs. Profits
Should business therefore be identified with maximising profits, as it so very often is? There are two important reasons why not. The first is that profits, like earnings per share, return on investment and all other accounting measures, are notoriously slippery. By determining the timing of a firm's actions, management can shape the reality that financial statements report. And given the opportunities for (completely legal) creative accounting and 'window dressing', those reports can also be 'massaged' to suit management purposes.[24] Even when managers are scrupulously pursuing

the owners' objectives, the ambiguity and flexibility of accounting standards allow external analysts to disagree significantly about what actual profit levels are.

The second reason why profits are an inadequate measure of owner value, is that they import an intrinsically but inappropriately short-term bias: 'profits' usually means 'current period accounting profits'. By referring only to a single, short, historical span, current period profits do not make allowance for the investments—in research and development, in capital equipment, in training, in restructuring— that may be necessary to improve the business over the long term. Current period profits are not designed to take into account the future consequences of present action.

A thing's value, in contrast, is normally influenced by its future potential as well as by its past and by its present. The value of a piece of land is typically determined not just by its historical cost and its location, but by the likely availability of planning permission. As a result, calculations of value automatically recognise the importance of investment now for generating improved results later. Equally, calculations of value require paying heed to the consequences of business actions. Improper action that yields immediate profits may lead to actual and opportunity costs in future, and produce a net reduction of financial value. Value is therefore more satisfactory than profit for specifying the definitive end of business.

Owner Value vs. 'Added Value'
Another possibility is a formula for 'added value' such as that advocated by the London Business School and *The Economist*[25]. Specifically designed to gauge the value added for shareholders, the 'added value' figure assesses the extent to which a firm's output is worth more than the sum of its inputs of materials, labour and capital. 'Added value' is calculated by adjusting a firm's operating profits for depreciation and the cost of capital, and avoids some of the difficulties posed by different costs of capital and accounting practice. It therefore provides better cross-border comparisons of value added for shareholders than traditional

accounting measures. But the components of the calculation are themselves still accounting measures that are slippery, fundamentally manipulable by management, and reflect only the current period's results.

Owner Value vs. Share Price
A much more plausible candidate for owner value, at least of public quoted companies, is the share price. Notionally, the share price reflects the present value of the future cash flows expected from dividend payments[26] over the indefinite future. And according to efficient market theory, the share price incorporates all the information available at a given time about a corporation's performance and prospects. Market capitalisation should therefore represent what a corporate business is worth to its owners, the shareholders.

Share price has two major advantages as a measure of owner value. Unlike accounting measures, it is not directly manipulable by management. On the contrary, it exhibits the market's assessment of managements, and of managements' likely achievements. In addition, since the share price reflects future cash flows, it automatically takes into account the future effects of current actions, and consequently does not suffer from the short-term bias of historical, single-period measures.

But though the share price may be the best surrogate available at any time, it is nevertheless not a fully adequate measure of owner value. First, the best information available at any given time may still be incomplete, or simply inaccurate. When, for example, the stock market Crash of 1987 expressed a major shift in investor sentiment, whole sectors were marked down indiscriminately; in the crisis atmosphere, the likely effects on particular companies of, for instance, changing exchange rates, were inadequately differentiated. Until corrections were made some time later, the share prices of individual companies did not accurately reflect owner value.

Such errors do not only arise in crises. Some firms coast on their reputations long after they have ceased to deserve them, and thereby command a price that exceeds their real value. Equally, a low share price may reflect an inadequately understood business product, process or policy. While poor communications to shareholders may be paralleled by equally poor sales descriptions to customers, they need not be. There may actually be 'fundamental' value that the market has failed to appreciate. 'Unlocking' such value is often the objective of acquisitions, 'de-mergers' and buyouts.

A second and more basic problem is that share price is only a plausible measure of owner value for quoted companies. Share prices are not readily available for private companies, and may be manipulable when a liquid market does not exist. Even more fundamentally, neither shares nor share prices exist for the very many businesses that are not corporate in form. So although share price may be a good surrogate for owner value in quoted companies, it cannot be the definitive measure of business.

Owner Value Defined

The best way to measure owner value is to use that component of share price that is transferable: discounted future cash flows. Owner value consists of the present value of the future cash flows that the owners will obtain from the business. Those cash flows are normally of two kinds: distributions from the business, in the form of dividends or other payouts, and the capital gains or losses that are realised when (the owner's financial interest in) the business is sold.

Though estimating such future cash flows is one standard way of valuing businesses, most business decisions do not require estimating the value of a business as a whole. All they require is estimating the marginal effects on owner value of alternative courses of action. Even calculating the relative contributions of specific programmes is not easy; such calculations still require reliable information, and careful judgement in the choice of assumptions and discount rates. They are, nevertheless, calculations that businesses are accustomed to making, especially in connection with evaluating major capital projects. They are less familiar in considering personnel or policy proposals largely because explicit calculation is not necessary when the answers are obvious or immaterial. Whether or not evaluating it requires a mathematical computation, however, 'owner value' serves as a valuable criterion: it indicates what considerations are relevant when business decisions have to be made.

Owners vs. Others

Shareholders

Why is the relevant value that of the owners? The purpose of business cannot be maximising shareholder value, because not all businesses are corporations: shareholders are only one kind of business owner. Sole proprietorships and partnerships abound, especially in respect of smaller businesses, and are as legitimate a form of business organisation as the limited liability company and its international equivalents. Maximising shareholder value is the purpose of corporate business, not of business as such.

Stakeholders

An equally popular but more pernicious mischaracterisation of business is that which defines business in terms of 'stakeholders' rather than owners. The term 'stakeholder' was originally used to designate those groups without whose support the business could not survive[27], those in which the business had a stake: not just its owners, who provided the initial capital, but its employees and its customers, its suppliers and its lenders, the community and even the legal system. Increasingly, however, the meaning of 'stakeholder' has been reversed, and the term has been used ever more widely, to include everything and everyone who might have a stake in the business or be affected by it[28]. In this extended sense it has been taken to include the media, competitors and terrorists[29], and even encompasses future generations and nameless sea creatures[30].

The stakeholder theory of business typically holds that business is accountable to all its stakeholders, and that the role of management is to balance their competing interests.[31] Though increasingly popular, and indeed sanctioned by law in some jurisdictions[32], this characterisation of business is nonetheless wrong: stakeholder theory incorporates at least four fundamental errors.

First, in maintaining that all stakeholders are of equal importance to a business, and that the business ought to be answerable equally to them all, stakeholder theory confounds business with government. Because of the nature of government, citizens are equal under the law, and are entitled to representation and a vote in the way things are run. As argued above, however, participants in a business are not. Stakeholder theory asserts that they are, by mistakenly regarding stakeholders in a business as citizens of that business.[33]

Second, and even more fundamentally, stakeholder theory rests on a confusion about the nature of accountability. Starting from the fact that business is affected by and affects certain groups, the theory concludes that the business should be accountable to them. But this is nonsense. Business is affected by all sorts of things—by gravity and the weather and interest rates—and it affects the Gross National Product and traffic conditions, but it is not accountable to them. Equally, the business is not, and could not rationally be, accountable to terrorists or competitors. That the business must take them into account, does not give them any right to hold it to account. Nor does the fact that they are affected by the business, give them any right to control it.

The same is true for suppliers and lenders, employees and customers. To recognise that a business affects them, and must to some degree be functionally responsive to them, is quite different from saying that it is accountable to them. The business must indeed take them into account. But it is answerable to them only insofar as its specific contractual arrangements or laws have made it so.

There are, of course, a variety of ways in which a business might have rendered itself accountable to those counterparties. It might, for example, have entered into written contracts: loan agreements, or contracts of employment, or long-term purchasing arrangements. The business might also have bound itself by creating expectations that it now should honour; some contracts are implicit and unwritten. In all such cases, however, the accountability stems from the nature of the specific contracts entered into, not from the stakeholder relationship as such. The only stakeholders to which the business is automatically accountable are its owners.[34] And the reason why the business is accountable to them, is simply because it belongs to them: it is their property.

The third reason why the stakeholder theory cannot be a proper account of business, is that it effectively destroys business accountability. In substituting a notional accountability to all stakeholders for direct accountability to owners, the stakeholder approach to business makes it impossible to hold business properly to account. And that is because a business that is accountable to all, is actually accountable to none: accountability that is diffuse, is effectively non-existent. This sad truth is known to all executives who have struggled with 'matrix management'. When several groups or individuals are theoretically in charge, each has an excuse for not taking responsibility; getting things right is always someone else's job. Multiple accountability can only function if everyone involved accepts a common purpose that can be used for ordering priorities.

But therein lies the fourth problem with the stakeholder account of business: it provides no such criterion. In rejecting the maximisation of long-term owner value as the purpose of business, and requiring business instead simply to 'balance' the interests of all stakeholders, stakeholder theory discards the objective basis for evaluating business action. How are those conflicting interests to be balanced? Are they all strictly equal? Are some more important than others? If so, which are they? And when, and by how much, and why? Since stakeholder theory offers no substantive business purpose, it provides no guidance at all as to how competing interests are to be ranked or reconciled. It consequently provides no effective standard against which business can be judged.

It is interesting to note that some of the most prominent advocates of stakeholder theory have been just those with most to gain from avoiding accountability: business managers.[35] By substituting a vague notion of 'balancing interests' for a measurable standard of financial performance, stakeholder theory frees business managers to pursue their personal ends. Stakeholder theory allows them to take lavish salaries and extravagant perks, and enables them to protect their powers by rejecting takeovers that would maximise owner value.

But though stakeholder theory may be fundamentally flawed and open to abuse, the concept of 'stakeholder' still has a useful role. 'Stakeholder' is a convenient shorthand way of designating those groups whose support is essential for the business's continued existence. It can even serve as a useful collective name for all those with whom the business regularly interacts. So long as the components are clearly identified, it does not much matter which groups are considered stakeholders, because stakeholders as such neither have any rights in respect of the business, nor constitute its purpose.

Customers, Employees, Managers
If the purpose of business cannot be to serve the interests of stakeholders collectively, might it not be to benefit specific stakeholder groups?

The customer is traditionally king; perhaps, as many commentators have claimed, serving the interests of customers is also the purpose of business. Customers are indeed vital for a business's very existence: there is no business without selling, and no selling without customers. And treating customers well is essential for achieving business success: the customer is not always right, but in most circumstances the business benefits from acting as though he were.

Nevertheless, serving customers' interests cannot constitute the definitive purpose of business. First, serving customers does not distinguish business from all the other sorts of organisations that also provide services: fee-paying schools, for instance. If it were claimed that business differs because its purpose is to serve customers' financial interests, that still would not do. For if that really were business's objective, it would give its goods away—and would not long survive. Even if it covered its costs, such an organisation would be conceptually indistinguishable from a consumer charity.

Similarly, an association whose purpose is promoting the interests or expressing the wishes of its employees, is not a business but an employee club. Consider the all too common phenomenon of shop customers' wanting assistance while oblivious staff chatter amongst themselves. If the purpose of business were furthering employee interests, the staff would be justified in serving their own convenience rather than the customers. But they are not, because promoting employees' interests is not the purpose of business.

Nor can the purpose of business be serving that subset of employees consisting of its managers. Given the disjunction between ownership and control that is characteristic of large corporations, and the remoteness of most shareholders, the managers and directors are frequently left free to treat the business as though it were their property. But this simply reflects a defect of corporate governance. Far from owning the business, or constituting its reason for being, managers are merely agents of the owners, charged with maximising long-term owner value.

The meaning of 'long-term'

Though the phrase 'long-term owner value' has been used throughout in characterising the defining purpose of business, inclusion of the words 'long-term' is, strictly speaking, superfluous[36]: a thing's value normally reflects its potential. A car that has been driven 100,000 miles normally sells for less than one with low mileage. And a business with a backlog of new products, or a well-developed and popular brand image, will normally represent greater owner value than one with overhanging litigation or exposure to declining markets.

Though strictly unnecessary, 'long-term' is included in the formula to highlight the simple but too frequently overlooked fact that actions have long-term consequences, in business as elsewhere. It is therefore vital for businesses to take into account the future effects of their current actions.

'Long-term' serves as a reminder that though consequences may be temporally distant, and correspondingly uncertain, they are nonetheless real.

'Long-term' is also included as a reminder that business is normally assumed to be a sustained activity, not a temporary one. An isolated transaction does not usually constitute a business; a fly-by-night operation is a business deviation. Owner value is normally to be maximised on the assumption that the business will be around to reap the consequences of its current actions. Accordingly, in determining whether to undertake a complex restructuring programme, the high initial costs must be netted against the benefits likely to accrue over future years. Equally, the increased current profits that may result from sharp practice must be weighed against the long-term costs of covering up and of alienating stakeholders. When courses of action are assessed, their future consequences must not be ignored.

In most circumstances a business will be able to generate greater owner value if it operates over an extended period: the sum of future values will normally be greater if there are more of them to aggregate. But though there is often a presumption that businesses are perpetual, the object of business is not survival at any cost. If a business is generating losses, and is likely to continue to do so, its disposal value may well exceed its value as a going concern. When that is so, then owner value is maximised by selling the business, or winding it up. Reference to the long-term provides no excuse for incompetence or lacklustre performance in the meanwhile: owner value is unlikely to be maximised if the business's short-term decisions are wrong.

The Importance of Maximising

It is essential that the objective be to maximise owner value, not just to increase or promote, secure or sustain it. Less stringent objectives than maximising fail to differentiate business from other activities. If there were no requirement for owner value to be maximised, any activity or association that increased owner value through occasional sales would thereby qualify as a business. Hobbyists making casual sales would constitute businesses, as would families selling their houses.[37] But, of course, they are not.

Only maximising[38] provides a sufficiently clear-cut, hard-edged criterion of business action. All sorts of things can create or conserve or even augment owner value; if business's goal were simply to further or to enhance owner value, there would be no business reason to choose one alternative rather than another. When, in contrast, the purpose is to maximise value, the choice is clear: the policy, project or course of action to be pursued is that which is likely to produce the greatest return over time.[39]

Maximisation reinforces business's long-term view: future periods must be included in the calculation. The very need to be forward-looking can, however, make maximising long-term owner value seem an awkward criterion to apply. The owner value of a course of action can only be definitively determined in retrospect; even then, the values that might have resulted from alternative programmes remain unknown. In the absence of a reliable time machine, it is therefore difficult to know which of several courses of action will actually produce the greatest value.

The difficulty of foreseeing the future does not, however, disqualify maximising long-term owner value as a useful business criterion. To the extent that forecasting outcomes is a practical problem, it is one that besets all forward-looking criteria: the effects of current action on future share prices, or profits, or sales would be equally hard to predict. In each case, the criteria operate by specifying the terms of reference for business decisions, the standard against which proposals must be measured. Since the ultimate outcomes cannot be known at the time decisions are taken, decisions are based on the extent to which proposed actions are expected to achieve the desired goal. And that is a matter for judgement based on reasoned argument and objective evidence. The outcomes may not be available, but the reasons why particular actions are expected to lead to them can be subjected to critical scrutiny.

By indicating the grounds on which business action must be justified, 'maximising long-term owner value' specifies the sorts of arguments and the kinds of evidence that must be adduced to justify business decisions. All assumptions, factual data and judgements must be evaluated against the objective of maximising long-term owner value. It is not enough to show that a project is expected to increase current profits, or that it exceeds a hurdle rate for return on investments, or that all the directors like it. To justify a course of action one must instead show why and how the action can be expected to maximise long-term owner value, taking into account all the factors, positive and negative, that are likely to affect owner value over the foreseeable future. A proposal whose connection with maximising long-term owner value is remote, or that seems likely to produce less long-term owner value than an alternative, is one that the business should not adopt. Satisfying the criterion does not, of course, guarantee that long-term owner value actually will be maximised, but it does ensure that action will be directed at the right objective.[40]

The Role of Rational Self-Interest

Long-term owner value is likely to be maximised when business owners pursue their enlightened self-interest.[41] The notion of self-interest is normally presumed to incorporate an element of optimisation. Moreover, the considerations that are essential for maximising long-term owner value are closely akin to those that qualify the pursuit of self-interest to be called 'enlightened' or 'rational': the future consequences of actions must always be taken into account, and immediate effects must be balanced against wider and more distant ones.

Rational self-interest and maximising long-term owner value require taking into account behaviour by, and to, all those who regularly interact with the business. One of the most valuable uses of 'stakeholder' is as a reminder of, and a convenient shorthand label for, all those groups whose actions and attitudes must be considered in assessing whether a course of action is likely to maximise long-term owner value.

Although its responsibilities to stakeholders are limited,

the business cannot afford to ignore any stakeholder concern that might affect long-term owner value. It is not just the actions of owners that affect the operations of the business, but also those of employees and customers, suppliers and lenders and regulators. Their tastes and preferences, including their moral preferences, will influence their willingness to deal with the business, and thus must be considered in assessments of long-term owner value. It is as important to be straight with suppliers as with shareholders, as necessary to be fair to employees as to customers.

Rational self-interest and maximising long-term owner value also require reciprocity: behaviour both by, and to, all stakeholders must be taken into account. In business it is as vital that owners behave responsibly as that employees do, as important for borrowers to be honest as it is for lenders. When the nature of business is properly understood, and the components of maximising long-term owner value are fully appreciated, it should be clear why it is normally true both that 'bad ethics is bad business' and 'good ethics is good business'.

CHARGES OF INTRINSIC BUSINESS IMMORALITY REFUTED

Though the close association[42] between business success and business morality should now be apparent, business has, nevertheless, often been accused of being intrinsically immoral. Sometimes the charges have focused on the activities of particular sorts of business. The selling of certain items— tobacco and alcohol, pornography, drugs and armaments, for example—has often been castigated as immoral. And the way to deal with such problems will be discussed below, in Chapter 10. Potentially more serious, however, have been the assertions that business itself is intrinsically unethical, regardless of the products or services sold.

If all that is meant by the alleged 'immorality' of business is that the purpose of business is something other than seeking goodness, then business is guilty as charged. In this sense, business is better described as 'amoral': the purpose of business is maximising long-term owner value by selling goods or services, not promoting moral virtue. It would, nonetheless, be wrong to conclude from business's not having an explicitly moral purpose, that business is necessarily immoral. That would follow only if the sole way to be moral were to take promoting goodness as one's exclusive goal, everywhere and always. But if that were so, then all activities whose objective was other than explicitly seeking goodness would be unethical, simply in virtue of their distinctive objectives. It would not be just business that would be immoral, but also art and sport, medicine and gardening.

That its purpose is not to further moral goodness does not mean either that business is immoral, or that it is exempt from moral judgement. What determines whether a business is moral, is how it conducts itself in pursuing the definitive business end: a business will be ethical if it seeks maximum long-term owner value in ethical ways. As will be argued in detail in the next chapter and demonstrated at length throughout the rest of this book, there is no reason in principle why long-term owner value cannot be maximised ethically.[43] Particular businesses and business people certainly do behave badly; sadly, business is no more free of villains than any other walk of life. But their wickedness is theirs alone: it is not a necessary feature of business itself.

But perhaps what is meant in charging business with intrinsic immorality is something more specific: perhaps what is alleged is that business is necessarily exploitative. If 'exploitation' is used in its main sense of 'turning to account', then business not only is, but should be, exploitative: long-term owner value is unlikely to be maximised unless the business makes the most of its assets and its opportunities. But if 'exploitative' is meant to suggest that business necessarily misappropriates value, or that it is inherently coercive or intrinsically unfair, then the charge is completely unfounded: misappropriation, coercion and cheating are no part of the business purpose, and are not necessary concomitants of business.

The charge that business in general is exploitative can only

be plausible if the nature of business is radically misconstrued. Coercion is not intrinsic to business, but to government; contrary to Marx, business can only be coercive if it
acts against the law, or with the law's connivance[44]. And
despite confused ideological claims to the contrary, profits
are no more theft than property is; business is not conducted
at the expense of its non-owner stakeholders. In the long-
term, owner value is unlikely to be maximised by an organisation that lies or cheats or steals, or even by one that is widely
believed to do so. Business is by its nature based on contractual exchanges of value, voluntarily entered into; to be successful, business must therefore act in ways that encourage
others to deal with it.

Similar considerations count against accusations that business is necessarily opportunistic, or guilty of expediency. If
the terms refer to being alive to opportunities, able to detect
and rapidly act upon changes in ways that are to the business's advantage, then being opportunistic is a good thing. If,
however, opportunism is meant to suggest snatching short-
term benefits regardless of their long-term consequences,
then far from being a necessary feature of business, it is contrary to its very nature.

Finally, charges of business immorality cannot be justified
by any necessary connection between business and greed.
Greed for money is a motive, whose link with business is at
best incidental. People start businesses, and work for them,
for all sorts of reasons unrelated to avarice: they enter business to find an outlet for their skills, to be with their friends,
to carry on family traditions, to earn an honest wage. Greed
no doubt motivates some business people, but equally, greed
leads people to gamble and steal and marry for money.

Cupidity is in fact responsible for far fewer business evils
than is commonly supposed. Greed for money is a relatively
clean vice, because it is, in an important sense, self-correct-
ing. Those who genuinely want to acquire and keep wealth
will avoid conduct, including unethical conduct, that reduces
wealth. When lying or cheating or stealing diminish wealth,
they are avoided by the truly avaricious; the amounts of
money the greedy seek may be unlimited, but the ways of

achieving wealth are not. Sadly, however, such considerations seldom restrain those who lust for power. Power lust is what actually underlies many of the serious business offences traditionally attributed to avarice. But power lust is hardly exclusive to business.

If, however, business is not necessarily greedy or coercive or exploitative, then why is the morality of business believed to be so low? It may well be that business conduct is no better or worse than other conduct, but that business wrongdoing is simply more noticeable. And that may simply be because business as an activity is so very pervasive. More people have had personal experience of business's failings than have had of government corruption or academic chicanery; victims of medical incompetence may not live to tell the tale. Hard sales, defective products and incompetent service undoubtedly exist, and undoubtedly contribute to business's egregiously bad reputation.

Furthermore, business is accessible. Not only is it more easily understood than the learned professions but, unlike medicine or law, business has no protective mystique of infallibility. People often feel freer to criticise business than medicine or law or government. It is hard to get a lawyer to sue another lawyer, or a doctor to criticise a colleague, but businesses are normally pleased to benefit from the failings of their competitors. Moreover, reprisals are unlikely. Unlike governments, businesses cannot legally gag their critics[45]. And since more businesses compete than collude, complainants are unlikely to be denied all access to products or services. Complaints against business are therefore more likely to be made.

Business's bad reputation may also stem from its large scale and high public profile; businesses may simply be under greater scrutiny than other institutions. Their doings are, by law, largely a matter of public record. Quoted companies must not only distribute their financial statements, but must disseminate all material information; many newspapers now offer detailed coverage of business activities. Accordingly, business wrongdoing is both easier to detect and better known than that of institutions shrouded in official or professional secrecy. It may also be that people are more likely to comment on, and criticise, the foibles and failures of the rich whom they rather envy.

Or it may be that, given the central importance of business to the welfare of the nation, and the levels of resources in business's care, irresponsibility in business is simply less tolerated than it is elsewhere. The operations of business can directly affect the lives of thousands and, indirectly, through their effects on other businesses and communities, the lives of millions. Given business's inevitable involvement with money and power, the opportunities for both minor and major wrongdoing are perhaps more prevalent and less accepted in business than they are in other activities. Simply in virtue of its scale of operations, business may have greater scope for doing ill that is noticed and censured.

It is therefore vitally important to determine what constitutes ethical conduct for business. Accordingly, the next chapter will explore the nature of ethics, and the values that are central to business ethics.

3

The Business of Ethics

'. . . we must . . . take pains to state [each set of principles] . . . definitely, since they have a great influence on what follows . . . and many of the questions we ask are cleared up by it.'

Aristotle[1]

'Business is based on trust and trust is based, in turn, on clarity and understanding.'

Sir John Harvey-Jones[2]

Just as making ethical decisions in business requires a firm grasp of the nature of business, so too does it require a clear understanding of ethical activity. 'Business ethics' does not refer to vague notions of being nice or doing good, or to general injunctions against wealth or profit. Nor does it refer either to a separate and inferior 'business ethic' or to the whole of the moral life. By identifying both what ethics is not, and what ethics is, this chapter will characterise the nature and boundaries of business ethics. In so doing, it will supply the theoretical basis for resolving actual questions of business ethics, and thus provide the moral framework for the rest of the book.

The arguments of this chapter are rather more abstract than those of the other sections. But they are also essential for achieving a very practical purpose: better decision-making. Muddled thinking inhibits productive action, and confusions about the nature of ethics are major impediments to proper business conduct. Too frequently, businessmen and others are deflected from doing what is right by focusing on false surrogates for what is ethical. Accordingly much of this chapter will be devoted to unravelling quite basic confusions.

In particular, ethics will be differentiated from law and religion, from suffering, sacrifice and struggle, and from altruism and prudence. Arguments for ethical relativism will be considered and rejected. Finally, the principles that are fundamental to resolving questions of business ethics will be identified, explained and illustrated. These are necessarily abstract matters, but ones that should help businessmen and others to pursue genuinely ethical conduct, free of unfounded inhibitions.

DISPENSING WITH DISPENSATIONS

The first confusion to be eliminated is the notion that there is a separate 'business ethic' that puts business beyond the range of ordinary ethical judgements. The notion is a dangerous one: not only does it divert attention from genuine ethical problems, but it seems to provide excuses for conduct that would otherwise, rightly, be considered unethical. Such a notion cannot be justified either by actual business practice or by the various inappropriate models of business or ethics that have often been employed by commentators on business ethics. Though resorted to both by those who would defend business and those who condemn it, such models neither characterise business accurately nor justify moral laxity.

The real meaning of business ethics is not illuminated by considering business as a game, a war or a machine, but by understanding that activities—including business—are properly differentiated by their purposes. When that is fully appreciated, it becomes clear that 'business ethics' is not like 'cooking sherry', an inferior, adulterated version of the real thing. Rather it is more like 'sports medicine': 'business' appropriately limits the problems addressed, not the rigour of the standards to be applied. Business's distinctive nature does not entitle it to any laxer moral treatment.

The game of business

Nevertheless, commentators concerned to protect business from inappropriate moral demands have all too often resorted to the metaphor of business as a game. Business cannot be subject to ordinary moral standards, they have claimed, because games typically are not. But they are doubly wrong: not only is business not a game, but even games are not immune to moral judgement.

In some respects, of course, the game model is revealing. The rules of both business and games must generally be understood for the activities to be played properly or considered fair. Furthermore, participation in both is normally voluntary, and winning is very important. Moreover, games are indeed outside the ambit of ordinary ethics in some fundamental ways. Conduct that might otherwise be morally required may actually violate the rules of the game. And from within a game, questioning the moral rightness of the rules does indeed make very little sense.

The reason that such questioning is absurd, however, is not just because the triviality of most games removes them from the realm of serious moral concern. Even more fundamentally, it is absurd because a game is defined by nothing but its rules; changing the rules, however slightly, results in a distinct and different game. Questioning the queen's powers in chess is odd not just because those powers pose no danger of tyranny, but because an ecclesiastical version in which the bishop was more powerful just wouldn't be chess. Business suffers from no such limitation: it is not a self-contained, purely formal activity. The activities that constitute doing business—buying, selling, making, managing—consist of more than just performing conventional moves. Both the conduct and the rules of doing business can be questioned without destroying the essential activity of business.

Moreover, even games are not removed from the demands of everyday ethics. Some games are clearly better than others, in terms of being more challenging, or more suitable for certain types of players or conditions. And rules are subject to moral judgement: a competition to kill the most people would clearly be unethical. Finally, all games, including the simplest, are necessarily subject to a very fundamental moral rule: the prohibition against cheating. Even games that depend on deception—poker, Call My Bluff—cannot permit their own rules to be flouted.

The ban on cheating rules out losing deliberately as well as seeking to win unfairly. Players participate in the expectation that they, and all the others in the game, are actually aiming at victory. Playing a game means playing to win; throwing a game deprives the other side of the chance to win fairly. A player may have all sorts of reasons for not winning; he may be trying to encourage a child to learn the game, or flattering the boss, or cheering up an invalid. Whatever the reason, however, within a game all behaviour that is not devoted to winning is either not seriously playing the game or is cheating. Much of what is ordinarily regarded as moral activity is therefore ruled out within a game: however much kindness and generosity may be virtues, exercising them in helping the opposing side to win is incompatible with playing properly.

Many ostensibly 'moral' acts are equally inappropriate in business. But that is not because business is a game: it is not. The exclusion of extraneous activities follows automatically from an activity's having a specific, limited purpose. The objectives of businesses and games are very different: maximising long-term owner value by selling goods or services is not the same thing as scoring points or eliminating pieces by acting in accordance with a set of self-contained rules. In both cases, however, the objectives identify what counts as performing the activity. As a result, all other behaviour, including explicitly moral behaviour, can be rightly excluded as not being directed to the objective in question. Moreover, because there is a purpose to be accomplished, one cannot fully engage in the activity without seeking to achieve that purpose. The inclusion of 'maximising' in the business objective imposes as stringent a requirement as winning does in a game.

It does not, however, justify a separate 'business ethic'. Certain categories of moral strictures are inappropriate in business not because ordinary ethical values cease to obtain, but because they typically apply in situations outside business's very limited ambit. Neither the nature of business nor the model of a game provides any justification for exempting business from moral judgement.

The battle for survival

Ironically, the very fact that business is not a game has also been cited in support of a separate business ethic. Focusing on the intense competitiveness of business, some observers have claimed that ordinary ethics are a luxury that businesses can ill afford. In a struggle for sheer survival, it has been suggested, less rigorous rules are appropriate.

This conclusion is equally wrong. Once the defining purpose of business is identified and understood, it is not necessary to postulate a lower ethical standard to free business people to go about their business. Even for those businesses that really do operate in a dog-eat-dog world, competition is not war: life goes on even if the business does not. It is no more the case that all is fair in business than it is in love, or politics, or art, fiercely competitive activities though they all may be. So again, there are no grounds for a separate business ethic.

The business machine

Nor can the image of business as a machine, and business people as cogs in it, exempt business from ordinary moral judgements. The impersonality of businesses, their size and complexity, the dispersal of power and the diffuseness of decision-making, may well present practical problems in assigning moral responsibility, and in getting businesses to act morally. It is sadly true that large collectives, be they businesses or official bureaucracies or barbarian mobs, seldom display the moral sensibilities of their constituent members.

But the appropriate response should not be to apply lower standards of ethical behaviour, in the hope that somehow, if the hurdles are lower, the group will be less likely to fall short. Rather, it should be to remember that the purpose of business is not promoting morality, but maximising long-term owner value; business's proper ethical concern is simply pursuing that business objective in an ethical way. The challenge is thus to set up systems and structures within the business that encourage its members to do the (morally) right (business) thing.

Professional standards

Accountants and lawyers do have such systems: their own professional codes of conduct. Don't they constitute a separate 'business ethic'? Once again, the answer is No. To the extent that those codes are morally relevant, they simply give guidance on those issues that are commonly encountered in particular professional activities.

There is therefore no justification for laxer standards in business; it is not the case that principles indefensible elsewhere are acceptable in commerce. Business may take 'The public good be damned!' and '*Caveat emptor*' as its rallying cries, but they are not signs of business depravity. They are simply succinct reminders that the focus of business is necessarily limited.

That is the crucial point. Whatever the public perception, there is no need to assume a separate business ethic either to condemn or to defend business practice: what is needed instead is a proper understanding of the concepts of business and of ethics. Since business is defined by its distinctive, limited purpose, things—ethical or otherwise—only pertain to business if they relate to that end. Whatever the subject of another concern, that subject can only relate to *business* if it relates to maximising long-term owner value by selling goods or services. The same logical restriction that applies to business expenses and business meetings applies equally to business ethics.

This sort of limiting condition is, of course, not exclusive to business; other subjects are similarly qualified, and also do not have a separate ethic. Medical ethics, for example, studies ethical problems confronted by the medical profession. It is the *problems*, however, and not the ethical principles, that are medicine-specific. Although the questions—when to turn off the life-support system, what sorts of embryo research to allow—may arise chiefly in a medical context, the extent to which they are considered together as a separate subject is mainly a matter of academic convenience.

What is morally important is not the problems' classification, but the ethical issues that they raise and their answers, both of which call upon ethical values and principles that transcend academic divisions. Indeed, ethical problems may easily arise in more than one context: the question of using animals for drug testing, for example, is as much a problem for pharmaceutical companies as it is for medical researchers, a subject for business ethics as much as for medical ethics.[3] Regardless of the subject heading under which problems are addressed, however, the moral values and ethical principles that apply are the same throughout.

In conclusion, putting the word 'business' before the word 'ethics' merely provides a focus: it identifies the range of problems to be addressed, not the stringency of moral standards to be applied. Although ethical questions are only questions of business ethics if they relate to the activity of maximising long-term owner value, the principles that apply in solving them are ethical principles that apply everywhere and always.

Common standards

That is because a consistent, coherent ethical life presupposes values that are not subject to arbitrary divisions. This accords with our ordinary understanding of morality, in which values are widely recognised to transcend specific interests and purely conventional bounds. Business ethics cannot make breaking promises right in business when it would not be right otherwise. What business ethics can do, is indicate in principle what sorts of promises a business should and should not make.

If, however, business ethics is just the application of universal ethical principles in business, why does it present such problems? The answer is, because all too often both the questions as posed, and the answers attempted, suffer from grave conceptual confusions, including confusions about the nature of ethics. It is therefore necessary to eliminate those confusions, so that actual decisions can be made free of the muddles that commonly plague them. To focus productively on the ethical problems of business, it is essential to identify what is ethical.

WHAT ETHICS IS NOT

Law

It is often assumed that compliance with law is essential for guaranteeing a business's moral rightness—and that compliance marks the limits of business's ethical responsibilities. In fact, however, far from being both necessary and sufficient to ensure moral rectitude, legal compliance is neither. Law does not and should not specify all that is ethical. Nor could it: acting ethically requires freedom of choice. And the right thing to do may well be other—more or less—than the law or regulation requires.

Nevertheless, business normally should comply with the law. Even when the law lives up to its reputation and is an ass, the law should still normally be obeyed. And that is because the framework of law is necessary for business's very existence. Without protection against physical violence, without property rights, without enforcement of contracts, business as we know it would be impossible. Furthermore, many forms of organisation depend for recognition on a particular code of law: limited liability companies are now typically artificial creatures of a legal system. Undermining the law would undermine their very being.

The nature of business provides another reason for the presumption being in favour of obeying the law: long-term owner value is seldom maximised outside it. It may be that violating the law can produce short-term advantages. But in a free, competitive world, the law-breaking business may find it hard to attract law-abiding stakeholders. The sanctions for illegality normally extend far beyond the penalties exacted by the law itself. Moreover, property rights are essential for protecting owner value over the long term.

But what if the law is bad? All too often, especially with the intrusion of government into so many areas of activity, and the proliferation of regulation from so many sources, what the law requires may be silly, or counterproductive, or even wicked. What then? Is the business bound to comply even so? Normally, Yes. In a democratic society, there are ways of attempting to change the law that do not involve breaking it. Should it be in the business's interests to bring about a change, the first response should be to try those means offered by the system itself.

The crucial point to recognise is that violating the law, even to provoke a test case, is normally a very costly undertaking: it involves not just potentially massive penalties and legal fees, but, at least as significantly, vast demands on senior management time and attention. Given the damage likely to be suffered by the firm's normal business as a result of breaking the law, legal challenges will seldom promote long-term owner value. But if they cannot be justified on business terms, then the business has no business undertaking them. Except in the most extraordinary circumstances, therefore, the presumption must be that if an activity is required or forbidden by law, the business should comply.

What if the laws of the land are so bad—either morally or practically—that the business is regularly led to break them? That is indeed a sorry state of affairs, but even generally bad laws do not make business criminality right. The correct business response is instead to realise that such a regime is not a suitable one in which to do business, and to seek a better-ordered jurisdiction in which to operate.[4]

Contractual compliance

The presumption in favour of compliance with the law is, if anything, exceeded by that in favour of honouring contracts: contracts are not only pervasive, but voluntary. Businesses depend on contracts both conceptually and practically, and a firm known to violate its contracts will not find it at all easy to do business.

But however crucial contracts are to business, their contents are nonetheless subject to moral review. Once entered into, contracts, like the law and regulation, are normally binding, even if what they require turns out after signing to be seriously inconvenient or commercially harmful. As a matter of course, however, all prospective business commitments should be carefully scrutinised and evaluated with respect to their ethical implications; a contract that enjoins the immoral should no more be signed than one that requires the illegal. Like compliance with law, however, contractual compliance is not the same as ethical conduct; it is one of the things that should be subject to ethical review.

Religion

Religion must also be differentiated from ethics, if business is to be able to concentrate on genuinely ethical concerns. Most religions have moral codes; many moral teachings stem from religion; the same conduct is often specified by both religious and non-religious ethical systems. Nevertheless, ethics and religion are not the same thing. What makes religion distinctive is its otherworldly focus, its connection with the divine or with the saving of souls. To the extent that a religion dispenses with such spiritual concerns, it is hard to distinguish from a social welfare movement.

Religion can affect business in many ways. Religious principles can rule out specific business sectors as unacceptable to the faithful: Muslims are not allowed to charge interest and therefore may not be conventional bankers. Religion can ordain that individual believers should not engage in business: business is the wrong career for those with a vocation elsewhere. Religion can even condemn the purpose of business as such: worldly aggrandisement may be incompatible with the divine purpose.

Religion cannot, however, alter the purpose of business or what counts in consequence as proper business conduct. Its ability to provide moral guidance for business is correspondingly limited. Insofar as religion prescribes that other values should take precedence over long-term owner value, it is not providing ethical direction for business, but preferring other activities to business.

Because the requirements of religion are, nonetheless, frequently believed to be identical with those of ethics, ethics is all too often misidentified with sacrifice or struggle or altruism. Equally, the role of prudence is regularly misunderstood. These mistaken beliefs result in so many damaging confusions, that the following subsections will take some trouble to argue otherwise; examples from outside the business arena will be used to make the points more forcefully. Sacrifice and struggle, altruism and prudence will all be shown to be at most only contingently related to what is ethical; none are necessary hallmarks of ethical activity. Business action need therefore involve no suffering or sacrifice, struggle or altruism in order to be ethical.

Suffering and sacrifice

One of the commonest confusions afflicting discussions of business ethics is the notion that suffering is essential to morality: if something helps a business, it must therefore, by that very fact, be less moral. But this is simply wrong. Despite being deeply embedded in the Christian tradition, the connection between suffering and morality is neither necessary nor sufficient. Far from being painful, doing what is right can be gratifying . . . and normally should be, for those of good character[5]. The physician need not suffer to make his saving a patient's life good; he may even take professional pride in his work.

Sacrifice and suffering are themselves morally neutral, and are associated with both good and evil acts. Some suffering, of course, is the result of moral forbearance and self-restraint. But equally, suffering may be the outcome of self-indulgence: consider hangovers as the wages of gin. Suffering can also be a consequence of immorality and irresponsibility: the pangs of guilt can hurt, as can toothache provoked by ignoring dental hygiene. Moreover, much suffering takes place without any clear ethical content or personal responsibility; pain may also be the result of accident. When an aeroplane crashes, there is no obvious moral significance to the pain suffered by the innocent passengers and their families, or those caught by flying debris. It is only when glossed by religion as divine punishment or providence, or as a path to redemption, that suffering acquires a necessarily moral dimension[6]; otherwise pain or suffering do not themselves indicate moral goodness. So suffering is not a condition of being moral; there is no reason why business need suffer for its acts to be morally good.

That is not to say that suffering has no role in morality. Hostile circumstances and the need for sacrifice may indeed test moral conviction and commitment. But what they measure is an individual's sincerity and determination, not the ethical content of his acts or beliefs: that Ku Klux Klansmen may suffer for their cause, does not make their cause right. Though moral strength may be conspicuously displayed in the course of dealing with disaster, moral conviction may be equally strong, albeit often untested, when it exists in an easier environment. Moreover, extreme good fortune can also present moral challenges. It is not just how one copes with ill health, but how one deals with sudden wealth, that measures the moral character: consider the pools winner or the rock star. Similarly, in the business context, how bonuses are awarded and how promotions are handled are ethical questions as important as who gets the sack. So suffering is no more necessary for displaying moral character than it is for being good.

Struggle

Just as sacrifice and suffering are not moral indicators, and are not required for business to be moral, nor is struggle. The ethical nature of an act is independent of the ease or difficulty of achieving it; there is no ethical merit in doing things the hard way. If fairness is good, then the fact that being fair may also be natural and easy, makes fairness no less right, for an individual or a business.

There is, of course, a commonly held model of morality in which good must struggle to overpower and conquer evil impulses within the soul. The suggestion is that the man who successfully battles against vice demonstrates a stronger commitment to virtue than the man who is not even tempted. But though struggle may make the achievement of virtue more visible, it does not *confer* virtue, any more than sacrifice or suffering do. Consider a confirmed sadist: he may manage to keep his vicious impulses under control only with the greatest of effort. If struggle really were a necessary component of morality, the sadist would be more virtuous than someone who did the right thing naturally, enthusiastically and wholeheartedly. But that can hardly be right: however good the sadist's discipline may be, his impulses are wicked. Struggle may test virtue, but it is not itself virtuous. There is, therefore, no reason why the business should not devise systems that make it easy and gratifying to do what is right. If it does, it is much more likely that right will be done.

So neither suffering nor sacrifice nor struggle is necessary for establishing that an act is moral. Nonetheless, benefiting the business may still be thought to constitute a moral disqualification, and so present an obstacle to doing the right thing. To show why it is not, confusions about ethics, prudence and altruism must also be untangled.

Prudence and altruism

The connection between ethics and prudence is subject to two common but diametrically opposed misconceptions. Whereas one school of thought claims that the ethical is nothing but the prudential, another asserts that being prudent automatically disqualifies an action from being ethical. Both of these views are wrong, and obstruct ethical analysis and correct action.

First, being prudent is not the same as being ethical. Checking for traffic before crossing the road is prudent, but is not necessarily either moral or immoral. The wicked may prudently try to conceal their villainy to avoid getting caught, but do not thereby become good. In each case, the prudent act is simply the sensible one to do in the circumstances, the judicious or reasonable thing to do. The ethical act, in contrast, is that which is morally right.

The ethical is not reducible to the prudential. Being prudent is not enough to make an action good. It does not, however, follow that the prudent cannot also be morally good. Although the ethical and the prudent are conceptually distinct[7], the same act can and often does fall into both categories. That which is prudent—and which may, therefore, be profitable for a business—can also be genuinely ethical: fairness to employees, for instance.

Just as a prudent act can be moral, that which is altruistic can be deeply immoral. Despite the very widespread belief to the contrary, altruism is no guarantee of goodness. An altruistic act is simply one that is done to benefit interests other than the actor's own; it is defined by the 'other-serving' nature of the actor's motive, not by the content of the act. Accordingly, all sorts of things, including evil things, can be done altruistically: the road to hell is notoriously paved with good intentions. The parent who dutifully beats the devil out of his child may have genuinely altruistic motives: his devout wish to save the child's soul may be both sincere and unselfish. But battering a child is simply wrong, whether performed altruistically or sadistically. Equally, the act of selling dangerously defective products is wrong, even if the motive is helping employees by saving their jobs. Altruism cannot confer goodness on the acts performed in its name; it is neither sufficient nor necessary for moral rightness. A business therefore need not be altruistic in order to be ethical; a business act can be both self-serving and morally good.

WHAT ETHICS IS

So ethics is not altruism or prudence, struggle or sacrifice, law or religion. What is it?

As commonly used, 'ethics' and 'morals' refer variously to moral codes, to the actions enjoined by them, and to the study of either or both. And in dealing with received opinion, these usages will be observed. When used more strictly, however, the term 'ethics' refers simply to a branch of philosophy, that which seeks to identify and clarify the presuppositions of human conduct having to do with good and evil.

As a purely theoretical discipline, ethics in this strict sense neither is nor can be practical. There is, however, an extended sense in which the techniques and principles of ethics proper can be helpful in dealing with real life problems: the clarity of thought and awareness of key concepts developed in philosophical study can genuinely inform action. It is in this extended, metaphorical sense that one may properly speak of 'applied ethics', or of the 'application' of ethical principles to practical problems, or of ethics 'enjoining' specific courses of action.

Business ethics applies ethical reasoning to specifically business situations and activities: it is an attempt to resolve or at least to clarify those moral issues that typically arise in business. Starting from an analysis of the nature and presuppositions of business, business ethics applies general moral principles in an attempt to identify what is right in business . . . everywhere and always.

RELATIVISM REJECTED[8]

Business ethics is universal, because the definitive objective of business is universal, and so are the ethical principles underlying it. And those principles are universal by their very nature. That which is not universal may be a useful rule of thumb, or a practical guideline, or a summary of common practice, but it cannot be a principle. It is precisely the point of principles, including moral principles, that they should identify the unvarying, essential features of diverse situations. Only then can they provide a unifying framework that can make sense of actual problems as they arise in all their unpredictable variety and complexity.

Once again, this accords with our ordinary understanding of morality. Ethical values are normally expected to transcend specific interests, be they national or cultural or economic, and business ethics is expected to provide a basis for assessing and guiding all sorts of business conduct. Just as money, by providing a common standard of financial value, permits making tradeoffs between items as diverse as Apple computers and apple pies, so principles, by constituting constant points of reference, make discussion and decision-making possible across widely different situations. Unlike assertions of mere preference, moral principles provide a criterion of acceptable business behaviour that can be argued for, and applied consistently over a wide range of actual people, places and times. So principles are essential: without them one might have statements of intent, or descriptions of preferred practice, but not business *ethics*.

Where are such universal ethical principles to be found? Are the values to be used those of the UK or the EU, the CBI or the TUC[9], the north or the south? In our pluralist society, there are apparently as many values as there are proponents, and no generally accepted way of choosing amongst them. But despite the widespread relativist prejudice that no one's ideas on anything are any better or any worse than anyone else's, it is simply not the case that all views, even moral views, are equally right. On the contrary, starting with a philosophical understanding of the nature of man and the world[10], it is possible to abstract out ethical principles that can be seen to be genuinely better than the alternatives at making sense of the moral universe, and that do indeed express eternal verities.

Lying, cheating and stealing are simply wrong. So are killing and cowardice, irresponsibility, breaking promises and betrayal. Justice and fairness, in contrast, are always right. Whether or not they are actually observed or enforced, these values hold good everywhere, be it in love or war, business or pleasure, life or art, Africa or Asia. These values may, of course, not always be easily reconcilable, and hard choices may sometimes have to be made amongst them; given the complexities of moral life, it may be necessary to forgo one moral value to achieve another. But the value forgone remains a value nonetheless: the need to rank values never transforms virtues into vices—or vice versa.

Can the genuinely differing ethical views and practices that prevail world-wide be reconciled with such universal principles? Yes: easily. First, practice may deviate from principle because the principles may simply not have been employed. Philosophy cannot rule out either hypocrisy or ignorance or error, knavery or foolishness. Unlike physical laws, moral principles can be violated[11], and sadly, they often are. Rules are flouted or forgotten or misapplied and people just do behave badly.

Second, even when principles are applied correctly, outcomes will necessarily vary: when a constant rule is applied to different inputs, different outputs are the natural result. Consider a non-moral example. It is a basic principle of physics that every action has an equal and opposite reaction. Accordingly, action A generates reaction –A and action B, reaction –B. No one imagines, however, that because the principle is universal, that –B and –A are thereby the same. Nor do they suppose that because they are different, the principle has either not applied or that it is any less universal. In like fashion, moral principles applied to differing circumstances produce correspondingly diverse results.

Third, most perceived diversity simply has no bearing on business ethics or its universality. As a theoretical understanding of what is right, ethics relates to the nature of man; it has no necessary connection to any existing system of religious belief, or any specific legal framework, or any particular moral code. As a result, commonly cited variations of actual practice are largely irrelevant; cultural diversity, even cultural relativism, do not and cannot justify ethical relativism. Much of the variety does, in any case, relate to ends that are beyond those of business: since the purpose of business as such is simply to maximise long-term owner value, it will not, except incidentally, involve sundry and diverse visions of social welfare, spiritual development or psychic gratification.

THE FUNDAMENTAL PRINCIPLES OF BUSINESS ETHICS

So what are the universal principles of ethics that apply in business ethics? Establishing the foundations of ethics from first principles is necessarily outside the scope of this book: in a work on business ethics, the grounds of ethical activity, like the existence of business, must be taken as given. Fortunately, given the strictly limited objective of business, and its extremely narrow role, the key principles of business ethics[12] can actually be specified quite simply: the principles of business ethics are those enjoining the basic values without which business as an activity would be impossible.

It is important to note that although action in accordance with these key principles naturally tends to promote long-term owner value, the fact that it does so is not their ethical justification: the principles' moral rightness is prior to their business application, and independent of it[13]. The principles would be ethically correct even if, in any particular case, they precluded a business activity or diminished owner value. The business of contract killing would be morally wrong even if it were conducted so as to maximise long-term owner value, and even if it were not illegal.

What then are the ethical conditions of conducting business? First, maximising long-term owner value requires considering the long term. But long-term views require confidence, which in turn requires trust. Moreover, owner value necessarily presupposes ownership, and so requires respect for property rights. Business therefore presupposes conduct that excludes lying, cheating, stealing, killing, coercion[14], physical violence and most illegality, and instead exhibits honesty and fairness. Taken collectively, these constraints embody the values of what may be called '*ordinary decency*'. Without it, '. . . there is no place for industry, because the fruit thereof is uncertain'[15]: without the minimum level of trust needed for the possibility of settled expectations, life would indeed be 'solitary, poor, nasty, brutish and short', and business would be impossible. So ordinary decency is a pre-condition of business.

Furthermore, since business is more likely to achieve its defining purpose when it encourages contributions to that purpose, and not to some other, classical *distributive justice*[16] is also essential. Although the components of ordinary decency necessarily extend far beyond the limited business realm, distributive justice incorporates the purpose of business into its very definition.

Distributive justice

In its most general formulation, the principle of distributive justice asserts that organisational rewards should be proportional to contributions made to organisational ends. Distributive justice stipulates *why* benefits should be accorded: for making contributions to the objectives of the association. And it specifies *how* benefits should be allocated: in proportion to those contributions' value in furthering the association's purpose.[17]

Consider some examples. The definitive purpose of a symphony orchestra is to play music; within it, therefore, the proper basis for reward is musical achievement. The distinctive purpose of a university is to extend and convey human knowledge; accordingly those who are best at doing original research and at teaching are those who deserve recognition. The definitive purpose of a business is to maximise long-term owner value by selling goods or services; promotions and pay rises should therefore go to those who contribute most to owner value. In practice, of course, organisations often have more than one objective, and these days even orchestras and universities can ill afford to ignore their finances. But to give the highest musical honours to the accountant rather than to the virtuoso soloist or the conductor, would be as perverse as rewarding the business's staff on their ability to whistle.

Distributive justice is an extremely powerful concept: it allows for the full range of divergent human purposes, and for rewards as diverse as payments and praise, honours and responsibilities. Distributive justice serves both as a principle of allocation and as a principle of selection. Although the term may be unfamiliar in business, the underlying concept of distributive justice is in fact commonly invoked. It is implicit in the widely accepted view that productive workers deserve to be better rewarded than shirkers; properly understood, both performance-related pay and promotion on merit are expressions of distributive justice. But distributive justice governs more than just remuneration. It also determines who should be hired and fired, and which bidders should be awarded contracts, and even, by extension, which products and plants and projects should be financed.

In each case, what is relevant for the judgements of distributive justice is not the nature of the contributor—his identity or his motives—but only the contribution itself. It does not matter if a potential supplier is the boss's nephew or a former employee or a start-up firm—unless it affects the ability to deliver; the contract should simply be awarded to the source that can provide the best product at the best price, reliably and promptly. Distributive justice is concerned essentially with achievements; dispositions and aspirations are relevant to the business only insofar as they actually or potentially affect long-term owner value.

The principle of distributive justice is so fundamental, that it is important to avert a number of common misunderstandings. First, since distributive justice relates only to contributions, it is wrong to extend its judgements to cover the characters or capabilities or general worth of the contributors. When, in a business, distributive justice decrees that A is more deserving of a pay rise (or a promotion) than B, it does not necessarily imply that A is morally superior, or a better person; it just means that A has made (or is expected to make) the greater contribution to maximising long-term owner value.

Second, what is fair or just according to distributive justice is always relative to the defining purpose of a particular organisation, not to some abstract, external standard. Distributive justice is not about some notional 'just wage' or 'fair price' or 'appropriate return'. Furthermore, distributive justice specifies only the relative, and not the absolute, rewards to be allotted. The basic unit of reward will vary from organisation to organisation, and within each organisation will vary over time depending on the organisation's circumstances.

Third, distributive justice holds only within an organisation, not between or among them: unless there is an association of associations, there is no common end to which contributions can be related. It is therefore not distributively just or unjust for one business to have higher profits than another, or for workers at different firms to be paid differently. Intercompany comparisons of distributive justice can only refer to the extent to which distributive justice governs each firm's internal allocation of rewards.[18]

Finally, distributive justice does not require equal treatment for everyone with the same job description. Quite the reverse: the principle of distributive justice asserts that those who contribute more, deserve more. But such contributions are a matter of actual achievement, not administrative category. There are typically wide variations in performance within any personnel classification, while those with different job titles may well make contributions of equal worth. 'Equal pay for equal work' expresses distributive justice only if the work is equated on the basis of its contribution to long-term owner value.

Ordinary decency

Nevertheless, 'treating equals equally' is indeed a requirement of moral business: it is part of what is meant by fairness, and as such is a component of ordinary decency. Like distributive justice, however, those components need clarification if they are not to be misconstrued. Ordinary decency is not generalised 'niceness'. Rather, ordinary decency consists of fairness and honesty and refraining from coercion and physical violence, typically within the confines of the law.[19] Taken together, these values represent the minimum necessary for the existence of business.

What about courage and responsibility and integrity: aren't they important? Indeed they are, but they refer mainly to ways in which the more fundamental values are pursued.

Consider courage. Since killing and coercion and physical violence are out of bounds, physical courage normally has little role to play in business. Business courage is therefore mainly moral, and is most commonly displayed in a steadfast adherence to the fundamental values of justice, honesty, and fairness. Businesses[20] should be neither timid nor foolhardy in responding to the various dangers and difficulties that confront them, and should be stalwart in maximising long-term owner value ethically.

Similarly, responsibility has to do with the ways in which a business pursues its definitive end, and the extent to which it respects the fundamental values in doing so. A responsible business is one that considers the consequences of its actions, and recognises that it may be held accountable for them. The responsible business will make sure that its actions to maximise long-term owner value, and their long-term, distant and indirect consequences, do not undermine the conditions of doing business. It will ensure that its actions are directed towards the business objective, that they are compatible with distributive justice and honesty and fairness, and that they are conducted without coercion and with respect for the law.

Integrity also has to do with the ways in which other values are pursued. A business displays integrity when its values are consistent with each other, and when its actions reflect its values. A business with integrity can be relied on to act in accordance with its principles and to stand by its actions: its actions and its values fit together in an integral whole. When, therefore, a business systematically maximises long-term owner value in accordance with justice and honesty and fairness, and avoids coercion and physical violence, and respects the law, it acts not only with distributive justice and ordinary decency, but also with integrity.

A business that characteristically respects the central components of ordinary decency will therefore also exhibit courage and responsibility and integrity. Conversely, cowardice, irresponsibility and a lack of integrity will almost certainly involve acting dishonestly or unfairly, coercively or illegally. The requirements of ordinary decency can accordingly be limited to the four basic components of honesty, fairness, refraining from coercion and physical violence, and respecting the law. These values act as constraints on business's legitimate activities, as specified by its defining purpose.

Fairness

What do these mean in practice? While fairness does require 'treating equals equally', it does not mean treating everyone, even everyone in the business, alike. Not all ways of being equal are relevant to the business objective, or deserve equal treatment by the business. People may well be equal in respect of their hair colour, but the business need not treat all redheads in the same way to be fair. What 'treating equals equally' does require, is simply that insofar as the organisation has rules, it should apply them systematically and even-handedly, without favour or capricious exception.

Fairness also requires honouring agreements. The ethical business scrupulously performs its part of the bargain[21] when it enters into contracts, whether they are explicit and written or implicit and based purely on trust. In order for arrangements based on trust to work satisfactorily, however, all the parties need to have the same understanding of the arrangements they have made. The ethical business is therefore extremely careful about the expectations that it engenders or that arise about it; inappropriate expectations are a major source of the perception that business is unfair. The ethical business does not encourage or condone unrealistic expectations about its activities, objectives or abilities. And it is equally careful to fulfil the realistic expectations that it has fostered, not disappointing them without good reason and good explanation.

Honesty

The meaning of honesty must also be made clear. In business as elsewhere, honesty means telling the truth. But contrary to widespread belief, failing to tell 'the truth, the whole truth and nothing but the truth' is not necessarily dishonest—even in business. 'The truth, the whole truth and nothing but the truth' is what one must swear to tell when answering questions in a court of law. To expect that same strict standard of truthfulness to apply in any other situation is inappropriate; indeed, it is normally a mark of social ineptitude or deliberate provocation. Just as context and purpose are crucial in determining utterances' meanings and appropriate responses to them, they are equally essential in determining what counts as honesty.

First, not all business utterances are meant to convey factual information. Those that do not are typically neither true nor false, honest nor dishonest.[22] 'Buy our product!' is an injunction to be ignored or obeyed, not a report to be evaluated for its truthfulness. A commercial dramatising the lives of product users may be fatuous or well-made or amusing, but it is honest or dishonest only in the way that fiction is.

Second, even business statements that do convey information have to be assessed within a specific context. The extent of information appropriate, and consequently what constitutes honest disclosure, depends in large part on the purpose of an utterance and on its audience. A newspaper headline is not normally dishonest or false for conveying less information than the full article. Nor is an English speaker ordinarily being dishonest or evasive if he responds to a casual 'How are you?' by saying 'Fine' . . . even if he is not feeling particularly well. Normally, he is just recognising that a conventional greeting does not call for the same medical evaluation that a physician's inquiry does. Similarly, the expert who refrains from revealing the full extent of his knowledge at a dinner party is usually being tactful, not dishonest. The everyday standard of disclosure in life, and thus in business, varies considerably, but it is almost always less than 'the truth, the whole truth and nothing but the truth'.

That is not to say that lying is right in business: it is not. Neither *caveat emptor* nor the argument above justifies any form of deceit: lying, cheating and stealing are simply wrong. Being honest means being accurate in description and keeping one's word, both when that word is enshrined in contract and otherwise. So business statements that express factual data should be factually correct: the product description, the expected delivery date, the terms of the warranty, are all bits of information on which one should be able to rely.

What about the half-truths and lies of omission that are so common: is it essential to mention the possibly better alternative on offer only elsewhere, the high running costs that might make the product bad value, the difficulty of getting planning permission? Is keeping silent about them morally acceptable? It all depends. If a customer asks the question direct, or if the business is making the provision of reliable advice one of its distinguishing features, then the business should offer full disclosure. So should it if non-obvious dangers are likely to result from the production process, or from using the product for its proper purpose.[23] Often, however, volunteering information is supererogatory.[24]

It is wrong to castigate sales pitches and advertising for not providing impartial consumer advice: that is simply not their function. Certainly they should be truthful, but it is inappropriate to expect them to tell the whole truth and nothing but. *Caveat emptor* can, in fact, be seen as a pithy reminder of the purpose of much business language: it is securing sales, not providing general consumer guidance. So strong, indeed, are the ordinary business conventions, that adopting a stronger, non-standard level of honesty may be positively counterproductive.

Consider 'estate agentese', for example, which is commonly recognised by both home owners and comedians[25] to constitute a sort of code, to which the appropriate response is not literal acceptance, but translation. Unless the 'honest' estate agent is recognised not to be using the code, he will put off both sellers and buyers and benefit no one. Similarly, the negotiator who opens with his target figure would normally be doing both his client and himself a disservice: when exaggeration is expected, plain speaking will not achieve the desired end.

Does this mean that high probity is a business liability? Far from it: a reputation for trustworthiness and reliability[26] should command strong customer loyalty and premium pricing. And that is because, contrary to popular belief, business doesn't depend on dishonesty: what generates sales and long-term owner value isn't lying, but paying attention to customers' needs and responding to them promptly, knowledgeably and helpfully. Some salesmen, of course, are blatant liars: they insist that the £2 sparkler they are peddling is a genuine diamond. But not for long . . . customers who are cheated are unlikely to return. So although the strategy must be understood in order to be effective, it can be argued that honesty is not just conventionally, but actually, the best policy.

'GOOD ETHICS IS GOOD BUSINESS'

That is because ordinarily, being ethical is good for business.[27] Although ethical conduct is, of course, not sufficient to assure business success, and business success is no guarantee of ethical conduct, distributive justice and ordinary decency typically do enhance long-term owner value. They do so in many ways, but chiefly by obviating the difficulties of operating without them. Stakeholders who doubt the good faith of the business, or of their colleagues, are more likely to spend time in protecting their backs than in performing their functions. Time, energy and resources that could be spent more productively and rewardingly are consequently diverted to basic self-preservation, with a direct opportunity cost to the business. Decent treatment, in contrast, permits and encourages stakeholders to get on with the job.

The costs of disregarding ordinary decency and distributive justice are far-reaching. In a business characterised by lying, cheating and stealing, disillusion and low morale typically replace initiative and enthusiasm; teamwork becomes difficult at best, and long-term commitments counterproductive. When exertions on behalf of the business are rejected or penalised rather than encouraged and rewarded, they are unlikely to be repeated. Distributive justice and a modicum of decency are therefore essential for the business to operate; without them, the business is unlikely to attract the best people or their best efforts. But when they are respected, the business will normally be characterised not only by responsibility and integrity, but by maximum long-term owner value.

A business seeking to be ethical must ensure that all its stakeholders treat each other with ordinary decency and distributive justice.[28] Corporate criminality and environmental disasters may grab the headlines, but it is business's ordinary, everyday conduct that matters most. The specific performance that business ethics enjoins is that of distributively just and ordinarily decent business behaviour—*all of the time, to* all those involved in the business, and *by* them all.

To perform optimally, stakeholders need to know what is expected of them, and need the assurance that they will be rewarded appropriately for doing it: in other words, they need to know that the key principle of distributive justice will be respected. Giving credit where credit is due is thus vital everywhere, not just in banks. So is loyalty, both up and down and, in respect of non-employee stakeholders, in and out. As a matter of principle employees should perform their functions in ways that serve the business end, and should put business first during business hours. But if the firm is to reap the maximum benefit from their presence, it must not only supply them with the equipment necessary to do their jobs, but also with the information and the freedom to do so: it is difficult to work in the dark or when one's hands are tied.

The well-run business should not allow its stakeholders to develop unrealistic expectations. Nor, having encouraged realistic ones, should it disappoint them: mutual support and reciprocity are essential. A supplier who goes out of his way to meet unusual specifications, and is encouraged to expand to meet a large order, should normally have the chance to bid next time round. But the responsibilities go both ways: if the quality specified has only been supplied in a fraction of the items delivered, the purchaser will in future rightly look askance and look elsewhere.

Good communications, both internal and external, are vital. A firm that allows rumours of impending reorganisation to circulate without comment is jeopardising its own future. An employee concerned about redundancy is unlikely to concentrate on the job, and a potential customer may justifiably worry about after-sales service. It may well be that the management have no good or comforting answers to offer, but the mere fact of their honestly acknowledging the existence of the problem can do wonders for morale and for productivity. Only if all the stakeholders, including employees, customers, suppliers and sources of finance, know that the firm is fair and honest and just in its dealings, can they have the confidence to deal with it openly, and to take the risks necessary to bring about improvements.

. . . even internationally

The fundamental values of distributive justice and ordinary decency apply to international as well as to domestic business, to the multinational conglomerate as well as to the small family firm. Cross-border, cross-cultural business can raise questions of business ethics: is it, for example, ethical to sell elsewhere, products that fail to meet the standards of the sophisticated home market? If the differences are those of taste, or of wealth, there is no obvious reason why not: it is a mark of the successful marketeer to vary his offerings to fulfil the needs of his customers. If the target market is too poor to afford colour televisions, it is good business, not moral condescension, to offer black-and-white sets instead.

But what about cases when the target market is genuinely less sophisticated, and the products are those that cannot be sold at home because they are considered unsafe or somehow defective? The answer then depends on a number of factors. If the danger is small, then it is a matter of tradeoffs. The car without rear seat belts that cannot be sold in Britain, may nevertheless be a positive boon in the Third World. And the lives of starving people can still be saved by food that is wholesome past its 'sell by' date.

If the products are seriously unsafe, however, then it would be wrong, and counterproductive, to sell them in *any* market. Selling a kettle that is prone to electrocute its user not only violates ordinary decency, but it is more likely to attract costly prosecutions[29] and distrust than profitable repeat business. Similarly, when the danger is such that, although not obvious, it is inescapable, then sales will continue only at everyone's peril. If the pollutants will irretrievably poison the planet, then it is not in the long-term best interest of the business to sell the product anywhere. It cannot help the business, or be right for the business, to do anything that would render the conduct of business impossible.

The short-term profits that may be available from dangerous practices or from selling dangerous goods must be weighed against both present and future consequences. Costs will likely result in the long-term, when perceptions in the target market catch up with those at home. But costs may be substantial well before then, as the home market reacts to the business's questionable practices abroad[30]. If the products are deemed dangerous, even when far away, then disapproving stakeholders are likely to vote with their feet. The business whose ethics are thought dubious anywhere at all may well find it harder to attract employees or suppliers or finance.

To sum up, business is not exempt from ordinary moral judgements; there is no separate 'business ethic'. Ethics is not the same as law, or as contractual compliance or religion, or as suffering or struggle; altruism is neither necessary nor sufficient to make an act ethical. The principles of business ethics are those enjoining the values without which business would be impossible. And those values—distributive justice and ordinary decency—apply everywhere and always.

The critical importance of distributive justice and ordinary decency will be demonstrated throughout the rest of this book. These two central concepts, and the proper understanding of business in terms of its definitive purpose, provide the key to resolving the ethical issues that arise in business.

II

RESOLVING ETHICAL
PERPLEXITIES

4

Ethical Implications

'We should state not only truth, but also the cause of the error—
for this contributes toward producing conviction, since when a
reasoned explanation is given of why the false view appears true,
this tends to produce belief in the true view.'

Aristotle[1]

The key elements of business ethics have now been
identified. To be an ethical business, an organisation must be
a business and must conduct its activities ethically. An organisation is a business if its objective is maximising long-term
owner value; a business acts ethically, if its actions are compatible with that aim and with distributive justice and ordinary decency. Taken together, these three conditions
provide the means for actually resolving substantive business
ethics issues. This chapter will illustrate just how powerful
these concepts are by addressing, and answering, a number
of general business ethics questions.

'IF IT'S GOOD FOR THE BUSINESS, CAN IT REALLY BE ETHICAL?'

Hard-headed though businessmen are supposed to be, they
are all too often perplexed and embarrassed by a very basic
question. Having struggled to present their ethical credentials, having proudly shown how they have treated their
employees fairly, and their customers honestly, and their
waste products responsibly, businessmen are nonetheless frequently stumped when the question is posed: if what the
business has done is good for the business, can it really be
ethical? They shuffle about, and examine their shoes, and

fall silent, unable to rebut the implied accusation that because the business has benefited, it and its good acts are somehow less moral.

But such moral diffidence is quite unnecessary. The answer to the question is simply, emphatically, Yes: if it's good for the business, it certainly *can* be ethical. The reason why the possibility is so often doubted, is because of a number of fundamental conceptual confusions. To untangle them, the differences between ethics and struggle, suffering, altruism and prudence have to be recalled. And the difference between acts themselves and the motives that people have for doing them needs to be examined. Finally, it is necessary to recognise that different criteria apply to the ethical evaluation of acts and those who perform them. These are necessarily abstract matters, but they are central to resolving this key ethical question.

Acts vs. Motives

A motive is that which induces someone to act. It often refers to the personal, usually emotional, satisfactions that a person may seek in pursuing the objectives that define activities[2]; a motive can also characterise the way in which definitive objectives are pursued. That which is *done*, the act that is actually achieved or accomplished, can usually be abstracted away from the doer's motive and evaluated separately. Although for the purposes of moral[3] discussion motives are often incorporated into the descriptions of actions, this is largely to facilitate judging moral agents.[4]

The same morally good act can be done from all sorts of motives. A man can, for example, save a child from drowning out of a love of children, or fear of being called a coward; he can do it because it is his job, or because it is his moral duty; he can do it out of hope for publicity or a spirit of protectiveness[5]; he can even do it to spite the child's murderous parents or to upset his rival lifeguards. Whatever the motive, however, a good act—that of saving a child's life—has been performed. That would be true even had the lifesaver been wicked and his motives thoroughly vicious: had he pulled the floundering child out of the sea only because he wanted to hold it for ransom or torture it, the child would still have been saved from drowning. Similarly, in business, morally correct acts can be undertaken for all sorts of reasons. A firm can offer equal pay for equal work in order to champion justice or undermine the unions or simply obey the law. The moral rightness of acts is perfectly compatible with the full range of motives—prudence and ruthless selfishness as well as duty and altruism.

Equally, all sorts of motives, even noble ones, can give rise to immoral acts; worthy intentions are no proof against ignorance or error or foolishness. Genuinely devoted to justice, and with the best will in the world, a jury may nonetheless send the wrong man to gaol and a manager may promote the wrong person. The moral quality of an act is not determined by the motive that inspires it.

'Ethical Acts' vs. 'Acting Ethically'

For an act or activity to be deemed ethical, all that is required is that it be the right thing to do. The judgement refers only to the thing done, to the accomplishment itself, and does not extend to the character of the person or business responsible for it. Accordingly, the assessment is independent of how or why or with what motive the act was undertaken.

Where motives and intentions are relevant, in contrast, is in connection with the conceptually separate exercise of evaluating moral characters. For an agent to be acting ethically, much more is required than mere performance of the right act. The right thing must be done, but it must be done in the right way—as an ethical agent would do it. And it must also be done for the right reasons: because it is the right thing to do. In order to be acting ethically, an agent must do the right thing freely, deliberately and characteristically.[6]

A person who performs an ethical act only out of self-interest, or just because it is required by law, will not deserve the same moral credit as the one who does the right thing *because* it is right. But 'because it is right' need only be among the agent's motives; it need not be the only one. Motives may be mixed and still be meritorious. One may be motivated to perform an act both because it is right and because it is gratifying, and deserve moral credit even so.

The question 'If it's good for the business, can it really be ethical?' can now be definitively answered. If the 'it' referred to is the act performed, then Yes, most certainly, it can be ethical. An act that is good for the business can equally well be an ethical act; 'being good for the business' does not disqualify an act from being morally worthy.

But what if the second 'it' is the business? If its acts are self-serving, if they benefit the business, can the *business* be considered ethical? Once again, the answer is a resounding Yes.

The ethical business

For what do we mean by an 'ethical business'? Ordinarily, what is wanted from business is, in fact, simply the performance of ethical acts.[7] The ethical business is normally just that business which does the right things—the one that, for example, provides fair treatment for employees, and honesty in dealings with customers. Like the lifesaving, these are outcomes whose goodness is independent of the motives with which they are performed. The fact that they were done 'for the good of the business' is therefore irrelevant: it is in virtue of their achievement, not its motivation, that the business will be deemed ethical.

Even if businesses can be understood to have intentions, not all intentions—even laudable ones—are suitable for a business. For businesses are fundamentally different from natural moral agents: business's defining purpose is very restricted, and sharply limits the ends that a business may legitimately pursue. An organisation that pursued moral goodness simply because it was good, and regardless of the consequences for long-term owner value, would simply not be acting as a business. The same prudential consideration that (as a motive) is irrelevant to assessing the morality of an act, is (as an objective) actually essential for establishing that a business is acting as a business. So getting back to the original question, the conclusion is unequivocally Yes: if it's good for the business, it certainly can be ethical. And what is more, if it's not good for the business, it normally isn't right for it either.

FIDUCIARY RESPONSIBILITY

Fiduciary responsibility is another subject that suffers from fundamental confusions. Fiduciary responsibility occurs in many areas of business. Morally, corporate directors have a fiduciary responsibility to their shareholders[8], and advisers— solicitors, accountants, merchant bankers, management and other consultants—often have a fiduciary responsibility[9] to their clients.[10] Fiduciary responsibility ordinarily arises when a client entrusts his assets or his affairs to the care of an adviser.

A fiduciary is ordinarily expected to pursue his client's best interests in the way a reasonable man would, had he the fiduciary's specific expertise. For the directors, this means ensuring that a business corporation pursues the objective of maximising long-term owner value. And for financial advisers, it normally means maximising the client's financial returns, within the terms of reference agreed.[11] Whatever the particular constraints, the essence of the fiduciary relationship is that the client expects, indeed relies upon, the adviser's taking the client's best interests[12] as his objective and criterion of action.

What determines whether the fiduciary responsibility has been fulfilled, is whether the criterion of client interest has indeed been used to govern decisions. Just as an action qualifies as a business action in virtue of the kind of arguments and evidence offered in its support, even if the outcome is disappointing, so too does an action satisfy fiduciary responsibility if the relevant decision criterion has been employed. Personal motivation is irrelevant: it does not matter whether the fiduciary's actions are prompted by a sense of professional pride, or financial self-interest, or by an altruistic wish to spite his client's rivals. So long as the operative *decision criterion* is the client's best interest, and the decisions taken could reasonably have been expected to produce the client's best interests, then the fiduciary responsibility has been duly discharged. Other, unrelated objectives, including financial objectives[13], may even be served[14] by the same action; what must be exclusive is the criterion used, not the effects caused.

While some ways of failing to achieve the shareholders' or the client's best interests do represent a failure of fiduciary responsibility, many others do not.[15] To understand why, it is useful to examine three distinct cases. In the first, the correct criterion of maximising long-term owner value or client best interest is employed and the director or adviser is genuinely expert, but the outcome is nevertheless disappointing. In the second case, the correct criterion seems to have been employed, but the director is inept or the adviser less than expert. In the third case, the wrong criterion of action is used. Although an unsatisfactory outcome is equally unsatisfactory whether caused by an honest bungler or a clever spiv, the degree to which the director or adviser is culpable nevertheless differs from case to case.

The first case is the simplest from the point of view of business ethics: it involves no unethical conduct. Markets are so complex and unpredictable that even genuine experts can misjudge them on occasion; sadly, it is possible for even the most scrupulous and sophisticated of directors and advisers legitimately and pardonably to get things wrong. When that happens, results will be disappointing, but no one will have acted unethically. And in such cases, unfortunate though the outcomes may be for the clients, the adviser or director will deserve no moral blame.

There is a difference, however, between making the odd misjudgement or mistake and being culpably ignorant or inexperienced. If the adviser or director does not understand how to apply the criterion—if he is not properly equipped, mentally or otherwise[16], to base his decisions on it—then the adviser has indeed acted unethically: it is as immoral for a director to misrepresent his abilities as it is to lie about the criterion employed. In putting himself forward as an expert, the honest adviser must have a realistic view as to what his abilities actually are. Self-deception may permit sincerity, but it is no excuse for lack of appropriate, necessary skill. When the 'expert' adviser is incompetent, he is morally at fault.

But so, possibly, is the client. For it is the client's responsibility to choose his expert: there is a sense in which *caveat emptor* applies even here. Although the client typically lacks the adviser's specific expertise, he will usually be capable of judging his probity and general competence. The client can, for example, investigate the expert's qualifications and reputation and track record; he can often seek a second opinion. A client need not be a motor mechanic to realise that an offer to transform a beat-up Mini into a brand-new Rolls is unrealistic; so, too, should he be capable of suspecting that a promise of enormous, risk-free financial returns is probably too good to be true. If the client fails to take adequate precautions in vetting and selecting his expert, then he is contributorily negligent, and shares some of the moral blame when things go wrong.

The most striking cases of business immorality are the third type, those in which the adviser or director simply employs the wrong criterion in pursuit of the wrong objective. Such cases are what most critics of financial practice take as standard. Even when this is an accurate diagnosis, however, the real immorality is seldom properly identified.

Consider an adviser who, though purporting to be seeking the best interests of his clients, instead seeks his own at their expense. What makes this sort of action unethical is not that the adviser has been greedy, or that he has served his own interests. His motives are irrelevant, and it is not inappropriate for his personal interests to be furthered[17]. Trustees often receive some remuneration for their labours, and performance-related incentives are both legitimate and sensible. What is immoral is not that the adviser's interests have been served, but that they have served as the criterion of action. In misrepresenting his objectives, in only pretending to seek the client's best interests, the adviser has lied; he has betrayed the trust that is the essential core of his fiduciary responsibility. In using anything but the client's best interests as his criterion of action, the adviser has been guilty of teleopathy, and has violated both fiduciary responsibility and ordinary decency.

CONFLICTS OF INTEREST

Part of the confusion surrounding fiduciary responsibility results from muddles concerning conflicts of interest. Business, like life in general, is full of conflicts of interest: the many parts played by one man in his time can run concurrently and sometimes incompatibly. Because conflicts of interest sometimes promote immoral action, conflicts of interest are often presumed to be intrinsically bad. But just as a business need not avoid self-interested works in order to be ethical, it need not automatically shun conflicts of interest.

A business conflict of interest is only unethical if it or its likely outcome fails to respect the business objective, distributive justice or ordinary decency. Conflicts of interest are, therefore, not necessarily wrong. Moreover, they are so very pervasive that attempts to eradicate them altogether are likely to do more harm than good: artificial barriers and rigid prohibitions are apt to impede perfectly moral and necessary business operations. The way to deal with conflicts of interest is ordinarily not to ban them, but to manage them, by being clear about which interests conflict and how they should be ranked or reconciled.

The classic model of conflict of interest occurs when an individual's own interests are pitted against those of the organisation for which he works. If, for example, the employee who is in charge of purchasing has received a substantial gift from a potential supplier, or has a family interest in a supply firm, the employee is presumed to have a conflict of interest. The worry is that the individual may allow his purchasing decision to be distorted by the favours he has received, or the profit his family could get: he has an extra, personal, incentive to do the wrong thing. While not unreasonable, that concern may nevertheless be unjustified in any particular case. Self-gratification and family feeling do not automatically overwhelm all other considerations; they are resistible, and can be subordinated to more impersonal interests. The employee may be wholly disposed to fulfil his business responsibilities with complete probity, and perfectly capable of exercising objective judgement in doing so.

Judging whether or not the conflict of interest has perverted the outcome is a straightforward matter: it requires examining the decision, not the motives of the decider. What determines whether a decision has been taken properly is not the presence of single-mindedness, or the absence of temptation, but the use of the correct decision criterion. If the appropriate procedures for obtaining competitive tenders have been followed, and the alternatives have been evaluated in accordance with the agreed standards; if those standards reflect ethical contributions to long-term owner value, and the decider is accountable for his decisions' effect in achieving that essential business end, then the fact that the decider has an interest in one of the competitors, or has accepted a gift, need pose no moral problem. So long, therefore, as all relevant interests are fully disclosed, and the business objective is properly understood and duly pursued, the existence of a potential conflict of interest need pose no actual moral difficulty.

Serious problems are more likely to arise when what is involved is not just a conflict of interest, but a conflict of obligation.[18] If the employee in charge of purchasing is a director of the family supply firm, then he has not just got an interest in furthering its aims, but a positive obligation to do so. And that duty, which ordinarily requires obtaining the highest price for goods supplied, is directly opposed to the obligation he has to his employer, to seek the lowest purchase price for those same items. Except by the greatest fluke, therefore, the two obligations cannot be satisfied simultaneously. Comparable conflicts occur in finance when, for example, two corporate finance clients are on opposite sides of the same bid; they may be rival bidders for the same target, or one client may be the target of the other. In such cases, the interests of both clients cannot simultaneously be served by the same adviser.

Even such conflicts can be managed, however, if the exclusive nature of the commitments is appreciated from the outset. The conflicts result from the broadness of the commitments given: to maximise long-term owner value, to support the client's interests. Since equally embracing commitments to other parties may be impossible to fulfil, no other such commitments should be undertaken without suitable disclosure and qualification. This does not mean that a corporate finance business must restrict itself to a single client. But unless it wants to end up with just one client, by deserting the others just when its services are most needed, it will ensure that all its clients are warned at the outset of what may happen if clients' objectives do conflict.[19] Equally, a business need not ban its employees from having outside financial interests. It should, however, require full disclosure of them as a condition of employment, and ensure that its business decisions are insulated from even the appearance of bias. Distributive justice is so important that it is sometimes not enough for it to be done: like justice itself, it must also be seen to be done.

The best way to achieve both the appearance and the reality of ethical conduct will depend on the nature of the business, the nature of the potential conflict, and the particular circumstances that obtain. Unless those remote from the decision-making process know as much about the safeguards as they do about the potential conflict, doubt may cloud even perfectly correct decisions. Accordingly, every care should be taken to ensure that standards are clear and clearly understood. In some cases, the most practical and efficient method may indeed be to eliminate the conflict by prohibiting those in particularly sensitive positions from a designated range of individual interests. Such prohibitions, are, however, a matter of prudential judgement, not ethical necessity. The moral requirement is simply to maximise long-term owner value, subject only to respecting distributive justice and ordinary decency.

Moral hazards

It is chiefly when the proper purpose of business is ignored that room arises for unethical behaviour. The conflicts that typically pose the most acute ethical problems, and cause the severest staff anxiety, are those that result from incompatible ends; for every employee at risk of being suborned by a tempting gift, there are many more who must deal with competing departmental priorities or with conflicting demands from senior management. The sales department's interest in lower prices and the engineering department's interest in leading-edge technology may both be reasonable, just incapable of being satisfied simultaneously. When, however, there is no agreed principle for reconciling such legitimate but conflicting interests, the manager charged with doing so faces a real problem. Even more distressing are the choices employees may have to make when the actual demands made on them diverge from the official ones, when the boss insists on speed though the memos require quality. Such choices can lead to much agonising, and to a costly loss of time and morale.

The key to managing such conflicts, and the more fundamental ones that can arise between managers and owners, is heeding the business purpose. When the definitive business goal is clear, and the principles of distributive justice and ordinary decency are enforced, legitimate interests can be differentiated from illegitimate ones and can be ranked. Conflicts can then be readily resolved: the right order or mix of interests is simply that which maximises long-term owner value, subject to distributive justice and ordinary decency.

Conflicts can actually be prevented, by ensuring that subordinate objectives are compatible with the main objective. The goal of the sales department should not just be sales, but profitable sales; the goal of the engineers not the most novel technology, but saleable technology. Care in framing objectives can do much to prevent instructions to employees from being or seeming contradictory. And care in setting the measures used in performance-related remuneration can help prevent the creation of a serious moral hazard.

Moral hazards exist when the rules of an institution provide a positive incentive to do the wrong thing. They typically arise in business when remuneration is based on something other than maximising long-term owner value. If bonuses are based simply on units produced, the likely outcome is high output—with correspondingly high fault levels. And when brokers are rewarded for the volume of transactions undertaken, or bankers for the numbers of new loans they book, it is not surprising that the result is churning and bad debts, and that clients suffer. But so do the businesses. The most insidious conflicts of interest, and the most inexcusable, are those that result when the firm's own incentive schemes encourage stakeholders to undermine long-term owner value.

BRIBERY

Whereas conflicts of interest can be perfectly moral, bribery is always wrong.[20] A bribe is an incentive offered to encourage someone to break the rules of the organisation he nominally represents and deliver an (unfairly) favourable outcome. Although commonly associated with governments and the Third World, bribery is a problem that can equally afflict private organisations and all locales. The defence contractor greasing the palm of the official in order to secure a government contract is guilty of bribery; so is the leisure group that gives travel agents backhanders to skew their clients' custom.

Bribery is always wrong because it violates distributive justice: by hypothesis, the benefit (the contract to do the business, the access to confidential information) is awarded in exchange for the bribe, not on the relevant merits[21] of the case. An individual or group, 'the bribed', receives the benefit of the bribe, but the organisation is expected to deliver the goods . . . typically in ways contrary to its best interests. Bribery creates a conflict of interest that necessarily results in a violation of business ethics. If the bribed individual does what he has been bribed to do, in violation of the business's interests, then he acts teleopathically. But if he does not, either because he respects the business purpose or because the bribe-induced outcome would have been the one coming about anyway, then he has taken the bribe under false pretences: he has lied. Bribes are also unethical for those who offer them, the bribers: by their very nature, they are attempts to cheat and violate ordinary decency.

Where corruption is endemic, bribery may seem unavoid-able. Even in such situations, however, the question is not whether circumstances can make bribery right: they can-not.[22] The proper question is instead whether those are appropriate markets, countries or societies in which to be attempting business. Though bribery is not involved if the local rules are duly observed, those rules may be incompati-ble with the rules of maximising long-term owner value. If the local goal is maximising family influence, or power, or prestige, then even ostensibly business transactions may well be conducted on the basis of contributions to those non-busi-ness ends. Benefits due to the business may be difficult to identify and enforce. And if what is done even *looks* like bribery, it may well, albeit unjustly, diminish both the briber's and the bribed's reputation with those who find bribery objectionable.

COMPETITION

Virtually everything that a business does can influence its competitive position. Competition is therefore a complicated matter, in which issues of business ethics often get confused with those of public policy and personal taste. Like all else that a business does, however, its competitive manoeuvres are ethical so long as they respect distributive justice and ordi-nary decency in their pursuit of maximum long-term owner value. Much competitive activity that is commonly castigated as unethical is therefore perfectly moral.

Charging what the market will bear, for example, is pre-cisely what a business should do—even if its products are life-saving drugs. Far from its being wrong to wrest maximum benefit from its products or market position, a business is obliged to do so, subject only to observing distributive justice and ordinary decency. 'Predatory' pricing that forces com-petitors out of business is also perfectly acceptable. Ordinary decency no more requires a business to be gentle with its competitors than it requires it to be charitable to its customers; all it demands is that the business avoid lying, cheating, stealing, physical violence and illegality. So long, therefore, as a pricing policy operates within those constraints, and is designed to maximise long-term owner value, it is correct: the business's obligations are to its owners, not to its competitors. Making life difficult for the competition by providing a better product or by pricing it aggressively is perfectly ethical.

What limits 'predatory' pricing and other aggressive competitive strategies is simply the definitive business goal: it is not current profits that must be maximised, but long-term owner value. The business must therefore carefully weigh the returns available from selling larger volumes at lower prices against those available from selling smaller volumes at higher prices. It must also consider that if potential customers go out of business for lack of an essential but too expensive item, or if patients die for lack of the medication they cannot afford, the universe for future sales may decrease. The business must also take into account the fact that higher margins will make the field more attractive to new entrants, whose presence may then reduce its ability to command premium prices. Finally, it must consider the extent to which public disapproval of aggressive practices might lead to stakeholder alienation, competitor litigation or official regulation; whether or not they are morally justified, such responses may nevertheless occur and undermine owner value.

The need to maximise long-term owner value also serves as a constraint on 'knocking copy' and 'hard sales'. Advertising that highlights the flaws or failures of the competition is moral so long as it is accurate. Equally, 'hard sales' can be ethical if they are merely insistent rather than coercive or deceptive. But though moral, both practices may easily be counterproductive. If more customers are repelled than attracted by what they perceive as pressure, or if their dislike of carping outweighs their appreciation of the information conveyed, then hard sales and derogatory advertising will not maximise long-term owner value, and should not be undertaken.

'Dirty tricks', in contrast, are unethical even if they increase owner value. Uses of coercion and physical violence are fundamental violations of ordinary decency. Attempts to intimidate customers away from the competition or towards the business are simply wrong; so is sabotage. Ordinary decency also rules out all stealing, including the theft of customer lists or proprietary information from competitors. Lying is equally wrong, including lying to customers about the product and the merits or demerits of the business or the competition.

PANDERING

What is a business to do if its stakeholders' values are, or are thought to be, immoral or wrong? What if racist customers refuse to deal with foreign staff, or feminist employees threaten to ostracise a male recruit? It is received wisdom that 'the customer is always right', and it can be seriously teleopathic for a business to disregard the views of its staff[23]. Is a firm therefore morally obliged to give in to the prejudices of its stakeholders? No: there is no ethical obligation for a business to accept its stakeholders' views.

First, not all stakeholders' views are of equal weight. It is the preferences of the owners that are paramount, since the business belongs to them. If the owners wish to sell propaganda to bigots, that is their right. They may not find many who are willing to join them in that endeavour—customers, employees and funding may all be in short supply and the business may, as a result, not succeed. Nevertheless, subject only to their consciences and what the law allows, determining the type and identity of a business is its owners' prerogative.

Second, a business need not, and normally should not, accept its stakeholders' views if they would undermine long-term owner value. The larger the business, and the broader its stakeholder base and aspirations, however, the more complicated the calculation becomes. It is necessary to take into account the preferences of many groups, and to estimate the distant and future reactions to current, local decisions.

Consider the English subsidiary of a major multinational

corporation: one of its production teams needs a new member. The team is well-established and close-knit, and has been notably productive. It also, incidentally, happens to be virulently anti-Irish: two of the team have lost family members in IRA terrorist attacks. If the team's strong preferences are ignored, and the Irish candidate who would otherwise be the best-qualified is hired, teamwork will suffer. So will the candidate, who is likely to be ostracised. In such circumstances, it might well seem that long-term owner value would be best served by accepting the team's prejudices. The argument for doing so would be even stronger if the team had been hired as a unit on the basis that it could remain an Irish-free zone, or if the firm had a policy that effective teams were allowed to vet and approve prospective members[24].

But the short-term advantages of not disrupting the team must be weighed against the wider negative effects. First, and most obvious, is the fact that, by hypothesis, a weaker candidate would be hired; though more readily integrated, he will nevertheless have less to contribute functionally to long-term owner value. Second, allowing prejudice to prevail may set a dangerous precedent: what if the adjacent team wants to exclude Catholic workers, or women? Third, observers may assume, however wrongly, that the team's views are shared by the firm. They may disapprove of intolerance on principle, or just fear that their own qualifications might be overridden by the prevailing prejudice. Whichever, employees elsewhere in the organisation may conclude that the firm is not the sort they wish to work for, and job-seekers that it is not one to which they should apply. Workers at the firm's Irish subsidiary are unlikely to be pleased by the team's discriminatory practices; the firm's chances of getting a development grant to build a new Irish factory will probably not be improved. And customers and suppliers of goods and sources of funds may also take offence, even if they are not themselves Irish: those in America, imbued with political correctness, may well withdraw in horror.

Given the diversity of human views, pleasing some stakeholders will often mean alienating others. The weight that should be given to each group, and specifically the importance that should be attached to the preferences of existing employees, will be a matter for careful deliberation. Distributive justice dictates that the greater a group's contribution, the more appropriate it is to please that group, subject to the owners' views being paramount. And the overall calculation of owner value must take into account the perceptions and implications of the firm's decisions as well as their immediate effects. What will happen when the decision becomes widely known within the business? In the local community? How will distant stakeholders with different values respond? What will happen if local views become more like those held elsewhere?

Finally, even if pandering to questionable tastes would maximise long-term owner value, the conditions of distributive justice and ordinary decency must also be satisfied. In a community of gangsters, murder and theft might be the accepted and the most efficient ways of maximising owner value. But they would still not be acceptable for an ethical business. Preferences that are intrinsically dishonest or unfair, coercive or illegal, should simply not be indulged.

In summary, then, understanding the purpose of business and the principles of distributive justice and ordinary decency enables problems of business ethics to be resolved quite straightforwardly. There is no reason why actions that benefit the business should not be fully ethical: motives have nothing to do with whether acts are moral. Fiduciary responsibility does not require purity of motives but applying the correct decision criterion. Bribery and 'dirty tricks' are always wrong, but competitive practices that are compatible with the business objective and ordinary decency are not. The need to respect that objective, ordinary decency and distributive justice also determine the extent to which a business should cater to stakeholder prejudices.

5

The Ethical Enterprise

Resolving Questions of Business Ethics

'. . . the solution of the difficulty is the discovery of the truth.'
Aristotle[1]

The time has now come to generalise the method of resolving business ethics issues that so effectively dispatched the problems of the last chapter. Systematised in the four straightforward steps of the Ethical Decision Model, that method can differentiate questions of business ethics from those of personal conscience and public policy, and can be used to resolve business ethics problems whenever, wherever and in whatever forms they may arise.

THE TELEOLOGICAL APPROACH TO BUSINESS ETHICS

The teleological approach to business ethics consists of recognising that it is business's distinctive purpose—maximising long-term owner value by selling goods or services—that differentiates business from all other associations and activities. In turn, that definitive goal identifies distributive justice and ordinary decency as the ethical values essential to business. Employing the teleological approach makes it clear that a great many of the problems that are supposed to afflict business are not problems of business ethics at all, and makes it possible to resolve those that are.

One of the commonest and most fundamental sources of wrongdoing consists of simply getting the ends wrong: an association that fails to be a business cannot be an ethical business. Teleopathic activity occurs whenever an organisation that is intended to be a business pursues non-business ends, or pursues business ends in ways that are routinely incomplete or incompetent[2]. Teleopathy is usually deceptive: an association that claims to be a business, but seeks something other than maximum long-term owner value, is trading under false pretences. Even when it is done openly, teleopathic action is wrong simply because it is directed to some end other than the business's intended goal; it represents choosing the wrong end, or pursuing the right end in the wrong way. Insofar as other ends utilise any business resources, even staff time or attention, they interfere with maximising long-term owner value, and thus are incompatible with the proper purpose of business.

To assert that an objective is unsuitable for business, or for an individual in his business capacity, is not to deny that objective's importance. Those other ends may be perfectly legitimate, even worthy, for individuals in their private capacities or for other sorts of organisations. Similarly, to deny that a problem is a matter of business ethics is not to deny that the problem is significant: it is simply to locate the problem in a more appropriate context, where it is more likely to be answerable. When a child wonders how giraffes manipulate their trunks, it is normally more productive to explain that it is elephants who have trunks, than to explore methods of animal baggage handling.

Many of the problems that seem most perplexing for business ethics are difficult precisely because they extend far beyond the realm of business: the problem of evil, for example, and the problem of injustice, the questions of why one should be ethical and how one can be moral in an immoral society. Such problems are vitally important, and need to be addressed, but both their sources and their solutions lie outside the confines of business ethics. The problems being addressed here are instead those narrower ethical concerns that arise for business as business.

THE ETHICAL DECISION MODEL

Those central issues of business ethics—what constitutes ethical conduct for business—respond readily to the teleological approach. However complex and varied actual businesses may be, determining whether the right end is being sought, and whether distributive justice and ordinary decency are being respected, can do much to untangle ethical perplexities and identify what course of action is morally right. So useful, indeed, is the teleological approach, that it can be generalised into an Ethical Decision Model, a schematic framework that can be used to tackle any ethical issue in business.

Applying principles in the form of a decision model is, of course, no substitute for moral or business leadership: morally right decisions still have to be implemented, and change is never easy. The Ethical Decision Model does not preclude the need for exercising careful judgement or for taking the full circumstances of actual situations into account; the Model can neither eradicate moral problems nor eliminate the need to make hard decisions.

What the Ethical Decision Model can do, is identify which problems businessmen in their business capacities actually need to address, and offer a way to resolve them. The Model indicates what information is relevant to ethical decision-making; it organises that information so that it will be more productive in leading to a decision; and it specifies the ethical principles to be employed in deciding what is right. The Model introduces conceptual clarity and structure to matters that are too often clouded by emotion and moral fervour. It thereby provides a way of managing and resolving ethical problems in business.

To make the Model as clear as possible, steps that are often combined in practice have been set out separately below, and illustrated briefly with examples drawn from the multi-faceted problems of business and the environment. The use of the Model is exhibited in greater detail in Chapters 6, 7 and 8, where it is employed to resolve problems of, respectively, personnel, finance and corporate governance.

Step 1: Clarify the question

The critically important first step in tackling all problems of business ethics is clarifying exactly what is at issue. In the forms in which they are commonly posed—by the media, by demanding interest groups, by disgruntled stakeholders— ethical questions often seem perplexing, either trivial or intractable. One reason why the answers frequently seem so elusive is because, in many cases, the questions themselves are fatally flawed. Like 'When did you stop beating your wife?', many questions of business ethics need to be unpacked before they can be sensibly answered.

Consider, for example, questions of how business is to stop shirking its responsibilities, whether those responsibilities are deemed to be towards poor workers or the underfunded arts or threatened species. Such questions are directly comparable to 'When did you stop beating your wife?' They cannot be answered directly, because any direct reply—that one hasn't stopped beating one's wife, or isn't going to stop shirking one's responsibilities—appears to validate the questions' central (false) presumptions: that the respondent is a wife-beater, that business is actually irresponsible. The correct way to respond to such questions is instead to correct their false assumptions: to assert firmly that one has never beaten one's wife (or that one has no wife), and that business's responsibility is to maximise long-term owner value.

Even when business ethics questions do not exhibit such logical defects, they must still be examined critically before they can be properly answered: as they are posed in the abstract, ethical questions tend to comprise not one but many intermingled issues. To deal with moral issues productively, it is essential to identify which of a number of possibly related difficulties is the one that is actually at stake—for this business, at this time. Consider the media favourite, 'What should business do about the environment?' As stated, the question potentially raises any number of issues—of public policy, power politics and science as much as of morality. The popular dispute may, indeed, not even be about the environment at all, but about technology or growth or free trade. Such questions are interesting and important, but they are not questions of business ethics. Failure to recognise the specific matter at issue is a major source of confusion in resolving ethical questions, both in business and elsewhere.

Broad rhetorical questions must therefore be analysed to determine exactly what is being asked. A useful start can sometimes be made by considering what the solutions are assumed to be. If, for example, as is often the case with respect to environmental issues, the alternatives are different forms of regulation, then the issues are ones of political philosophy and public policy, not business ethics. The questions that actual businesses need to resolve are normally very limited and specific ones, which must be considered with a view to practical action. Though obscured in the general form, the environmental questions 'Which solvent/cleaner/paper should we use?' and 'What should we do with by-products?' are not only more directly relevant to real businesses and much easier to answer, but may well not give rise to any particular ethical perplexity.

The first step, then, in addressing any question of business ethics, is simply to identify what is actually being asked. And that may be made clearer by determining: Who is asking? What has prompted the issue? What precisely is at stake? Who will be affected by the outcome? What sort of decision or action might be called for? Why are there differing views? Over what period—short, medium or long-term—is the decision to apply? Who is responsible for taking, implementing, reviewing the decision? How long is available for making it? What objective is being sought?

Step 2: Determine its relevance for this *business*

Having analysed the question, the second step is to determine whether it actually is a problem for this business; if it isn't, then there is no business ethics issue for this business to resolve. Questions about business conduct often come from outside of business, and are presented in forms that are remote from business concerns. Addressing such abstract questions can be a worthwhile activity, but it is seldom one appropriate for business: pontificating and philosophising normally add little to owner value[3]. To avoid wasting business time and resources on non-business concerns, it is therefore important to confirm that the ethical point at issue is genuinely a problem for this business.

That inquiry has three parts: Is the issue relevant to *business*? Is it relevant to *this* business? Is it a *problem* for this business? The first question is the most basic: does the issue relate to maximising long-term owner value? Unless it does, there is no business concern at issue, and nothing to be evaluated in terms of distributive justice and ordinary decency. Avoiding teleopathy is the primary, and often the most stringent, condition of business ethics. Only when an organisation is seeking to maximise long-term owner value is it a business; only then can distributive justice and ordinary decency be invoked as ethical constraints on business activity.

When, therefore, questions arise as to how or in what way business should pursue such goals as social welfare, environmental activism or personal development—or indeed any objective other than maximising long-term owner value—the way to handle them is clear. The proper response is not to agonise over the proposals' comparative ethical merits or their individual moral worth. The right response is instead to point out that such activities are not legitimate for business as business. They properly engage business attention only if, and then only to the extent that, they can contribute to maximising long-term owner value: insofar as they help the business to attract useful stakeholders, for example, or reduce the threat of regulation. Otherwise, they should be strictly avoided. Many activities that are commonly recommended for business, indeed endorsed as business's 'social responsibility', fail this fundamental test. They are in fact teleopathic, and should simply be rejected outright: business fulfils its responsibilities in scrupulously avoiding such ends, not in pursuing them.

If an issue is relevant to business, however, the question still arises as to whether it actually is an issue for any particular firm. Purely domestic English businesses seldom face problems of Third World bribery. And environmentally, machine tool manufacturers usually have no more need to consider the saving of species than London launderettes have to deal with nuclear waste. Bribery, species diversity and atomic debris raise important questions of ethics and public policy, but unless they directly relate to a particular business's maximising of long-term owner value, they can be dismissed by that business.

Even if a concern is relevant to a particular firm, it remains to be determined whether it represents a problem. The matter may, for example, be easily soluble through the application of ordinary business criteria. If even on the most ruthless assumptions a potential takeover or a proposed pipeline is unlikely to increase long-term owner value, there is no need for the business to ponder the ethics of asset stripping or toxic spills; if recycled paper is cheaper and of the same or better quality, its use is prescribed on straightforward economic grounds. Equally, the ethical issue may not be problematical simply because it is subject to legal or regulatory constraints. Food companies in the UK need not agonise about whether to list ingredients on their product labels, because ingredients lists are required by British (and EU) regulation.

Step 3: Identify the circumstantial constraints

Once the question has been established, the next step is to identify the constraints that may limit solutions. Business decisions are constrained not only by law and regulation, but also by contractual, cultural, economic, physical and technical considerations. Even though the principles of ethical conduct are constant over time and place and industry, what businesses actually can do is crucially affected by their individual circumstances.

Contractual commitments represent a fundamental constraint on business conduct. Contracts, like laws, should never be broken lightly. Indeed, so critically important is trust to business, that business should normally respect legitimate[4] expectations whether they are based on formal contracts or promises or less stringent forms of unwritten understanding. If, therefore, the business has contractually committed to buying certain components for its products, it cannot unilaterally switch to a 'greener' alternative: that a substitute may be cleaner or less wasteful is no excuse for reneging on an agreement with a supplier. Similarly, if a business has undertaken to maintain 'smoke-free' zones for its employees, it must normally honour that commitment, even if implementing it requires incurring greater expense than anticipated.

Business conduct is also constrained by the culture of the firm and the larger community in which it operates: both may have a significant effect on what will in fact maximise long-term owner value. Rigid rules may be counterproductive for entrepreneurial firms; individual responsibility may be hard to implement in bureaucratic organisations. A small business, dependent on the patronage of a local community, may find that the acceptance of local tastes is a fundamental condition of survival.[5] Even large, cosmopolitan businesses cannot ignore cultural norms: as greenery has become an increasingly popular concern, even firms with no natural sympathy for the cause have found it necessary to establish their viridity.[6]

In addition, the classic business constraints of cost, availability and physical capability must always be taken into account, even in the context of ethical decision-making. There is no point in choosing a greener product if it cannot perform the required function, is too large to fit the allotted space, or cannot be supplied on time. The limitations of the physical world and of human nature do not disappear just because the issue in question is perceived to be ethical.

Step 4: Assess the available options

The next step is to see how alternative solutions measure up against the three key conditions of maximising long-term owner value and respecting distributive justice and ordinary decency.

Assessing a proposal's potential effect on long-term owner

value is a straightforward business calculation, which differs from estimates of profitability over time only in employing the sounder criterion of long-term owner value. All the potential costs and consequences, including those that are distant and delayed and indirect, must be weighed against all the potential benefits.

In making environmental choices, for example, the possibly greater initial costs of a green alternative must be weighed against the expected long-term gains; conversely, the instant gratification of seeming green must be weighed against the continuing costs. Although cleanliness and conservation are not in themselves suitable objectives for business, selling tuna caught by dolphin-friendly methods may well increase long-term owner value if it attracts dolphin-friendly stakeholders. And some ways of being green contribute directly to owner value: eliminating waste and saving energy normally save money.

A business that introduces its own environmental policies may enjoy other indirect benefits. It may be able to avert or influence proposed regulation, and make it less onerous and costly. It may be able to introduce changes at its own pace, and avoid the need to respond hastily and expensively to externally imposed requirements. It may get a head start on providing the sort of environmentally-friendly products or services that may later be required, and thereby improve its potential market share. Being seen to be green may also help the business by making it easier to attract those productive employees who favour greenery, and to obtain official permits. Finally, it may make finance more readily available, both from green investors and from the bank lenders who are increasingly being held liable for the costs of environmental depredations associated with their borrowers[7].

Once a proposal's likely effects on long-term owner value have been assessed, the next stage in ethical decision-making is to judge the proposal against the other two conditions of ethical business conduct: distributive justice and ordinary decency. Unlike assessments of owner value, the judgements of distributive justice and ordinary decency that a business must make are not normally ones of degree or extent[8]. Alternatives either do, or do not, satisfy the conditions; those that do not are not ethical for the business.

Distributive justice is respected when business rewards are bestowed on those who actually contribute to achieving the business end, and the levels of reward are proportional to their contributions. Since distributive justice is chiefly concerned with the allotment of rewards, not all aspects of business life involve considerations of distributive justice. Many explicitly environmental questions—how much packaging to use, for example—do not. When, however, pay and honours and responsibilities are being allocated, distributive justice must govern their distribution if the business is to be ethical. The bonus for energy-saving should therefore go to the energy-saving suggestion that contributes most to long-term owner value, not to the one that saves more energy at the expense of owner value. Similarly, the job should be given not to the greenest applicant, but to the candidate whose overall skills, aptitudes and character seem likely to contribute most to achieving the definitive business purpose.

Ordinary decency imposes even broader restrictions. When considering alternative courses of action, the business must determine if they are fair and honest, and if they involve any form of lying, cheating, stealing, coercion or physical violence. A course of action that violates any of the requirements of ordinary decency should simply be rejected, even if it might increase profitability. Ordinary decency thus obviously rules out kidnapping the competition, and killing complaining customers. Equally, it excludes reneging on agreements, and stealing a competitor's formula or a subordinate's glory; it precludes lying about the extent of environmental benefits or dangers, and cheating on specifications, and punishing scapegoats.

Conclusion: The right course of action

Once the relevant question and the operative constraints have been identified, and alternative proposals have been assessed, the ethical answer should be clear. The business should choose that alternative which is likely to contribute most to long-term owner value, so long as it satisfies distributive justice and ordinary decency. If either of those conditions is not met, then even if the proposal appears to maximise long-term owner value, it should not be adopted. Equally, satisfying distributive justice and ordinary decency is not enough: the purpose of business is not pursuing distributive justice and ordinary decency, but maximising long-term owner value. The morally right course of action for the business must satisfy all three conditions: it is that which aims at maximising long-term owner value *while* respecting distributive justice and ordinary decency.

In presenting the Ethical Decision Model, an attempt has been made to break the ethical decision-making process into discrete and sequential steps. In practice, however, unethical alternatives are eliminated most efficiently when the criterion that is expected to be the most difficult to satisfy is considered first. Given the widespread misunderstanding of business, substantial progress in resolving questions of business ethics can often be made just by identifying and eliminating teleopathic objectives. Once those have been dispatched, and the real question clarified, the number of true business alternatives to be evaluated tends to be manageably few. Screening them for distributive justice and ordinary decency is then comparatively straightforward.

The relative importance of the three conditions in analysing questions of business ethics depends on the particular problem being addressed. Some issues, like those of remuneration, involve considerations primarily of distributive justice; others, like advertising, involve issues mainly of ordinary decency. Ultimately, however, most do involve both. Moreover, the hardest part of ethical decision-making typically is not applying the principles of distributive justice and ordinary decency, but determining which action will actually maximise long-term owner value. But however difficult it may be to project outcomes, estimating long-term owner value cannot be avoided: it is the core not just of ethical decision-making, but of business as such.

Costing ethical choices, however, poses no particular problem[9]: with the Ethical Decision Model, it is not necessary to calculate the benefits of honesty or fairness or distributive justice. The need to respect distributive justice and ordinary decency is not the outcome of a cost/benefit analysis; it is a condition of being ethical. Moreover, whether an action accords with distributive justice and ordinary decency is largely a function of the concepts involved.

Employing the Ethical Decision Model permits any number of standard business ethics issues to be resolved quite readily. Should a business contribute to charity? Should it sponsor artistic extravaganzas? Should it slow down global warming? In each case the answer is simply No; not unless, and then only to the extent to which, the proposed activity helps to maximise long-term owner value. Does the head of personnel want to be generous to the employees? Fine—so long as his generosity enhances their productivity, or the company's image, or its ability to attract the best staff, and the rewards are proportional to contributions. But does the business have a responsibility to save the whale? No: managers' duty is to maximise long-term owner value, not to protect species diversity.

Stakeholders, be they employees, customers or neighbours, have no right to expect the business to be seeking anything but long-term owner value. A supplier offering shoddy goods must expect rejection, not charity; a customer who wants to help the unemployable should not expect the business to put them on its payroll. Nevertheless, given the importance of well-disposed stakeholders to maximising long-term owner value, only a seriously short-sighted business will ignore stakeholder interests. Properly employed, the Ethical Decision Model not only permits supposedly difficult problems of business ethics to be resolved quite straightforwardly, but also shows why ethical behaviour by all stakeholders is essential in everyday business dealings.

Why, then, is ethics perceived to pose such difficult problems for business? The answer is partly that identifying the right course of action is only the first step: it must still be implemented, and change is often hard to achieve. The main reason, however, is simply that business's obligation to maximise long-term owner value is often forgotten or ignored or resisted. When that happens, the business's refusal to pursue some ostensibly 'moral' but non-business end may be seen as a commitment to immorality, and its business goals seen as an impediment to doing the 'moral' thing. But, in fact, quite the reverse is true: in focusing on the limited end of maximising long-term owner value, the business is not being immoral, but true to its proper purpose.

This needs to be kept very clearly in mind with respect to environmental issues. There may well be those who protest that the teleological approach somehow misses the point, that the really *moral* issue is precisely the extent to which environmental concerns should supersede business ones. That is indeed a serious moral question, and one that cannot be ignored by individuals or polities. But the issue it raises is the very fundamental one of ranking business against other human goals; as such it is necessarily outside the realm of business and business ethics. Expressing their own views, owners who value greenery may, of course, specify that their firms pursue explicitly environmental objectives independent of their effect on owner value. To the extent that the firms do so, however, they will simply not be operating as businesses.

If the challenger protests again, and asks to what extent a *business* should increase its costs to achieve green objectives, the answer has already been given. Business should pursue green objectives only insofar as they help maximise long-term owner value, subject to respecting distributive justice and ordinary decency: business as business has no moral obligation (or right) to do anything else. But even this may not satisfy the questioner. It may be that the real question troubling him is a more general one: if the business's environmental acts benefit the business, can they really be ethical? But that question has already been answered, and answered positively: there is no reason why not.

The rest of this book will use the Ethical Decision Model to analyse key issues of business ethics. The focus will be on those issues that potentially affect all businesses, be they retailers or manufacturers, purveyors of goods or services. Accordingly, the next two chapters will address some basic issues of personnel and finance.

6

Personnel

'. . . in the area of remuneration it is the avoidance of unfairness which is the most important single factor. . . .'[1]
  'It is certain that every individual not only expects, but should be entitled to, a reward that recognizes his contributions.'[2]

Sir John Harvey-Jones

'The worst crime against the working people is a company that fails to make a profit.'

Samuel Gompers[3]

INTRODUCTION

One of the most revealing indicators of an organisation's ethical character is the way it customarily treats its staff[4]. The fashion in which a business deals with its secretaries and its supervisors can be as important as the way it deals with its suppliers or its bankers; employees ordinarily affect both the product and relations with customers. Accordingly, their expectations and preferences cannot be ignored. Treating employees ethically is not an optional extra, but an essential ingredient in maximising long-term owner value.

Recognising the importance of treating employees ethically does not, however, mean that the business should be 'soft'. Nor should it put its employees first: a business should no more be run for the benefit of its employees[5] than for the benefit of its bankers. Being ethical does not mean giving in to muddled thinking or pandering to the absurd demands that so often beset discussions of personnel matters. Specifically, despite widespread notions to the contrary, it is not the role of business to give meaning to the lives of its employees or to provide social welfare or full employment; business is not a substitute for family or community, the church or the state.

Treating employees ethically simply means treating them with ordinary decency and distributive justice. The ethical business rewards contributions to the business objective, and is honest and fair to its staff; it avoids lying, cheating and stealing, coercion, physical violence, and illegality. And crucially, since trust is so dependent on expectations, the ethical business is extremely careful about the expectations it engenders. Neither by action nor by omission does it encourage its employees to have inappropriate expectations concerning the business. Conversely, having encouraged realistic expectations, the ethical business does not disappoint them without good reason and explanation. Finally, the ethical business rightly demands comparable treatment from its employees: the need for ethical conduct is reciprocal.

Businesses are, however, not free to operate unconstrained by law and regulation. The restrictions that apply to personnel matters are many, and vary widely across geographical jurisdictions. Although these restrictions will normally be observed by the ethical business, it is nonetheless important to distinguish clearly between the requirements of the legal and those of the moral. Throughout this book, the focus will be exclusively on the universal requirements of ethics, not the local requirements of law.

Motivation

It is equally important to differentiate the ethical from the psychological: maximising owner value is part of the definition of business, not a principle of human motivation. Given the diversity of human values and objectives, expectations and experience, what actually motivates employees can vary enormously. Depending on the group involved, financial gain may actually be a less effective incentive than job satisfaction, job excitement or departmental rivalry, providing customer service or producing quality products.

In motivating its staff a business may use whatever works,

subject only to respecting distributive justice and ordinary decency. Ordinarily, the demands of motivation are compatible with those of ethical conduct. Indeed, academic studies have shown that staff tend to be 'de-motivated'[6] when they are treated unfairly, and when rewards are disassociated from achievements. But even if particular stakeholders were more effectively motivated by unethical incentives, the ethical business would be bound not to use them.

Consultation

The ethical problems of businesses always arise in the context of particular situations, which must be addressed in all their actual complexity. The questions that businesses must confront are not 'What shall be done to help the handicapped?' or 'How should old people be treated?', but 'Which of these accountants, one of whom happens to be in a wheelchair, shall we hire?' and 'What sort of pension scheme should we arrange for our local line managers?' In considering the ethical issues that concern personnel, it is therefore vital to take into account the specific circumstances of a business and its staff.

The need to deal with issues in all their particularity does not, however, mean that 'consultation' with employees is essential: consultation is justified only insofar as it helps to maximise long-term owner value. It is not necessary for a business to have workers' councils, or to hold opinion polls or to give employees votes, in order for the business to be ethical.[7] Indeed, far from being necessary, consultation as it is typically understood is often neither ethical nor productive.

Why, then, is consultation so widely regarded as a moral necessity? One of the standard justifications for consultation is its supposed contribution to productivity[8]. The very act of being asked, it is alleged, makes employees feel important to the business: by helping to engage their interest and intelligence, consultation *per se* increases worker productivity. And this 'Hawthorne effect'[9] has been supported by some famous academic studies.

Other academic studies, however, have concluded quite the reverse: consultation can seriously reduce productivity.[10] And this is scarcely surprising.[11] The act of consultation may waste time that would otherwise be devoted to more directly useful activities. Or the suggestions garnered may be misguided or impractical. Furthermore, when those consulted have little to contribute outside of the areas of their specific expertise, seeking their views will be both subversive of sound practice and deeply counterproductive. To ask cleaners for their opinions on financial technicalities would normally be both foolish and patronising. And to let them determine corporate strategy, would be for the board of directors to abdicate a primary responsibility.

It can, however, be eminently sensible to seek factory workers' recommendations concerning the organisation of the factory. Those closest to a situation may well have useful views as to how it might be improved: they may be able to spot and correct difficulties not even suspected by managers attempting to supervise from a distance. Moreover it is reasonable and prudent to solicit workers' opinions on how changes affecting them might be structured. Often the most efficient way to get information on how to achieve a desired result, and the most effective way to secure willing cooperation in bringing it about, is just to ask.

The degree to which consultation will improve productivity or morale or motivation depends on the circumstances of the specific case. The nature of the business, the character and attitudes and expectations of the employees, the sensitivity of the management, the responsibility of the directors—all are factors in determining the value of any proposed consultation. Assessing that value is important, because as it is ordinarily understood, consultation is only justifiable in terms of its contribution to maximising long-term owner value. No institutionalised form of 'employee involvement' is required by either distributive justice or ordinary decency.

There is, however, a genuine ethical requirement that is closely related to and easily confused with consultation. Maximising long-term owner value normally requires that a business base its decisions and its actions on the best information it can obtain within realistic time and cost constraints. In doing so, it cannot ignore any source of information, particularly one as potentially valuable as its employees. Failing to take offered information into account is morally wrong: it is ordinarily teleopathic, and violates both distributive justice and ordinary decency.[12]

Distributive justice demands that an organisation recognise contributions made to its objectives. It therefore requires that contributions in the form of information supplied or suggestions proffered be duly acknowledged. The business may simply receive the suggestion with thanks, or it may implement it—preferably also with thanks—or it may give some sort of special payment or award; the form of acknowledgement appropriate will be a function of the specific firm and the employees involved. The business might even reject the suggestion: however constructive and useful a proposal might seem, there may be good business reasons why it cannot be implemented. To use the idea but to deny its source, however, would be both unjust and dishonest. Giving credit where credit is due is required by both distributive justice and by ordinary decency. Similarly, simply to ignore the suggestion would be to do justice neither to its proposer nor to the business.

Ignoring employee suggestions can give seriously teleopathic signals. If a sensible suggestion is simply ignored, as opposed to rejected with good reason, the employee who made the suggestion will be justified in doubting the good faith and good sense of those in charge. His doubts will be even more justified if the suggestion is rejected for the wrong reason—because the boss did not think of it himself, or because it came from the shop floor rather than the expensive management consultant, or because the more efficient methods proposed would reduce the boss's power. In such cases, the employee will correctly conclude that his best efforts are not really wanted, and that, whatever might be said, the firm's true goal is something other than maximising long-term owner value.

And that is why, despite expensive efforts, most

'consultation' is at best counterproductive: it is because it is fundamentally dishonest. When employees' suggestions are sought but are then ignored or scorned or stolen, employees' natural response is to become disillusioned; they respond to management hypocrisy with a wholly justified cynicism. Regardless of whether it is called worker participation or employee involvement or 'empowerment', consultation will not produce trust or long-term owner value unless it is realistic . . . and real. It is therefore best confined to areas where it can be.

Employee 'rights'

But don't employees have a moral right to be consulted? Absolutely not. The only rights that employees have *as employees* are those that are specifically conferred on them by law or contract. In their capacity as employees, they have no special moral rights.

Moral or natural rights[13] are those that arise from, and depend for their justification on, the nature of man: they pertain to human beings in their capacity as moral agents. Logically, therefore, they are not a function of any particular social, historical or economic sub-category. Although the people who are employees enjoy the same natural rights as everyone else, they have no extra moral rights *as* employees. Specifically, they have no special moral rights to a particular wage or a particular job, to collective bargaining or to union representation, to job security or organisational information or privacy.

To understand why this is so, it is important to distinguish the concept of *having a right* to something, from the quite separate notion of that thing's *being right*. A thing can be right in a variety of different ways: it can be morally correct or socially acceptable, it can be best suited to accomplish a stated objective, it can be in accordance with the rules of a practice. To have a right, in contrast, is to have a justified claim, an (enforceable) entitlement. Americans, for example, have a right not to have their freedom of speech limited by the US[14] government. Such genuine rights are, however,

extremely rare: most things that are correct nevertheless confer no entitlements. It is (morally) right to do one's best, but
one nevertheless has no right to demand that people do so.

What connects the two concepts of right, is the notion of a
qualifying condition. When membership of a category is con-
ditional upon achieving a stipulated standard, one is normally entitled to assume that members of that category will
meet that standard: one has a (logical) right to expect it. If it
is necessary to have passed certain medical exams to qualify
as a doctor, one is right, and one has a logical right, to expect
that someone who practises as a doctor will have passed those
exams.

Similarly, since only organisations whose goal is maximising long-term owner value by selling goods or services qualify
as businesses, one has a right to expect that businesses will be
seeking to maximise long-term owner value. And since to be
an ethical business it is necessary to respect distributive justice and ordinary decency, one also has a right to expect distributively just and ordinarily decent conduct from business
organisations that purport to be ethical.

It is in this very limited sense that rights other than those
conferred by law or contract might be said to exist against
business. The sense is limited, because if the 'right' is violated, all that happens is that the organisation disqualifies
itself from being deemed ethical.[15] Even these limited logical
rights, however, are not *employee* rights: they are a function of
the concepts involved, and apply as well to other stakeholders. So in their capacity as employees, employees have no special moral rights—to consultation, or anything else.

The general notions of motivation, consultation and
employee rights having been clarified, it is now appropriate
to examine in detail a variety of specific ethical issues that
commonly arise in connection with the personnel function.
The rest of this chapter will therefore be devoted to applying
the Ethical Decision Model to sorting out ethical ways of dealing with hiring and firing and remunerating.

HIRING

The Principle of Ethical Selection

The central issue in hiring is choosing who should be hired. Fortunately, understanding that business has a defining purpose makes the correct principle of selection very clear: the business should hire that candidate who is expected to contribute most to its purpose of maximising long-term owner value. This principle of selection applies very widely: it indicates who should be hired and who promoted, who should get a rise and (negatively) who should be fired; it even indicates which supplier should be chosen and which procedures should be implemented. Since the principle awards the job or the contract to the candidate whose contribution to maximising long-term owner value is expected to be greatest, it automatically satisfies distributive justice. In order to be ethical, therefore, selection in accordance with the principle simply needs to be implemented with ordinary decency: honestly, fairly, non-coercively and legally. The business should therefore not lie about the requirements or the benefits of the job, it should apply the same criteria to all candidates for a given post, and it should not illegally or forcibly exclude anyone from competing.

In applying the principle, it is, of course, important to recognise that contributions may be made in all sorts of different ways. Despite their mutual chagrin at acknowledging the fact, the marketing man's contacts may be as valuable to the business as the technician's scientific expertise. As a result, assessing potential contributions to long-term owner value may in fact be a complicated process. Even when choosing between candidates for the same job, it is necessary to take into account the nature of the particular post to be filled, the different ways in which various candidates might fulfil it, their potential for progressing to fill other roles in the firm, the ways in which they are likely to fit in with existing and future staff, etc. But however complex that assessment may be in practice, the principle of ethical selection is clear and straightforward: the right person to hire is the one expected to make the greatest contribution to long-term owner value.

This fundamental principle has direct implications for personnel practice. The first is that, contrary to custom[16], the task of the recruiter[17] is not just to eliminate the wrong candidates, but positively to select the right ones. It is, of course, important not to make mistakes in hiring. Creating a body of unsuitable or disaffected employees wastes both the firm's resources and the lives of those unwisely recruited. It fails to fill the job properly, and may embitter the recruits who are wrong for the job; having dissatisfied staff is bad both for present business and for future prospects. Nevertheless, avoiding risk is only part of the recruitment task. To achieve the business purpose, it is necessary not just to make the safe choice, the one that minimises risk: it is vital to make the right choice, the one that positively maximises long-term owner value.

This does not mean, however, that the business must scour the globe to find the ideal candidate. The hiring question facing the business is not the general one, 'Who, in all the world, is the absolutely best candidate for this job?' The proper question, the one that requires an ethical response, is simply, 'Which of these actual applicants should we choose?' When, as is often the case, there are many candidates who would be capable of making substantially the same contribution to long-term owner value, the business is correct to choose from among those who are readily accessible. Conducting a more comprehensive search would only be justified if the contribution expected from the elusive, ideal recruit were to exceed the costs of the search.

A second major implication of the principle of selection, is that many of the considerations that are commonly assumed to be essential to ethical recruitment are either beside the point, or else are related to ethical conduct in ways other than are normally supposed.

Discrimination

Consider discrimination, for example. The prevention of discrimination is a cornerstone of most employment law: the US, the UK and the EU have extensive regulations prohibiting discrimination of various sorts. Far from being inimical to ethical recruitment, however, discrimination is absolutely essential to it: a business must carefully discriminate (i.e., observe the distinction) between that applicant who is most likely to maximise long-term owner value and all the others.

To be ethical, however, discrimination must be on the basis of *relevant* considerations, those that relate to the applicant's ability to maximise long-term owner value. Discriminating on the basis of other considerations is immoral. But it is not immoral because it violates any moral rights of the applicants—the applicants, as such, have no special rights against the business. It is immoral because, by wasting the business's resources and opportunities, or by supporting some end other than long-term owner value, it is fundamentally teleopathic. What is unethical is not discrimination as such, but teleopathic prejudice, that which excludes candidates on the basis of considerations extraneous to their likely contributions to maximising long-term owner value.

Which features are relevant to maximising long-term owner value? Amongst the factors that will always be relevant are the functional abilities or qualities that are directly necessary to perform the job in question: the ability to drive for a chauffeur, the ability to sell for a salesman, the ability to listen attentively and analytically for an interviewer. Such job-related characteristics may, of course, include those that relate to the candidate's personality and character: a supermarket cashier should not only be able to operate the cash register, but should also be honest and able to deal with customers.

Functional abilities and qualities are usually independent of age, sex, religion, ethnic origin, hair colour, sexual orientation, family connections, social background and smoking habits. And to the extent that they are unrelated, such circumstantial considerations should be ignored. The business that does not ignore them will normally fail to maximise long-term owner value, because it will artificially limit the universe of candidates from which to make its selection. The firm will either fail to recognise the best candidates, because they happen to belong to an excluded group, or it will increase its costs, by demanding that all its candidates come from a smaller source of supply. With population densities shifting away from the traditionally most favoured category—young white men—a business that fails to tap other categories is likely to lose out.

Moreover, if an organisation only hires, or always excludes, applicants from a particular religious group or ethnic background or social class, it thereby redefines itself as a club. It may be a commercially successful club, but since by hypothesis its decision criterion is something other than simply maximising long-term owner value, it is not, and cannot be, a business. Similarly, an association that hires the disabled simply because they are disabled, and regardless of their job-related abilities, may well perform a useful social role, but it is not the role of a business.

Does this mean that circumstantial characteristics can never be relevant, that it is always wrong to eliminate candidates automatically just because they are a member of some category? Of course not. Sometimes circumstantial characteristics are necessarily associated with the functional qualities that are sought. Men, for example, lack the essential equipment to be wet nurses, and women to be sperm sources, and they do so simply because of what they are: it is not necessary to interview applicants individually to make sure that they cannot do the job. Sometimes what looks like a circumstantial characteristic may, because of the nature of the job, actually be functional. Being a particular shape and size is irrelevant to fulfilling most jobs, but it is essential for being a fashion model. And sometimes circumstantial characteristics may directly affect long-term owner value: being HIV-positive or overweight, for example, may give rise to unacceptably high private health insurance costs.

It can also be entirely appropriate to reject candidates simply because they are members of certain religious or affinity groups, if their creeds prevent them from doing that which is necessary for the job. Committed sabbatarians, for example, can automatically be rejected for jobs that require work to be done on their holy days. Conversely, conforming to a religious or other practice may be a legitimate requirement for filling a position: a cook in a vegetarian restaurant must do without meat on the job.

Whether a particular circumstantial characteristic is relevant to maximising long-term owner value is determined in part by the business's circumstances. Since long-term owner value is normally maximised when a firm makes itself and its products attractive to potential customers and other stakeholders, the conventions of the industry, the market and the community must normally be taken into account. The business will, therefore, ordinarily reflect stakeholder preferences and prevailing values in its choice of personnel, subject to those preferences being compatible with distributive justice and ordinary decency. When targeting the teenage market, a business may well find it useful to feature adolescents in its advertisements and to employ youthful counter staff in its retail outlets. Those same workers, however, might be counterproductive in marketing fashions for the elderly. Similarly, a regional or class accent that may attract some customers, may easily repel others. Circumstantial characteristics can legitimately be considered when they affect maximising long-term owner value.

But they should not be when they simply constitute pandering to management prejudices. Is pandering really a problem? Yes, though in ways not often suspected. One common kind of pandering is that which discriminates against applicants whose 'faces don't fit'. Firms regularly reject candidates who are not in the image of the recruiter or the management to whom they will report. They do so largely because accepting divergent applicants would unsettle or inconvenience the current staff. The greatest contributions, however, may well come from unfamiliar or 'difficult' sources: from eccentrics, or mavericks, or gadflies. Indeed, unless the existing staff, and particularly those charged with recruitment, are themselves ethical maximisers, cloning them is almost guaranteed to produce the wrong choice.

'Old Boy Networks'
Does that mean it is unethical to use the 'old boy network'?

Of course not. There is nothing wrong in an 'old boy network' as such: it is natural and valuable for mutual support systems to exist amongst those with much in common. Moreover, such networks can be extremely useful to business. They can constitute a reliable source of employees who are relatively easy to evaluate; their informal social sanctions can be productively used to promote ethical business objectives[18]. And homogenous backgrounds and shared values can foster harmony and easier communication.

The only occasion when an 'old boy network' should provoke concern is if it is regarded as the *sole* acceptable source of recruits. When only 'old boys' are considered, better-qualified candidates without access to the network may well be overlooked. What matters ultimately is not how the applicants are found, but what principle of selection is applied. So long as there is unimpeded access to the selection process, and the selection is made on the basis of expected contributions to long-term owner value, then there is nothing wrong in tapping any source of potential applicants, including the old boys: the candidate in the old school tie might just be the best one.

'Overqualification'
One of the most teleopathic forms of pandering is that which rejects applicants for being 'overqualified'. Given the ethical requirement to hire that candidate who will contribute most to maximising long-term owner value, it is hard to see how a candidate could be overqualified: the description suggests that a contribution to long-term owner value could somehow be too great. Yet applicants are regularly rejected because they have too much experience or too much education, even when it would cost no more to hire them than a less qualified applicant.

The explanation that is typically given, is that applicants with superior abilities or higher expectations will disrupt the balance of the firm. If most of the team are school-leavers, a recruit with an advanced degree will, it is alleged, be unlikely to fit in comfortably. And this may well be so. Whether the fit is comfortable, however, is a different matter from whether it *should* be comfortable. Unless the status quo is ideal, unsettling it can be a good thing . . . and normally will be, if the changes lead to greater contributions to long-term owner value.

All too often the equilibrium that would be upset by hiring a superior applicant is that of the manager to whom that candidate would report. Managers fear that candidates with extensive experience, or good minds, will be difficult to manage and may threaten their positions. They might reveal the manager's hitherto hidden inadequacies, or be obviously better able to perform the manager's responsibilities than he can himself; they might even aspire to the manager's own job. But these are reasons for hiring the 'overqualified' applicant, not for rejecting him. Having to maintain superiority over a particularly capable subordinate may be a good way of keeping a manager alert and focused on the job. The purpose of the business is maximising long-term owner value, not providing a refuge for staff in search of a quiet life.

This is not to say, of course, that those with the most experience, or even the greatest skills, are necessarily the best for the business. If the well-qualified candidate feels the job is beneath him, or if he is bored or keen to move on, he may not give the job his proper attention or stay long enough to repay the costs of recruitment and initiation. If the candidate's previous experience has engendered bad habits, his experience may be counterproductive. And if his skills are irrelevant to the job at hand but expensive to hire, they will probably not be worth the cost. The MBA who believes he knows it all, and that the business owes him both a living and a senior position—instantly—should obviously be avoided. But not all MBAs fall into that category. Holders of MBA degrees do not automatically lack business sense, and candidates with Ph.D.s may be both practical and canny—and a source of significant contributions to long-term owner value. To assume otherwise is to exhibit teleopathic prejudice.

Candidates should be evaluated on their individual merits. The mere fact that a candidate may have proven abilities in one sector does not mean that he lacks comparable skills in another. A quick learner or an all-rounder can be particularly valuable to a business operating in an environment of rapid change. What is important in each case is determining how well the individual candidate can satisfy both the specific requirements of the job to be filled and the long-term needs of the business. When other things are equal, having the best staff possible is likely to contribute significantly to maximising long-term owner value.

'Ageism'

A similar, and equally unrecognised, kind of pandering is associated with 'ageism', the practice of artificially restricting the age ranges that are deemed acceptable for job applicants. All too often, trainees are required to be under 25, while prospective managers are required to be less than 45 years of age.[19] The arguments for such restrictions usually depend on associating age with the presence or absence of functional qualities. Older workers[20] are presumed to be less capable of adapting to new circumstances, or to be less willing or less able to learn new skills[21]; conversely, they are expected to be more experienced and responsible. Such correlations are, however, highly questionable.[22] Older applicants may be flexible and inventive; having learned to distinguish the essential from the accidental, they may actually master new skills faster than their juniors. Equally, younger workers may be both conscientious and diligent. Educability, responsibility and resistance to change are qualities of character and mind, not functions of age.

Nor are commitment or enthusiasm necessarily age-related. Air traffic controllers and bond traders may perhaps burn out after a very few years: the degree of concentration required may be difficult to sustain. Cooks and connoisseurs, in contrast, normally get better with time, as their greater experience translates into greater expertise. The lack of enthusiasm sometimes exhibited by older workers may be a result of natural laziness and slowing down, or of shifting priorities. But it may also be a reflection of the job concerned. It is notable that those with interesting occupations, those who are in positions of the greatest authority, and those who see their work as making a difference, tend to continue working efficiently and productively until very late in life: politicians and entrepreneurs are renowned for their professional longevity[23]. Finally, youth does not even guarantee that a candidate will be available to work longer for the firm: given the trend to multiple employments that has obtained since the 1980s, there is no assurance that any recruit will last. Indeed, youths with no domestic responsibilities may be amongst the most mobile.

If age is at best a contingent and highly unreliable guide to valuable contributions[24], why then is it so often stipulated as a hiring requirement? One reason is that older employees can cost more, not least in respect of their pension provisions. An equally significant reason, however, is that having employees of a standard age normally makes life easier for their managers. Like those who are 'overqualified', recruits who are significantly younger or older than the norm may be more difficult to control than those who fit the usual pattern. Candidates who achieve the necessary skills at a precociously early age may be disconcerting, or a reproach to those around them; high-flyers often have high expectations that can be difficult to satisfy. Moreover, older workers may resent being told what to do by comparative youngsters. Conversely, an older-than-average applicant may be disturbing evidence that careers, like shares, can go down as well as up. Or the older worker may simply be harder to boss around[25]: someone who has seen it all before may be less willing to accept the boss's word unchallenged.

In summary, therefore, 'ageism' is often simply another form of teleopathic prejudice, of pandering to the wish of managers to have a quiet life. Age should therefore normally be ignored as a criterion of employment. The reason why, however, is not because business has any obligation to help the aged, or because it is right for the workforce to reflect the prevailing demographics. The only reason to hire an aged applicant—or a youthful one—is because that candidate is the one likely to contribute most to long-term owner value.

Short cuts

How are businesses to evaluate candidates' likely contributions to long-term owner value? Scarce resources seldom permit an in-depth assessment of every candidate who applies for a job. As a result, businesses typically employ short cuts to screen out the least promising applicants. What sorts of short cuts are ethical? The difficulties of using the 'old boy network' and age have already been addressed. Is the use of credentials any more appropriate? What about utilising 'objective' tests for specific aptitudes, or psychometric tests for revealing personality and character? And is screening for disease or drug use ethical?

Credentials

Credentials—degrees, certificates, examination results—are at best surrogates for the actual qualities that the business needs. Recruiters typically rely upon credentials because they are easier to assess than the underlying qualities: it is simpler to screen for academic qualifications than for intelligence, for vocational qualifications than for genuine expertise. But although excluding people because they lack specific credentials may simplify the recruiter's job, it does not necessarily serve the best interests of the business. Despite the common belief to the contrary, credentials may be more like irrelevant circumstantial characteristics than they are like relevant functional skills.

Unless possession of a particular credential is a regulatory requirement (as a driving licence is for drivers), relying on credentials to eliminate candidates may well be arbitrary and counterproductive. The most creative and effective computer programmer may not only lack an advanced degree in mathematics, he may not have been to university at all. If, therefore, having a first or a Ph.D. in mathematics has been specified as a requirement for the job, the best candidate will be excluded. Screening on credentials can also be needlessly expensive: if the qualifications are not essential for the job, hiring people who have them incurs an unnecessary, continuing expense. This is, of course, not an argument against well-qualified candidates: a business should normally hire the candidate best qualified to maximise long-term owner value. But when the business needs a candidate with intellectual curiosity and perseverance, or one with a cultivated first class mind, it should demand precisely those characteristics, not possession of a piece of parchment.

Testing
Perhaps then, the solution is to use 'objective' tests? Tests have sometimes been regarded as the most ethical basis on which to make recruitment decisions, because they are assumed to be reliable, consistent and unbiased. And some tests are: typing and driving tests are reasonable indicators of candidates' ability to type and to drive. Such tests are unusual, however, in that they directly examine the skill in question, albeit under somewhat artificial conditions. Most tests, in contrast, involve only surrogates for the real thing, and at best measure some proxy for the actual skill or quality sought. Intelligence tests typically measure test-taking ability and vocabulary rather than intelligence; lie-detector tests measure physiological responses, not honesty. Like credentials, therefore, test results are normally a second best, a substitute for good judgement in evaluating candidates' ability to contribute to long-term owner value.

Unless tests genuinely enable the business to select better candidates, they waste business resources and are teleopathic. The extent to which tests do improve selection will depend on their design, the skill with which they are administered, and the skill with which the results are interpreted and translated into hiring decisions. Even when tests do identify the best candidates, however, the benefits may be offset by the hostility of candidates and stakeholders to the fact of testing.

Tests, particularly lie-detector, personality and drug tests, are commonly thought to violate candidates' privacy. But just as the business has no right to information about candidates, candidates have no right to privacy in their dealings with the business: the level of disclosure is a matter for negotiation between them. What limits the legitimacy of business probes into candidates' or employees' personal lives is not their nonexistent rights to privacy, but the business's obligation to maximise long-term owner value. If the business seeks information it does not need, it will be wasting resources and acting teleopathically. Most intrusions that are offensive are also irrelevant to, or actually undermine, long-term owner value.

Subject, however, to maximising long-term owner value and respecting distributive justice and ordinary decency, a business may legitimately use whatever aids it likes in making its own choices. Distributive justice is automatically satisfied when the principle of ethical selection is used in recruiting. If the subjects of the tests are existing employees, distributive justice will be at issue only if exemption is allowed selectively on the basis of something other than contributions to long-term owner value.

Equally, there is no reason why testing cannot satisfy the requirements of ordinary decency . . . however often actual tests may fail to do so. Making a test a condition for getting or holding a job involves no coercion: candidates can just say no and walk away. Testing is honest when those requiring the tests are frank about what is being tested and about how the tests employed are expected to work. And testing is fair when the tests genuinely measure what they are intended to, and they are properly, i.e., professionally and impartially, administered and interpreted.

The requirements of distributive justice and ordinary decency can be met not only by tests of typing and critical reasoning; they can also be satisfied by the more controversial psychometric tests, and even by polygraph[26]—lie-detector—tests. However intrusive they may seem, even tests for drugs make sense when business performance[27] is affected. Psychometric tests, which attempt to measure personality traits such as extroversion and stability, can be very helpful in prompting businesses to identify the character traits most relevant for maximising long-term owner value. They can also provide comparable, numeric data about large numbers of candidates. Accordingly, psychometric tests have been found productive by significant numbers of large firms.

Nevertheless, psychometric and polygraphic tests should only be used warily. They do not violate applicants' (non-existent) right of privacy, but they do often alienate those who are asked to take them. The more opaque or dubious a test is to those being subjected to it, the greater their resistance is likely to be. And rightly or wrongly, it is the candidates who have most to offer who are most likely to find psychometric tests offensive and insulting. The more intelligent and discerning the candidates, the more they may resent questions that seem in every way impertinent, especially when the questioners' ability to understand the answers seems limited.

Reliance on tests of unclear or dubious soundness may properly evoke scorn from candidates. It is not just graphology, astrology and clairvoyance[28] whose predictive validity in the workplace is seriously doubted by academic psychologists.[29] Even conventional psychometric tests may reveal more about the characters of the businesses that use them, than they do about the candidates who take them. Often, what the use of such tests demonstrates is a lack of confidence in the recruiters' judgement. The wrong sort of testing can therefore undermine belief in the firm's business ability as well as in its justice and decency. Equally, if applied to existing employees, tests purporting to measure integrity may indicate a fundamental lack of trust in the workforce. The more substantial the negative reactions to testing are, the greater the positive contribution the tests will have to make if their business use is to be justified.

Equality of opportunity

Though short cuts often undermine ethical recruitment, equality of opportunity is essential for it. Fortunately, however, equality of opportunity automatically results when a business respects distributive justice and ordinary decency in pursuing long-term owner value. There are only three conditions that must be satisfied for equality of opportunity to exist. The rules that allocate the good—be it a job or a rise or a promotion—must be applied equally to all comers. Applicants may not be rejected except by reference to the rules. And prospective applicants may not be forcibly prevented from subjecting themselves to the rules. The first and second conditions are general requirements of fairness; the third is satisfied when a business refrains from coercion and physical violence.

Violations of equality of opportunity typically occur when the rules for allocating a good are not applied impartially, or when individuals or classes of candidates are prevented from even entering the competition for it. Such restrictions result either when the law, or those who use or threaten physical violence outside the law, bar candidates from subjecting themselves to the rules, or when those administering the rules simply refuse to consider prospective applicants from certain categories. Equality of opportunity was genuinely violated when non-whites were prohibited by the laws of South Africa from even applying for certain sorts of jobs.

It is, however, important to recognise what equality of opportunity does *not* involve. First, equality of opportunity does not preclude discrimination on the basis of circumstantial criteria, so long as those criteria are explicitly incorporated in the selection rules applied; there is no ethical, as distinct from legal, reason why a job description should not specify that candidates be of a particular sex or nationality. Equality of opportunity is a purely procedural requirement; it governs how rules are administered, not what their content or their outcomes should be. The rules that must be applied fairly, and to which access must not be denied, can be of any sort. It is indeed a condition of ethical business that goods be allocated on the basis of relevant characteristics, but that condition is imposed by business's definitive purpose and by distributive justice, not by equality of opportunity.

Second, equality of opportunity specifically does not require that either the candidates or the outcomes be equal. The fact that, for example, all successful applicants may have gone to the same school does not necessarily mean that equality of opportunity is lacking. There may be only one school that teaches the relevant specialised skill, or one school may be outstandingly better than all the others. Equality of opportunity specifies how rules should be applied; it does not determine the results of applying the rules. If candidates of varying abilities are impartially screened by the same criteria, their successes will naturally be as varied as their abilities.

To the extent that equal outcomes are sought, what is

required is not equality of opportunity, but its opposite. Equal outputs can be secured in only two ways. The inputs themselves can be equalised, or the rules can be adjusted to compensate for the candidates' inequalities. If inputs are equalised by denying access to those who exceed or fall short of the stipulated standard, the definitive condition of equality of opportunity will explicitly be violated. If, instead, the inputs are given unequal assistance, or different criteria are applied, the selection procedure will be unfair. Either way, the principle of ethical selection is violated: the criterion employed in the recruitment choice is not the candidate's contribution to maximising long-term owner value, but equality. Any programme that is designed to provide preferential or remedial treatment, or that operates on the basis of quotas or even 'targets' for outcomes, is accurately described as 'reverse discrimination'. Far from promoting equality of opportunity, such efforts do the reverse, and are normally teleopathic as well.

In summary, then, the basis for ethical recruitment is not replacing old boy networks with objective tests, or relying on qualifications or outlawing discrimination. Discrimination amongst candidates' abilities to contribute to long-term owner value is essential to ethical recruitment. Invasions of privacy, 'ageism' and rejecting applicants for 'over-qualification' are typically teleopathic. Equality of opportunity follows automatically from observing ordinary decency and does not involve equality of inputs or outcomes. All that ethical recruitment does require is that the business hire the candidate likely to contribute the most to long-term owner value, and that it observe ordinary decency in its recruitment procedures.

REMUNERATION

Not surprisingly, since remuneration is all about allocating rewards, the key element in ethical remuneration is distributive justice: the ethical business rewards its employees in proportion to their contributions to the business goal. As the fundamental principle of ethical allocation, distributive justice governs all the rewards that the business has to offer its staff. It covers not just wages, salaries and bonuses, but praise and perks and promotions, honours and responsibilities.

Though the term 'distributive justice' is little used, the concept is nonetheless familiar in personnel matters. The distinction between workers and shirkers implicitly calls upon the concept; so does the notion of 'pulling one's weight'. Independent studies have confirmed that equity and fairness are crucial to workers, who typically assess their rewards against their contributions[30] and become disillusioned when their rewards fail to reflect them.[31] Distributive justice also helps to explain why people can think they are paid too much[32]: they are aware of the disparity between what they earn and what, based on their contributions, they actually deserve.

Standard deviations

Rewarding anything other than contributions to long-term owner value not only violates distributive justice, but is usually teleopathic. Accordingly, many considerations that are commonly taken into account in determining remuneration should be recognised as being at best irrelevant.

Need, Effort and Ability
Contrary to Marx, for example, neither need nor ability are appropriate bases for worker compensation. Just as employees' race and religion are normally irrelevant to remuneration, so too are their personal economic circumstances. That a secretary is an unmarried mother with triplets may perhaps be a reason to sympathise with her plight, or to respect her stamina and organisational ability in coping with a difficult challenge. But it is no reason to grant her a pay rise: rises are earned by producing contributions to the business end, not by producing offspring.

Similarly, ability and effort must result in long-term owner value if they are to count towards remuneration: distributive justice and the ethical business reward results, not talents or exertions. No matter how capable or clever or good an employee is, unless his sterling qualities are directed to achieving the business end, they are properly disregarded when determining remuneration; the employee's talent as a pianist and his piety are in themselves both normally irrelevant to his pay. Equally, the employee who works hard to get the job done deserves no greater reward than the person who achieves the same result effortlessly; the person who tries hard, but fails, deserves less.

It may be objected that this policy is too harsh. Employees aren't just human resources or machines, the protest goes, they are people, whose humanity ought to be respected. And so it ought: to be ethical a business must operate in accordance with ordinary decency as well as distributive justice. Nevertheless, the purpose of business is to maximise long-term owner value, not to reward moral character. To consider people's characters or qualities independent of their effect on long-term owner value would be to waste the business's resources: it would be less businesslike, not more moral.

Of course, people's characters and qualities and circumstances often do influence long-term owner value, both positively and negatively; when they do, they should correspondingly influence remuneration. Courtesy is a productive trait in a receptionist, and should be rewarded as such. An employee who characteristically attempts to get things right is more likely to maximise long-term owner value than one who can't be bothered; he is thus a more suitable candidate to send on an expensive training course. Conversely, if an employee's personal problems distract him from his work and reduce his effectiveness, the business may well be justified in chastising or penalising or dismissing him.[33] Whether doing so is indeed the best way to maximise long-term owner value, or whether the business might benefit more from helping the employee to resolve his problems, the better to restore him to full productivity, depends on the particular circumstances of the case.

If the business does help the employee, however, great care

must be taken to keep 'remedial' benefits separate from standard remuneration. If the assistance is to achieve the entirely appropriate goal of helping the business by helping the employee, the basis on which it is granted needs to be perspicuously clear to all concerned. If it is not, it risks giving the wrong signals to the workforce and being seriously counter-productive.

Consider emergency help for an indebted employee. Providing financial assistance could enhance long-term owner value if, for example, it alleviated the worker's productivity-diminishing distress and promoted an atmosphere of support and confidence. In such circumstances, disguising the assistance as a pay rise might seem a kindly way of saving the recipient's face. But the pretence could easily backfire. Since by hypothesis the recipient's productivity has suffered, awarding him a pay rise could well lead to confusion and discontent amongst his colleagues. However much they might sympathise with his plight, they might nonetheless legitimately object to inferior performance being rewarded. Remedial assistance should therefore normally be provided via special *ex gratia* loans or grants[34], and kept quite distinct from standard remuneration.

Seniority and Loyalty

Another factor that should normally be recognised as largely irrelevant to ethical remuneration is seniority. Like an employee's age, the number of years he has spent working for a business is seldom, if ever, what determines his contribution to owner value. His years with the firm may perhaps be correlated with useful experience; when promotion is mainly internal, seniority may well be correlated with rank in the business hierarchy. Even when it does, however, seniority is at best a surrogate for estimating contributions: experience is no guarantee of expertise. Familiarity with a firm may, of course, make it easier to fit in and to accomplish routine tasks in the accepted way. Unless the accepted way is a particularly good way, however, experience of it may be more likely to generate bad habits than to maximise long-term owner value. Precisely because they see things differently, new staff can often make significant improvements and thus contribute greatly. Even a relative newcomer can therefore be more deserving of reward than the employee with long but undistinguished service.

Nor is contribution necessarily correlated with hierarchical position. Chairmen and chief executives should normally make the greatest contributions to their business corporations, and thus merit the greatest rewards. Sometimes, however, even quite junior staff contribute, and should therefore be paid, far more. After London's 'Big Bang', for example, it was quite often the case that a salesman would be the highest paid employee in a securities firm, earning more than its chief executive or even the head of the firm's clearing bank parent.[35]

Recognising the limited relevance of seniority for remuneration doesn't mean that faithful service shouldn't be rewarded: it should be. The key element in business loyalty is, however, not longevity but productive commitment to the business purpose. When distributive justice is properly observed, loyal service is not only recognised, but is rewarded when the contribution occurs: the more closely rewards accompany contributions, the more likely they are to reinforce the right conduct.

There is nevertheless a widely held notion that long-serving staff deserve something extra. Having given the business 'the best years of their lives', long-serving staff are assumed somehow to have made the business 'theirs', and to be entitled to a special say in how it is run. Is this right? No: when employees have simply been time-servers, the traditional gold watch is probably an all-too-appropriate acknowledgement, and possibly more than their inertia deserves. But what if employees really have thrown themselves into the business, devotedly sacrificing their private lives in doing so: don't they deserve recognition? Yes . . . if their sacrifices have genuinely contributed to maximising long-term owner value. But as always, what deserves reward is the contribution, not the sacrifice. Too many managers are like self-martyred mothers, and wrongly expect to be rewarded for sacrifices that were neither sought nor wanted nor useful: they confuse unceasing toil with increasing owner value.

When, however, the business really has made exceptional demands of its staff, and they have responded in kind, then special rewards may indeed be in order. A firm might, for example, have asked its employees to defer taking their contractual entitlements so that the funds saved could be used elsewhere in the business. If, as a result, employees have forgone pay rises or perks that they were otherwise due, then they deserve to get not only the rewards that they initially earned and deferred, but also credit for their patience, loyalty and commitment. And the longer and the more often that staff have agreed to such deferrals, the more the business owes them. By deferring their entitlements, the employees have made a kind of equity investment in the business[36]; to the extent that they have acted like owners, they deserve to be treated like owners. It is in this way that long-serving employees might legitimately acquire a proprietary interest in their firms.

Deferrals are commoner than normally supposed. Occasionally they are public and the subject of written contracts. More often, however, they are the result of informal agreements: 'Don't insist on the rise just now and we'll see you right next time'. When such verbal arrangements are real and not just imagined, it is vital for the business to honour them. Failing to do so violates ordinary decency: lying and breaking promises are dishonest. Not fulfilling agreements is also seriously teleopathic: in undermining trust, it hampers the attainment of long-term owner value. Employees who can understand longer-term goals and are prepared to defer gratification in order to achieve them are the sort of employees who are capable of making the greatest contributions to the business. To alienate such exceptionally valuable employees harms the business doubly. It not only deprives the business of their specific contributions, but it gives a clearly counterproductive signal to the rest of the staff: grab what you can when you can; the firm's word can't be trusted. If a business wants its employees to be loyal, it must be loyal to them.

Inflation and the 'Going Rate'
Do inflation and the 'going rate' have any place in determin-

ing ethical remuneration? Yes . . . but only indirectly. Firms have no automatic obligation to maintain the purchasing power of the remuneration they offer. But economic circumstances can affect whether (and how much) a given performance adds to long-term owner value. In times of high inflation, the services of a cash management specialist may be absolutely essential, and worth more to the business than those of a salesman. When, in contrast, prices are stable but competition is fierce, the salesman might well be more important.

Does this mean that in inflationary times the cash manager will automatically be paid more than the salesman? Not necessarily: the amount paid will depend as well on the labour markets for each category. If the importance of cash management has only recently come to be recognised, and experienced cash managers are in short supply, then they are likely to command a premium in the market and from the firm. If, however, the market has been flooded by cash managers hoping to cash in on the trend, then they might be available for less than salesmen. The key determinant of the 'going rate', the pay and perks that must be offered to secure the services of a type of worker, is the interplay of supply and demand. That 'going rate' may, of course, reflect inflation in other ways; it might, for example, require indexation of pay or pension benefits. Whatever the 'going rate' is, however, it represents only one side of the equation.

Though conditions in the labour market determine the price of labour, individual firms must still decide whether that price should be paid. The firm must therefore estimate what value any particular individual is likely to add. If and only if that contribution sufficiently exceeds the price paid to secure it, should the candidate be hired or the 'going rate' be paid.[37] It is not enough for the business to know what things or people cost; it is also essential to consider what they are worth.

Differentials
What they are worth is a function of their specific contributions to long-term owner value, not their titles or positions in the official hierarchy. As ordinarily used by UK labour

unions, the notion of 'differentials' is therefore incompatible with ethical remuneration. The 'differentials' that the unions typically seek to preserve are those that define the remuneration levels of types of jobs. Such differentials require that each category of job receive different remuneration, and that all the workers in a given job be treated alike.[38] Distributive justice, in contrast, requires that individual performances be evaluated and remunerated on their merits.

Within any job classification, there are likely to be discernible differences in the qualities of performance: the best manager will contribute more than the worst manager. Moreover, contributions to long-term owner value do not necessarily correlate with job titles: a bad manager may well contribute less than a good secretary. Conversely, employees in different job classifications may well make contributions of equal value: a machinist and a telephonist may therefore deserve the same pay. Actually assessing contributions is notoriously difficult in practice, but the principle is nonetheless clear: in the ethical business, remuneration relates to long-term owner value.

Performance-related pay

Does this mean that performance-related pay is essential? Yes, ordinarily it does. Indeed, since pay represents only a fraction of most employees' remuneration, what is required is not just performance-related pay, but performance-related remuneration[39]. In basing remuneration on performance, however, it is crucially important that the right sort of performance be identified and rewarded.

In the ethical business, the right sort of performance is that which maximises long-term owner value while respecting distributive justice and ordinary decency. Consequently, three conditions must be satisfied for performance-related pay to be structured properly. The activities that are measured should themselves enhance owner value and respect distributive justice and ordinary decency. Wherever possible the measures should build in reference to the consequences of current actions over the long-term. And the measures employed should promote maximisation, both quantitative and qualitative.

Most of the measures that are commonly used for determining performance-related pay are, accordingly, altogether unsuitable; they range from the merely counterproductive to the positively perverse. If the measure used is simply the number of units processed, for example, then the numbers of units will likely rise—but so, most probably, will the number of faulty units. Similarly, if the measure is turnover, then current sales may well increase, but quite possibly at the expense of realistic sales descriptions, customer satisfaction, and short and long-term profits. If the criterion for managers' rises is the numbers of subordinates managed, or the size of budget controlled, then staff numbers and expenditures will most probably grow—often with no regard for, and quite possibly at the expense of, long-term owner value: when executives are actively rewarded for increasing costs, costs are likely to increase. And when business size is the determinant of pay, managers gain a strong personal incentive to pursue acquisitions independent of their effect on long-term owner value.[40] The moral hazard is further exacerbated when rewards are ratcheted and do not decline in line with performance.

Given the inappropriateness of the most commonly used measures for determining performance-related pay, it is not surprising that independent studies should have found performance-related pay to be at best marginally useful in promoting business achievement.[41] Such studies do not, however, invalidate the concept of performance-related pay. What is defective about the schemes examined is not their ability to motivate employees, but their design: performance-related pay has been shown to be all too effective, albeit in promoting the wrong sort of outcomes.[42]

The response, therefore, is not to despair of performance-related remuneration, but to improve its structure: the end that it promotes should be the end that is actually wanted. The measures on which the performance-related remuneration is based should be tied much more closely to maximising long-term owner value ethically. The performance measured should not be simply the number of units processed, but the number of saleable units processed within time and cost and fault constraints. The appropriate criterion for salesmen will not be just making sales, but making sales that satisfy customers and generate profits and repeat business. Similarly, bankers should be rewarded not simply for booking loans, but for booking loans that are profitable to the bank and get repaid on time. Finally, managers should not be rewarded for just increasing the business's turnover, or even its current profits or its earnings per share: such measures are key causes of 'short-termism'. Managers' remuneration should be linked instead to increasing owner value[43] *over an extended period of time.* That way, even if managers are not themselves owners, their interests and those of the owners will coincide more closely.

When properly structured, performance-related pay promotes good corporate governance. It does so because, by identifying the contributions made and the employees making them, it increases accountability. Accountability should, however, always be accompanied by responsibility; fairness demands that people should be held accountable only for those things that are under their control. It is therefore important to take into account the degree to which an individual's contribution depends on external factors: on team co-operation or the franchise of the business, on the supply of equipment or the nature of the market. Such considerations will inform the decision as to whether the basic unit for performance-related pay will be an individual or a team, a profit-centre or a division. And when the basic unit for performance-related pay is a group, that group should be allowed to choose and discipline its own members[44]. Whatever the unit, however, the criteria must be clear and clearly conveyed. If performance-related pay is to work, there must be no room for excuses.

Perks and paternalism

There are three ethical questions relating to perquisites: what level of perks should the ethical business offer its staff;

to whom should the perks be offered; and which perks, if any, should business not offer. The answers follow directly from the conditions of ethical business.

The ethical business should offer those and only those perks that promote the maximisation of long-term owner value, subject as always to respecting distributive justice and ordinary decency. The level of perks appropriate will therefore normally be that which is needed to attract and keep good staff, who typically have their choice of potential employers. That 'going rate' for perks will, however, be qualified by distributive justice, which will also govern their allocation. Which perks are most likely to maximise long-term owner value will depend on many factors: the nature and conventions of the industry, the types of employees, the state of the market, the legal and tax regime, even the geographic location of the firm. But what determines whether a particular perk is ethical, is simply whether it respects distributive justice and ordinary decency while maximising long-term owner value.

A number of perks that are commonly thought morally dubious can therefore be seen to be perfectly moral. There is, for example, nothing necessarily wrong with 'golden handshakes', which are simply front-end payments used to secure an employee's services. The more volatile the industry, and the more uncertain the recruiting firm's future, the more likely it will be that a potential recruit will want concrete assurance that investing his time with that firm will be worthwhile. Although ideally a business should seek employees who are sufficiently confident in its prospects to do without financial guarantees, the circumstances of the business or of the industry may make them necessary. Equally, a substantial initial payment may be required to compensate the recruit for benefits he would lose by leaving his current employer: a bonus that has been earned but not yet paid, for example, or stock options that would be forfeited. Such payments have nothing to do with bribery and are perfectly legitimate.

In all cases, however, the 'golden handshake' will be appropriate if, but only if, it is consistent with distributive justice.

The amount paid must be warranted by the recruit's expected contribution to long-term owner value, and the costs of providing it must be outweighed by the expected benefits. That calculation must take into account not only the actual amount of the payment, but also its possible effects on existing employees' morale and future recruits' expectations.

The same ethical conditions apply to 'golden handcuffs'. If the services of key executives are necessary for maximising long-term owner value, then contractual arrangements to ensure their continued presence may be appropriate. Similarly, if employees have been given expensive training, it is sensible for the business to try and protect its investment by keeping them. Despite their name and their explicit attempt to limit employees' freedom, such contracts can be entirely consistent with ordinary decency: they typically result from hard negotiations freely entered into, and involve no coercion. And they are compatible with distributive justice if the amounts paid to retain the employee's service are justified by his expected contribution.

The ethical problem presented by 'golden handcuffs' is normally not whether they interfere with the employee's liberty, but whether they unjustifiably constrain the business.[45] Given the practical difficulties of estimating future contributions, and the very substantial costs to the business of long-term employment contracts, 'golden handcuffs' may diminish long-term owner value. Staff who are tied to the business by contract instead of enthusiasm or loyalty may not be worth their keep; those bound by perks may be more resentful than grateful. It therefore makes sense to require explicit approval by the board or even the shareholders for material 'handcuffs' and 'handshakes'.

It is also important to recognise that most perks are intrusive or controlling in some way. Perks that are obligatory rather than optional are obviously restrictive. 'Golden handcuffs' explicitly make it more difficult for employees to change jobs. But so do tied cottages, subsidised mortgages and company cars, albeit more subtly. The fact that a perk is controlling or intrusive, however, does not automatically make it immoral. No compulsion is involved in even the most restrictive of legal perks: staff consent to the perks in accepting the job, and can rid themselves of unwanted interference by resigning. When, therefore, the arrangements are represented honestly, entered into freely, implemented fairly and allocated justly, intrusive and controlling perks are wholly compatible with ordinary decency and distributive justice.

As with other contentious perks, the problem with counselling is not that it is intrinsically immoral, but that the contribution it makes to long-term owner value is strongly affected by employee attitudes. Delving into employees' private lives can benefit long-term owner value if it alleviates distracting distress, or reduces absenteeism. But it can also prove offensive to just those employees who are most valuable to the business. Competent, responsible adults have little need for assistance in their private lives, and may well resent any business attempts to interfere; privacy is often protected jealously even if it is not enjoyed as a matter of right. The proffered assistance may therefore be regarded as unwarranted and annoying rather than as valuable; what is meant as a perk may be perceived as impertinence. The resentment will be even stronger if the business's intrusive attempts to help are handled insensitively or unprofessionally. And when firms repudiate their legitimate business interest in resolving staff problems, and represent their efforts as pure altruistic interest in staff welfare, they make things even worse. If their claims are false, then the business is hypocritical. But if they are true, the firm's interference is both teleopathic and grossly presumptuous.

The business should therefore consider very carefully the composition and likely reaction of its workforce before introducing measures that might be considered intrusive: a perk that is not understood or is not wanted is unlikely to maximise long-term owner value. One way round this problem is to offer employees a 'menu' of benefits from which to choose. In such flexible benefit schemes, sometimes known as 'cafeteria benefits', employees may pick the perks that best suit their individual needs. An even simpler and better solution, however, is to incorporate the money that would be spent on perks into higher wages or salaries, and let the employees use them as they wish. Giving employees the money not only maximises individual choice and personal responsibility, which in themselves are useful to the business, but is normally more efficient than providing perks directly. Unless the perk is a reflection of the business's own activities (discounted airfares from an airline, for instance), or there are significant tax or volume advantages in providing the perk centrally, the administrative costs of direct provision are likely to outweigh any business benefits.

In conclusion, then, the level and kind of perks will reflect the nature of the business and its circumstances, and particularly the sensitivities and preferences of its staff. Though most perks are controlling and intrusive in some way, they may nevertheless be perfectly moral. The right perks are those that maximise long-term owner value, subject to respecting distributive justice and ordinary decency.

FIRING

Contrary to popular belief, firing workers can be positively ethical. The purpose of business is maximising long-term owner value, not providing full employment or promoting employee welfare; whatever legal or contractual rights workers may have, they have no natural rights to continued employment with a business. Firings may be unfortunate; they may even be devastating. But they are not necessarily immoral.

What determines whether firing a particular worker is ethical or not is simply whether the dismissal is directed at maximising the long-term owner value of the business while respecting distributive justice and ordinary decency. If a worker's contribution to long-term owner value does not exceed the costs of employing him, then it is both economically and ethically correct for the firm to dispense with his services ... so long as the dismissal is consistent with both distributive justice and ordinary decency. Distributive justice is respected if it is contributions to long-term owner value that determine who gets fired and what gets offered in discretionary termination packages. Ordinary decency is respected if the firing is conducted with honesty, fairness and legality, and involves no coercion or physical violence. Firing is ethical when the right person is fired for the right reason and in the right way.

Unfortunately, there are many ways of getting it wrong. Often, dismissals are conducted in ways that clearly violate the principles of ethical business. Cruelly playing with staff is wrong; so is leaving them unnecessarily in doubt about their future with the firm; so, too, is callously abusing power. When staff have been given their notice it is prudent to ensure they have no opportunity to damage the business; it is seldom appropriate to see them off the premises like criminals, without time to bid their colleagues goodbye. And there are more courteous as well as more productive ways of notifying staff that they are being sacked than by leaving black plastic bin bags on their desks.[46] Insensitive firing can seriously impair long-term owner value; it lowers the morale of remaining staff, and makes it more difficult for the business to keep[47] and recruit good workers in future. Employees who are badly treated in the course of dismissal are likely to harbour and spread resentments that may last far longer than their jobs ever did; the bitterness may well outlive the firm.

'At will'

Amongst the most damaging sorts of firings are those which seem to be unjust or capricious. To maximise long-term owner value, a business must be able to dismiss any employee who ceases to serve the business end, whatever the reason[48]; in the terms of the common law, it must be able to fire 'at will'. It is, however, exceedingly unlikely that capricious or whimsical or random sackings will promote the business objective. Action that is arbitrary cannot, by its very nature, be directed at maximising long-term owner value; it is necessarily teleopathic. Equally, capricious firings are unfair and make even the shortest-term planning impossible; by creating an atmosphere of fear and uncertainty, they undermine the trust that is essential for business to exist and prosper.

A firm is unlikely to get the best staff or their best efforts if employees believe (rightly or wrongly) that they are being treated unjustly or dismissed lightly. Firings must normally not only be fair, but be seen to be fair, if they are to be productive. It is only sensible for staff to be given clear guidelines about what constitutes unacceptable behaviour, and allowed the chance to explain their actions before they are dismissed. The firm should apply its rules evenhandedly and impartially, and should be clear how the dismissal will help to maximise long-term owner value. All too often, it would seem, firms undertake mass layoffs without understanding why[49]; when the criteria are obscure, the benefits may prove correspondingly elusive.

Though intrinsically teleopathic, arbitrary dismissal is, fortunately, relatively rare. Even the worst managers seldom dial telephone extensions at random and fire whoever answers. The closest that most firms come to capricious firing is allowing the destructive whims of a key manager to operate unconstrained; when such a situation obtains, it may indeed be that looking the wrong way or wearing the wrong tie will constitute grounds for dismissal. No matter how productive a member of staff might otherwise be, such capriciousness should not be allowed: internal terrorism cannot be in the best interests of long-term owner value.

'For cause'

Firings are not arbitrary, however, when they are 'for cause', if they result from a worker's performance being poor or his services no longer being required for the business. The grounds that give rise to ethical dismissal are actions or dispositions[50] that undermine the business purpose, or that represent violations of distributive justice or ordinary decency. Those grounds apply whether offences occur on the shop floor or in the board room: in an ethical business, no one can be exempt from business discipline. Breaches of trust and confidence, sabotage, dishonesty and illegality are all legitimate firing offences. So are abuses of power and bullying[51]. Employees are also justifiably dismissed for incompetence, both absolute and relative, and for having a 'bad attitude' if it affects long-term owner value: an employee who is lazy, irresponsible, drunk or disorderly on the job is not furthering the business purpose.

Restructuring: reorganisation, rationalisation, redundancy

Most mass dismissals and many charges of unethical conduct against business result from restructuring: reorganisation, rationalisation, and redundancy. Many of the worst moral misunderstandings regarding layoffs, 'right-sizings', 'down-sizings' and 'de-layerings' can be eliminated if the purpose of business and the conditions of ethical business are kept firmly in mind. Since the purpose of business is not to promote full employment or social welfare, there is nothing intrinsically unethical about discharging workers or closing a plant: business exists to maximise long-term owner value, not to sustain the community or support the workforce. Subject to complying with relevant regulation, and honouring the specific explicit and implicit obligations it has undertaken, the ethical business not only can, but should, dismiss staff if they are surplus to requirements. That is so regardless of whether the business is contracting in response to economic adversity or market changes, or simply because it decides to change direction.

The key ethical issue in such large-scale layoffs is determining which workers should be dismissed. The basis for that decision should be the familiar principle of ethical selection—applied in reverse. Just as the ethical business recruits those candidates whose contributions to long-term owner value are expected to be the greatest, it dismisses those workers whose contributions to long-term owner value are likely to be the smallest. The right principle for discharging staff is therefore neither last in first out, nor first in first out. The operative consideration should not be the duration of the worker's tenure with the firm, nor his political vulnerability. Nor should it be just the cost of keeping the employee: the most expensive staff may be those who are most productive and most worth keeping. What should determine who gets fired is the quality of actual and potential contributions:

those contributing least should be the first to go.[52] And that principle must apply to managers and directors as well as to other employees: if executive inadequacies were responsible for creating or exacerbating the firm's problems, then executives deserve the axe.

But what about those loyal workers who have given their lives to the business? Doesn't the business have obligations to them? It depends . . . on the industry and its conventions, on the specific agreements, implicit as well as explicit, that the business has accepted, and on the business's circumstances. In some sectors—US-style investment banking, for example—executives have traditionally enjoyed little or no job security; employees' high salaries and jobs may be terminated at any time, reflecting conditions in the fast-moving markets in which they work.[53] In other industries—UK-style clearing banking, for example—life-time employment formerly used to be at least tacitly assured. The more that the business has encouraged or allowed its staff to expect job security, the greater its responsibilities to them. Its responsibilities are not, however, to keep the surplus or substandard workers on the payroll, but, if possible, to provide them with some compensation for disappointing the expectations that it has fostered.

The most resented mass discharges are perhaps those in which workers are dismissed on the grounds of economy while the executives' large remuneration packages continue undisturbed. Despite popular protests, even such actions can be perfectly ethical. It may be that unskilled labourers are no longer needed because of technological developments or changes in the structure of the industry, and that executives' contributions have actually risen as a result; managing change and increasing productivity are key managerial responsibilities. When, however, the contraction is in response to a general economic decline, it may be counterproductive as well as unfair for executives not to share in the firm's reduced circumstances.

In all cases, the business must be careful that savings made by dismissing staff are not outweighed by the costs, which may go far beyond the statutory redundancy pay. The costs may well include reduced morale and productivity in the remaining workforce, as confidence in the future and the management are undermined. And unless the staff cuts have been made in accordance with a clear strategic plan, they may well handicap the business's ability to take advantage of improved circumstances when they occur. Great care should be taken that savings in the short-term not deprive the business of resources it needs for maximising owner value over the long term. What is unethical is not firing, but undermining long-term owner value, distributive justice and ordinary decency.

7

Finance

'. . . two basic principles govern the provision of information on the company . . . First, that the company should be as open as it sensibly can about the financial state of the business and, second, that it should treat equally all those whom it has a duty to keep informed.'

Sir Adrian Cadbury[1]

'Turnover is vanity, profit is sanity and cash is reality.'

City of London maxim[2]

Guinness . . . Blue Arrow . . . Ivan Boesky . . . Michael Milken . . . Joseph Jett. . . . On both sides of the Atlantic, business has been the subject of major financial scandals. Contrary to popular belief, however, the most serious ethical problems concerning finance are neither those of the financial services industry, nor those associated with high-profile business failures; they are, instead, those issues which relate to financial reporting, and thus concern all businesses everywhere. Once the underlying questions are clarified, those problems, like the issues raised by mergers and acquisitions, junk bonds and insider trading, can be resolved quite straightforwardly using the Ethical Decision Model.

THE PROMINENCE OF FINANCIAL PROBLEMS

Why do financial matters seem to present so many ethical problems? One key reason is the sheer pervasiveness of finance. Since all business dealings involve finance, so do most business problems—including business's ethical problems.

Though finance is not exceptionally problematical, it is, in business, virtually inescapable; everything a business does has financial ramifications. Finance also suffers from many of the same features that make business itself seem ethically suspect. It is the locus of decisions that can involve vast sums and equally strong temptations, and its practitioners are often presumed to be clever manipulators of money and of men. And sadly, some prominent examples of financial loss have indeed been the consequence of moral wrongdoing, of deceit and outright theft.[3] Even in such cases, however, the misconduct is simply reflected in finance; it is not intrinsic to finance.

Major business scandals tend to be associated with finance, because they are associated with financial losses. But it would be wrong to conclude either that financial wrongdoing is the cause of those losses, or that finance is especially unethical. Businesses typically lose money because their products or their marketing are misjudged, or because their operations are badly managed. Such failures always have financial consequences, and are ordinarily expressed in financial terms, but they are not themselves financial shortcomings. Even when financial problems are at fault, and businesses suffer from bad debts or mismatched funding or undercapitalisation, the failings involved are more often the result of folly than of fraud. Indeed, unethical conduct in finance may be as much a response to financial losses as a source of them; it is when businesses are weak that the temptation to falsify results may be the greatest.

THE IMPORTANCE OF FINANCIAL STATEMENTS

There is, however, a context in which financial misrepresentation constitutes a genuine problem, and where it is more common than is ordinarily supposed: in businesses' own management accounts. The primary ethical challenge relating to finance is making sure that businesses' internal financial reporting is honest and fair and reliable.[4]

Businesses often keep two sets of accounts: financial accounts, which companies use to report to their shareholders, and internal management accounts. The role of management accounts is to show how the different operations of the business are functioning, to record what they do, what they cost and what they earn. Management accounts are a fundamental management tool: they provide the information necessary for evaluating the performance of business activities and for identifying operational problems.

All a business's accounts must be trustworthy if the business is to be ethical; honesty and fairness are essential if ordinary decency is to be respected. But however important it is for a business's public report and accounts to provide a true and fair statement of its financial position, it is even more essential that its internal, management accounts do so. And that is because having trustworthy internal accounts is a necessary precondition for running a business ethically. A business must have a dependable guide to long-term owner value if it is to be able to apply the Ethical Decision Model, implement the Principle of Ethical Selection or satisfy distributive justice.

But there is an even more fundamental reason why internal accounts must be trustworthy: accurate numbers are necessary for a business to function at all. Finance is the language of business; expressed and recorded in accounts, finance underpins or undermines all that a business does. If the language of finance is corrupted, if it is systematically used in ways that are incorrect or not meaningful or inconsistent, it will be impossible for those managing the business to understand what the business is doing or what it should be doing; the fundamental decision criterion of maximising long-term owner value cannot operate if the components of owner value are misrepresented. It is therefore absolutely essential that a firm's internal accounts be true and fair and reliable: unless the management accounts have integrity, all management decisions based on them will be distorted.

For management accounts to be true, fair and reliable, three main conditions must be satisfied. First, the rules according to which the accounts are drawn up must make sense and must accurately reflect the realities of doing business. Determining how key elements are defined and measured, and particularly how costs and earnings are allocated internally, is one of the most powerful ways management have of shaping the course of a business: which rules are adopted significantly affects which business activities will seem worthwhile. Setting the rules is, accordingly, one of the management powers most open to abuse.

Consider what happens if favoured projects or groups are allotted less than their fair share of costs, or an unfairly high share of earnings.[5] Most obviously, those projects will appear more profitable than they really are: they may even seem to be profitable when they are actually generating losses. Deprived of their fair shares, operations elsewhere in the organisation will appear to be less profitable than they actually are; perfectly healthy operations may look like losers. As a result, operations that should be expanded may be curtailed, and those that should be cut may instead be encouraged. Performance-related pay will be a travesty: however carefully the right performances may have been identified, if the rules for measuring and reporting them are faulty, those performances will not be properly recognised. And when the contributions made are misattributed, distributive justice will not be done. If from ignorance, error or deliberate misrepresentation the rules adopted do not accurately reflect the underlying realities, the resulting accounts will be worse than useless.

The second condition that must be satisfied for trustworthy management accounts to be produced is that the rules must be applied appropriately and consistently. If different departments are allowed to use different rules, or if the rules used within a department change every accounting period, or some groups just don't bother, a coherent picture of the business will be difficult to achieve.

Finally, the data to which the rules are applied must themselves have integrity. Whether the numbers are the result of simple counting or of applying sophisticated formulas to complex variables, 'hard financial data' do not produce themselves. The methods used for assembling them must be consistent and comprehensive: a financial statement is only as strong as its least reliable entry.

Given the scope that exists for things to go wrong, and the grave consequences for ethical business of having unreliable internal accounts, it is vital that the integrity of accounts be safeguarded. Contrary to popular belief, however, keeping accounts honest is not the job of financial auditors. Management accounts are seldom audited, and even in respect of those accounts that auditors do review, the role of financial auditors is very limited. Financial auditing is rather like a Ministry of Transport car inspection. The MOT only checks whether a vehicle can pass a few functional tests; it examines the brakes, tyres and emission levels. The MOT does not guarantee that the vehicle is either generally road-worthy or that it is good value. In like fashion, an auditor confirms that financial statements have been drawn up in accordance with Generally Accepted Accounting Principles. Financial auditors do not determine which of the many variants allowed by those principles should be employed; far less do they guarantee the general health or viability of the underlying business.[6]

Keeping accounts honest is, instead, one of the key functions of an ethical audit, a key business ethics tool that will be described below.[7] Like a financial audit, an ethical audit evaluates the rules used in compiling internal financial statements, and the way they are applied. Unlike a financial audit, however, the ethical audit evaluates the rules not by reference to official accounting standards, but by reference to the purpose of the financial statements. To satisfy the ethical audit, the accounts must make it possible to judge whether the business's activities are actually maximising long-term owner value. Accordingly, the ethical audit checks whether the rules used in drawing up the accounts properly reflect the underlying realities of the business under review. It checks whether the information that is being provided about the business is adequate for properly managing and controlling the business. And it checks whether the information is true, fair and comprehensive, and presented in such a way that it can readily be used.

But however important ethical audits are for determining whether accounts are properly compiled, the responsibility for maintaining honest accounts is first and foremost that of the business itself.[8] To guard the integrity of its accounts, a business should make sure they are, to the fullest extent possible, transparent. The rules used for drawing up the accounts, together with their assumptions and underlying rationales, should be fully disclosed within the business. Finally, it should be made easy for the accounts to be challenged: if it can be shown that the rules or their application do not properly reflect the realities of doing business, the rules should be changed.

When a business has reliable management accounts, external reports that genuinely reflect those accounts will give a true and fair picture of the condition of the business. Given their different purposes, external reports and accounts will typically be less frequent and less detailed than management accounts. But the principal function of both kinds of accounts should be the same: they should provide readers with the information necessary for assessing how well owner value is being maximised, how well the business purpose is being achieved.

MERGERS AND ACQUISITIONS

Focusing on the purpose of business is the key to resolving most of the ethical concerns associated with mergers and acquisitions ('M&A'). Mergers and takeovers, buyouts and buyins have regularly been subject to scathing criticism. They have been castigated for destroying industries, communities and proper capital structures, for causing losses of jobs and careers, for unsettling suppliers, customers and traditional power relations . . . they have indeed been blamed for most of the ills of modern economies.

But though such criticisms are extremely widespread, and are often couched in moral terms, they are almost never genuinely ethical in nature. Mostly they are either protests from the displaced, or disguised statements of preference as to public policy. Or they are simply expressions of regret, wistful or waspish, that business's objective is not some variety of social welfare. Typically, they reflect a fundamental misunderstanding of, and sometimes outright hostility to, business as the maximising of long-term owner value.

In order properly to evaluate these criticisms, it is necessary to identify exactly what is at issue, bearing in mind that the morality of takeovers[9] is not a function either of their economic efficiency or of their contributions to social welfare. The rest of this section will examine in detail a number of the criticisms commonly levelled against takeovers, to determine whether what is attacked is indeed unethical, and if so, what should be done.

Common criticisms

Stakeholder Upheaval

One common charge is that takeovers are by their very nature destructive of the interests of stakeholders: they eliminate jobs, threaten communities, disrupt relationships with suppliers and customers. In evaluating such criticisms, the crucial point is that not all stakeholders' interests are equally legitimate. The purpose of business is maximising *owner* value; the interests of the other stakeholders are relevant to the business only insofar as they contribute to that definitive end. The disruption of stakeholders may pose matters of serious business concern to an acquiror; such disturbances may, if severe enough, even raise questions of public policy. But the mere fact of stakeholder disturbance is irrelevant to assessing the morality of takeovers. The ethical status of takeovers, like that of all other business activities, is a function solely of whether they respect distributive justice and ordinary decency while aiming to maximise long-term owner value.

However much one may sympathise with those suffering radical change as the result of a takeover, it is nevertheless wrong to think that the victims have any 'rights' to a continuation of the status quo. Change is a fact of life and *a fortiori* of business life. All stakeholders must regularly deal with disruptive changes, whether they are caused by takeovers, adverse economic conditions or political coups. Businesses

have no right to continued existence; when they fail to maximise the value of their owners, they are properly wound up
or taken over. And merely abolishing jobs is not immoral, for
workers do not have jobs as of right; business's obligation is to
maximise long-term owner value, not to provide full or even
partial employment. Indeed, despite the widespread British
belief to the contrary, it can even be a good thing—for business, for the economy, even for employees' own self-esteem
and pocketbooks—when workers are released from unproductive employment, and freed to make a greater contribution to long-term owner value elsewhere. Change is
positively beneficial when the alternative is death or decay.

The relevant matter in assessing the ethical status of
takeovers is not the fact that they may cause major changes,
but how those changes are handled: well or ill, ethically or
otherwise. If they are to be ethical, business actions must be
directed at maximising long-term owner value and conducted with distributive justice and ordinary decency. Simply
recognising the definitive purpose of business can do much
to prevent the worst excesses: when the objective is accepted
and the counterproductive effects of unethical conduct are
understood, sheer prudence can promote ethical conduct.

A prudent target will, for example, give its stakeholders as
much information about their likely prospects as it can, as
early as possible. Similarly, a prudent acquiror will encourage
displaced workers to apply for vacancies elsewhere in the
enlarged organisation; it may even offer them training so as
to take advantage of their local presence and familiarity with
the industry. But equally, if unproductive, disruptive or
inflexible workers were the reason why the target was under-
performing, the acquiror pursuing long-term owner value
will be right—ethically as well as economically—to fire them
as fast as contracts and regulation permit.

The disruptions caused by takeovers can be altogether
moral, or partly so, or not at all: it all depends on how they are
handled. By precipitating major changes, takeovers provide
significant occasions for behaving badly. But opportunities for
misconduct are, unfortunately, provided by any major source
of change, be it growth or restructuring or regulation.

However unfortunate the bad business behaviour associated with takeovers may be, the takeovers themselves are merely the occasion for such lapses; they are not the cause. As methods of transferring control, takeovers are no more intrinsically immoral than elections are.

Reversal of Fortune

But perhaps the problem isn't simply that takeovers cause change, but that they replace pillars of the community with ruthless asset strippers. Takeovers, it is claimed, undermine the very foundations of society, since they allow smaller companies and relative unknowns to gain control of major businesses. But there is no reason why they shouldn't. Substantial power inversions no doubt come as an unpleasant shock to those who are toppled, but they are not intrinsically immoral. What determines whether a particular change of business control is ethical is, as always, simply whether it is compatible with maximising long-term owner value subject to respecting distributive justice and ordinary decency.

The possibility of reverse takeovers, in which a smaller company takes over a larger one, can in fact be positively beneficial, both to the businesses involved and the communities in which they are situated. Power that cannot be challenged is more likely to ignore ethical constraints; by helping to keep large businesses accountable, takeovers and the threat of takeovers can perform an essential ethical service.

Breach of Trust

A more serious charge against takeovers is that they transfer wealth to shareholders by violating implicit contracts with other stakeholders[10]. Businesses often lead their stakeholders to expect that certain sorts of behaviour will be rewarded over the long term. The reliable supplier expects a chance to match competitors' bids, the faithful employee expects job security, the important customer expects flexibility on credit terms. The charge is that takeovers divert the expected rewards from the stakeholders who have earned them to the shareholders.

Since honouring obligations is a crucial part of observing ordinary decency, the accusation of breach of trust is a grave one. For such a charge to be valid, however, three conditions would have to be satisfied. The specific agreements entered into by the target would have to have been legitimate arrangements. They would have to have been wrongly breached. And for takeovers to be condemned as intrinsically unethical, such violations of trust would have to be a necessary feature of takeovers. How do takeovers fare against these conditions?

The first point to be recalled is that not all undertakings are legitimate for a business. All stakeholders have a responsibility to understand what business is about, and consequently to be wary of making or accepting unbusinesslike undertakings in their business capacities. Indeed, ordinary decency requires that a business not encourage inappropriate expectations in its stakeholders.

Having encouraged realistic ones, a business should, however, not disappoint them without good reason and explanation. So critically important is trust to business, that legitimate expectations should indeed normally be respected whether they were created by formal contracts or promises or by less stringent forms of unwritten understanding. If the firm has elicited low base wages and flexible work schedules from its workers by verbally promising them performance-related bonuses, it would be unethical, as well as deeply counterproductive, for an acquiror to renege on that undertaking. But that is because it is generally wrong to lie and to break promises.[11]

Far from being a necessary element of takeovers, breach of trust is likely to damage the ensuing business, and render the takeover unworkable. Normally, a business will benefit from violating undertakings only if the undertakings themselves violate the purpose of business or distributive justice or ordinary decency. Unethical breaches do take place, of course, but sadly they occur rather more often in the course of ordinary business than as a result of acquisitions; many an incumbent manager has benefited from unethically exploiting the loyalty and trust of his staff.

The most problematical situation occurs when management have actively encouraged *inappropriate* expectations. The moral question then is: what obligation is there, in a takeover or otherwise, to satisfy undertakings that are contrary to maximising long-term owner value, distributive justice or ordinary decency? Management may have led workers to expect job security come what may, or regular pay rises unrelated to productivity; they may have led their historical suppliers to believe that they would always remain so, regardless of their performance or competitiveness; they may have recruited expert staff with the lure of technical support whatever the expense. Insofar as what they offered was contrary to ethical business, however, those undertakings should never have been made; whoever made them exceeded their legitimate authority. The extent to which they should be honoured thus depends largely on the form which those undertakings took. If they were embodied in contracts, or were actually promised, the standard arguments for keeping promises and contracts apply, and the commitments should normally be honoured. Care must be taken, though, to explain that they are being honoured because of their form, and in spite of their content.

If the unjustified undertakings were simply suggested, however, then there is no ethical obligation for the business to fulfil them[12]—whether or not any takeovers occur. That such inappropriate arrangements are more likely to be identified and corrected after an acquisition, does not make takeovers themselves unethical. Quite the reverse: it is a point in favour of takeovers, not against them. Nevertheless, the disappointment of even inappropriate expectations is likely to produce a sense of grievance, especially if the implicit undertakings were instrumental in luring the stakeholders into dealing with the business. Unfortunately, those responsible for creating the problems, the old managers, can seldom be made to rectify the damage and provide compensation to those wronged; it usually falls to the acquiror[13] to suffer and correct the consequences of the previous managers' irresponsibility.

The right course of action in such circumstances will be a

matter of careful judgement, combined with clear explanation. The acquiror will need to consider a number of points: How long and how strong were the expectations? What did the stakeholders give up in exchange for the expected benefits? How obvious should it have been to the stakeholder that what was expected was unrealistic and illegitimate? What are the long-term economic consequences of fulfilling/disappointing the expectations likely to be? How will the breach be regarded by potential stakeholders?

In the interests of goodwill, the acquiror may sometimes decide to offer the aggrieved stakeholders some compensation for their disappointment, or to satisfy some of the inappropriate expectations it has inherited. If it does so, however, it should make it perspicuously clear to all involved that it is doing so only to fulfil vestigial, inappropriate commitments. The business must be extremely careful to relay that message unambiguously, or what was intended to promote the business, by preserving trust, will instead undermine the business, by reinforcing and perpetuating inappropriate expectations.

In summary, then, the charge that takeovers must be unethical since they necessarily involve breaches of trust, does not survive examination. Since trust is so critical to business's ability to maximise owner value over the long-term, violations of trust normally harm the business as much in the context of takeovers as they do at any other time. Breaches are therefore only likely to occur when those involved focus on short-term gain at the expense of long-term owner value. Such deviations do sometimes occur prominently in the course of takeovers. But when they do, the perpetrators have not just violated business ethics, they have denied business itself: it is the teleopathic deviations, not the takeovers, that are unethical.

Misallocation of Resources
Another common charge against takeovers is that they transfer resources from productive enterprises into power games. Time, money, energy and attention that should be devoted to capital investment, to long-term research and development,

to managing the business generally, are, it is alleged, diverted
into pursuing or repelling wasteful takeover bids, or paying
off the vast amounts of debt incurred in doing so. On the sur-
face, this seems a devastating criticism: if takeovers necessarily interfered with doing business, if they were intrinsically
incompatible with maximising long-term owner value, then
they would indeed be something to be avoided.

Once again, however, the valid moral criticism applies not to
takeovers as such, but only to those takeovers that are not
justified even on straightforward financial grounds. Takeovers
undertaken just to prevent management boredom[14], or to satisfy managements' imperial ambitions, or to follow commercial
fashion, are indeed unethical. By diverting resources from
proper business ends, such takeovers represent gross teleopathy, and often cause enormous damage both to owner value and
to stakeholders' lives. Because their objective is other than maximising long-term owner value, however, such takeovers are also
strictly unbusinesslike; they violate not only ethical principles,
but those of accepted takeover theory. Such unbusinesslike
takeovers are rightly to be deplored, and the managements who
initiate them should be removed by the owners of the businesses
whose resources they so egregiously waste.

What about the businesses that are the targets of bids or
that fear they might be? Isn't it unethical that their resources
should have to be diverted to dealing with the threat? Not
necessarily. However unfortunate it may seem that attention
has to be paid to an unsolicited and unwelcome development, change is an inescapable part of doing business.
Furthermore, even a bid that is contrary to the owner value of
the bidder may, despite—or sometimes precisely because
of—that fact be in the best business interests of the target:
when an ambitious buyer is willing to pay over the odds, willing sellers can profit.

Each bid must be examined on its merits, from the point of
view of the target as well as the bidder. Some bids are in the
best interests of all concerned. When, for example, the bidder is better run than the target, the target will typically
benefit, ethically as well as economically, from the bidder's
attentions; they force it to consider and improve its former

ways. Those bids that are ill-judged, trivial or initiated mainly for their nuisance value are indeed unfortunate, and may seem like extortion to their targets. But such bids are also, by their very nature, likely to be bad business for the bidders initiating them. Fortunately, however, since takeovers do still have to be approved by owners (at least in well-ordered jurisdictions[15]), businesses that have genuinely maximised long-term owner value are likely to be protected against such bids: they are less obvious targets, and are better able to defend themselves.

'Short-termism'

But doesn't the need to keep share prices up contribute to unethical 'short-termism'? Only if business and the stock market are misunderstood.[16] The best way to bolster share price, and to avert unacceptable takeover bids, is normally to make just those investments and commitments that maximise long-term owner value. 'Short-termism' that seeks current period accounting profits at the expense of long-term owner value is teleopathic. And it is much more likely to hurt than to help the share price: unlike managers, investment analysts and professional investors typically look at long-term sustainable cash flows[17].

What about 'short-termism' on the part of investors: isn't it unethical for investors to sell their stake and allow a takeover to happen? No: there is normally no moral obligation to own, or to continue to own, a business. The reasons for selling ownership interests are many, and are as varied as owners' reasons for investing. But insofar as decisions to sell are business decisions, stakeholders cannot legitimately expect that they will be based on anything but considerations of maximising long-term owner value.

Hostile takeovers

But perhaps it's not takeovers generally, but hostile takeovers that are unethical. Once again, the answer is No, not necessarily. The key to the moral evaluation of hostile takeovers is understanding exactly what hostile takeovers are. Takeovers are not labelled 'hostile' because they are inimical to the interests of stakeholders. Nor are they called 'hostile' because they are intrinsically damaging. What renders a takeover 'hostile' is simply opposition—for whatever reason—from the board of the target business: if the board does not welcome the bid, then the bid is deemed hostile. Since, however, (UK) boards are normally dominated by executive directors, hostile takeovers are typically just those takeovers to which the *managers* of the target are hostile[18].

Managers have all sorts of reasons for opposing bids. They may be trying to provoke a higher offer price, and accordingly acting in the interests of maximising long-term owner value. Or they may be protecting their own vested interests; if the business is taken over, their very jobs are likely to be at stake. Each takeover must be examined on its individual merits, and judged ethical according to whether it observes distributive justice and ordinary decency while pursuing maximum long-term owner value. The moral status of hostile takeovers is no different than that of other takeovers.

Why then are hostile takeovers so widely reviled? Mainly for the wrong reasons. It is not a legitimate criticism of business X that it does not take as its objective the interests of an unrelated business Y. Yet that is what is asserted when bidders, in such contexts normally called 'predators', are charged with not preserving or protecting the interests of their targets, often referred to as the 'prey'. It is not even the function of business X to maximise the long-term owner value of business Y. What X's objective should be, is simply to maximise the long-term owner value of X.[19]

That is not to say that hostile takeovers are never the occasion for immoral activity. Fierce contests with high stakes often provoke deplorable conduct, and contested bids are no exception. Given the different interests that are involved— predators and targets, managers and boards and owners, minority and majority shareholders—the likelihood of conflict is great, and the potential for abuse of power is enormous. So some of the criticism of hostile takeovers is justified. But most of it is not.

Consider the two-tier tender offer, for example, one of the

most aggressive of American bidding techniques.[20] In it, the first 51% of shareholders to tender their shares to the bidder receive a premium over the then market price, while the remaining 49% receive only promissory notes for the tender amount, typically payable at some distant future date. Staunch defenders of owners' interests have condemned the technique as 'unconscionable', as 'all-out robbery of share-holders' and as 'inherently coercive'.[21] But is that description justified? And how, if at all, is the technique unethical?

Perhaps the technique is unethical simply because it offers different shareholders different prices for their shares. But in principle there is nothing wrong with that: even when share-holders sell their shares through the stock exchange, they receive different prices depending on market conditions at the time of sale. The price of a share, like that of any traded good, is simply what a purchaser is willing to pay at the time. When demand is constant, prices normally decline as supply increases ... it is a sad but commonplace fact that not everyone can benefit equally from limited opportunities. In such circumstances, 'first come, first served' is a standard principle of allocating commercial goods.

But doesn't the fairness element of ordinary decency require that equals be treated equally? Here, it would seem, all shareholders are offering the same good—their shares—to the same purchaser, but they still do not get the same value in return. Isn't that unfair? It may indeed seem so to those receiving the lower value, but in fact the shares aren't all worth the same to the bidder[22]: it is only a subset of the total (and indeed probably considerably less than 51%) that confer control and that therefore command a premium. The amount tendered for a controlling interest is normally (and appropriately) greater than the ordinary market price.

Finally, though the technique may seem compelling, it is so only in the metaphorical sense that any extremely attractive, short-lived opportunity is. The tender is not coercive so long as none of the shareholders is forced to accept, so long as no physical violence has been used or threatened to secure their acceptance. So although the two-tier tender offer may well appear harsh, it is not intrinsically unethical.

'Shark repellents'

A defensive technique prompted by the two-tier tender offer
is even more controversial: the 'poison pill'. The name itself
is provocative, suggesting some form of murderous device. In
fact, 'poison pills' are nothing but the common designation
for 'shareholders' rights plans'. When companies with such
plans are the subject of a hostile bid, their shareholders automatically gain rights or warrants to buy shares from, or sell
shares to, their own company and/or the potential acquiror,
and to do so at a non-market price. The effect of such plans is
to dilute the value of the acquiror's stake and to make the
mooted acquisition prohibitively expensive.

Once it is clear what poison pills actually are, however, it
also becomes clear that, as with other financing techniques,
their ethical status depends on precisely how they are structured and used. If used to protect shareholders against
unwanted bids, poison pills are a good thing. If, however,
they are used to protect managements at the expense of
shareholders, they emphatically are not.

Unfortunately, poison pills have all too often been used
unethically, to disenfranchise owners and to diminish long-
term owner value. Insofar as they prevent hostile bids, poison
pills effectively transfer voting rights from owners to managements. Owners normally get to vote—if at all—only on those
takeover bids that have formally been presented to them by
their boards of directors. It is the management-dominated
boards, however, who decree bids hostile and thus automatically trigger poison pills. As a result, many bids are simply not
made, or are quashed long before they reach a shareholder
vote.

Given the conflicts of interest that often exist between
managements and owners, poison pills can thus be extremely
dangerous. By enhancing managements' power to prevent
takeovers without reference to shareholders, poison pills
lessen proper management accountability. And by allowing
managers to reject takeovers simply because they are contrary to their own interests, they seriously increase the potential for subverting the definitive purpose of business. Their

introduction without explicit owner approval is, therefore, clearly immoral. If they are properly structured, however, even poison pills can be ethical. When they are explicitly approved by owners, and those owners are represented by boards that are fully committed to maximising long-term owner value, poison pills can legitimately help protect businesses from unwanted distractions.

The key issue in the ethical evaluation of all 'shark repellents' is shareholder approval. 'Poison puts', 'people pills' and 'pac-men', 'golden parachutes' and voluntary recapitalisations are normally acceptable if approved by shareholders and used to combat bids that owners actually oppose. When they are not explicitly approved by shareholders, however, 'shark repellents' prevent owners from exercising their fundamental rights to dispose of their property as they see fit; used by boards to thwart bids that owners might accept, they are positively unethical.

Consider 'greenmail'. Greenmail occurs when a company agrees to pay more than the market price to buy its own shares from a potential predator, to stop the company's being 'put into play' as a takeover target. Why is greenmail so reviled? Partly, perhaps, because of the presumed parallel to blackmail. In blackmail, a genuine or imagined wrong is tolerated in exchange for silence money. What is averted by paying greenmail, in contrast, is simply a takeover bid that may be positively advantageous to the shareholders. Alternatively, the target may perceive greenmail as a threat to 'hijack' the business. But the greenmailer's 'alien' objective is just a takeover bid: since takeovers, even hostile takeovers, are neither intrinsically inimical to business nor unethical, nor yet is greenmail.

Indeed, most common criticisms of greenmail miss the point. First, the fact that the greenmailer may be getting riches beyond the dreams of avarice, and for what looks like little effort, does not constitute a moral criticism of greenmail, however much envy it may provoke. Second, it is normally those who *pay* greenmail, not those who demand it, who act unethically. Buying shares in a company is not in itself immoral[23]; nor is offering to sell them at a premium.

Neither is it intrinsically unethical either to moot a takeover or to withdraw from one.[24] Finally, greenmailing is not a form of extortion: no one is forced to pay the greenmailer's price. The alternative to paying greenmail is not violence, but a potentially beneficial takeover bid.

What makes greenmail unethical is the use of company money to undermine achievement of the company's objectives. Not only are the funds not being employed in productive business activities, but the purpose of the purchase is precisely to avert a takeover bid that might well increase owner value. Owners are thus doubly deprived: they are robbed of both funds and of choice. Greenmail that is paid by managements without shareholder consent is thus subversive of long-term owner value and genuinely unethical. Greenmail that shareholders explicitly approved, in contrast, would not be teleopathic: it is up to the owners to set the objectives of their corporation.

Buyouts

Problems similar to those posed by greenmail are presented by buyouts[25]. 'Management buyouts', 'MBOs', are a kind of takeover in which the principals making the bid are the existing managers of the target business; in 'management buyins', 'MBIs', the managers making the bids come from outside the target firm; combinations of the two are sometimes called 'BIMBOs': buyin management buyouts. Buyouts are typically supported by large amounts of debt, and are therefore sometimes known as 'leveraged buyouts', 'LBOs', especially when the transaction has been initiated by the financial backers rather than the management themselves.

The key business ethics issue posed by management buyouts is that of conflict of interest: the interests of the bidding management and of the owners of the business appear to be directly opposed in several ways. Most fundamentally, if the bidding managers believe that they could generate greater value from the business than it currently produces, it would seem that they should be extracting that value for the benefit of the existing owners.

That essential conflict is exacerbated by the mechanics of making and responding to takeover bids, in which the management are typically policeman, prosecutor and judge. It is normally management who have sole control over the content and timing of the information provided to the board of directors, which itself largely consists of and has probably been selected by those same managers. Furthermore, with their intimate knowledge of the workings of the firm, the management are in a very much better position than the shareholders or any competing bidder to know exactly what the business might be worth. They have even been in a position to run down the firm, so that their offer will appear more attractive. Given the immense benefits that the bidding management stand to reap if the buyout is successful, they are unlikely to be impartial judges of the shareholders' best interests.

These are serious considerations and, sadly, managers proposing management buyouts sometimes do act unethically. If the managers devote their energies to promoting their own interests instead of long-term owner value, they are in violation of their fiduciary responsibilities to the company and its owners. If they attempt to cheat the owners of what rightfully should be theirs, if they reveal confidential information in their attempts to secure financing for the proposed buyout, then they are indeed violating the conditions of business ethics. But what is immoral is their deviant conduct, not the buyouts themselves: the possibility of unethical use does not make an instrument unethical.

It may be, for example, that the subject of the management buyout is not the whole business, but some subsection of it. That subsection might indeed be more productive if freed from the bureaucracy of the rest of the group, or from strategies that might be incompatible. Or it might be that the managers proposing the buyout are not the firm's senior executives, but managers whose efforts on behalf of the business have been thwarted by inefficient, incompetent or teleopathic management at the top. Although all employees' energies should, of course, be focused on maximising long-term value for the existing owners, it may be the owners' own stewards who have prevented them from doing so.

When the board (and the shareholders) allow less than maximum performance, it is appropriate for those who could do better to make an attempt to improve matters . . . whether they come from outside or inside the firm. It would be preferable if managers could simply compete to manage the firm better for the existing shareholders. Until arrangements exist for doing so, however, or mechanisms are introduced that ensure stricter management and board accountability, a management buyout can help to alert owners to the unrealised potential of the business. If the price offered by the bid is greater than the value likely to be realised otherwise, it is sensible for the owners to demand why . . . and to accept if they cannot restructure the business to achieve a comparable value internally. If the price offered is not sufficient, then the owners can, as always, mount what has been called the 'Nancy Reagan'[26] defence: they can just say No.

The best antidote to conflict of interest, with respect to buyouts as elsewhere, is full disclosure and arm's-length negotiation. Although in most jurisdictions, conditions do unfairly favour the interests of incumbent managements over those of shareholders, this is an argument for better corporate governance, not an argument against corporate buyouts. Shareholders should be willing to consider buyouts on their merits so long as they[27], and all competing bidders, have equal access to information[28], and so long as all the development costs of the management buyout are borne not by the company, but by the managers who are making the bid—as they would be if the bidder were an unrelated company.[29] To prevent managements from initiating nuisance bids and wasting time that should more properly be devoted to furthering the business's interests, it might even be appropriate to insist that when management-led bids are unsuccessful, the costs of defending the business against them should also be for the personal accounts of the internal bidders, just as UK court costs for both sides are normally for the account of the loser.

In summary, then, takeover techniques, whether aggressive or defensive, are only unethical if they undermine the definitive business purpose, or violate the requirements of distributive justice or ordinary decency. So long as shareholders have the chance properly to review and vote on bids and 'shark repellents', such techniques can be perfectly compatible with the demands of business ethics.

JUNK BONDS

It was in connection with takeovers that 'junk bonds' had their most visible and controversial use. Junk bonds are simply (high yield) straight debt securities with a less than investment grade rating[30]. 'Less than investment grade' ratings can be achieved in two ways. Traditionally, most junk bonds were 'fallen angels': bonds which were originally of investment grade, but whose issuers had fallen on hard times. The innovation of the 1980s was the development of a market for debt securities that were less than investment grade from the outset, because they were issued by small, young or heavily indebted companies.

Reflecting media frenzy, public reaction to junk bonds changed from scepticism to enthusiasm to vituperation in less than a decade. Sadly, some of those most prominently associated with the issuing and trading of junk bonds were engaged in activities that were both illegal and immoral.[31] But one can regret the misdeeds of Michael Milken and Drexel Burnham, and deplore extortion and market manipulation, without attaching any moral criticism to junk bonds themselves. As an inanimate instrument, however sophisticated, a junk bond can no more be moral or immoral than a spoon can.

Like takeovers, junk bonds have usually been condemned for being seen in bad company, and for being used in ways that have been widely, though inappropriately, resented. Junk bonds were conspicuous in financing management buyouts and in funding the takeovers of large firms by small ones. By allowing established power structures to be overturned, such transactions attracted violent, albeit largely undeserved, criticism; the criticism was often, and even less appropriately, extended to junk bonds themselves. Similarly,

junk bonds were often blamed for the US savings and loan
crisis, because S&Ls invested unwisely in (loss-making) port-
folios of junk bonds. The source of the moral hazard was,
however, not the junk bonds but inappropriately structured
US deposit insurance.

The first step in evaluating the moral status of junk bonds
is to identify what exactly is at issue. As stated, the query 'Are
junk bonds a good thing?' potentially raises any number of
issues . . . of public policy, power politics and finance, as much
as of morality. The question needs refining: for whom, for
what, are junk bonds a good thing? For fund managers or
hostile bidders or 'white knights'? For investment bankers or
commercial bankers? For investors? For regulators with political ambition? For MBOs? For MBAs? For the economy? In
aggregate for all of the above? Often, the popular debate is
not about junk bonds at all, but about takeovers or leverage,
insider trading or upstarts' gaining power.

Many of the questions embedded in the general query are
actually ones of economic and public policy. 'Are junk bonds
a safe/productive/economically efficient way of financing
assets/takeovers/MBOs/corporate restructurings?' 'Do the
transfers of wealth and power permitted by junk bond
financed takeovers of large corporations by smaller ones contribute to instability?' 'What controls are appropriate for preventing abuses of near-monopoly power in securities'
markets?' 'Is the high level of debt associated with junk bond
financed projects advantageous for industry in the long
term?' Such economic and public policy concerns are often
confused with, and get in the way of, genuinely ethical assessment.

The questions that are relevant to the conduct of individual businesses are much narrower: 'Are junk bonds a suitable
investment for this portfolio?', 'Are junk bonds the best way
of financing this project?' Such questions are much easier to
answer, and may indeed not give rise to any particular ethical
perplexity. For the managers of equity funds, junk bonds are
inappropriate investments just because they are not equity
instruments. Conversely, the manager of a junk bond fund
must invest in junk bonds: doing anything else would violate

his portfolio's very reason for being. And the appropriateness of junk bonds for financing a particular project is a function of the markets and the alternatives available. If interest rates are prohibitively high, junk will not be a sensible option. But if the price is right, and the amount of debt is acceptable, they may be the best possible choice.

Whether a particular use is moral will depend, as always, on whether it is compatible with maximising long-term owner value subject to distributive justice and ordinary decency. That judgement is distinct from the moral assessment of the project being financed: the use of junk bonds can be unethical even if the project is perfectly moral. If, for example, taking on large amounts of expensive debt will jeopardise long-term owner value, then issuing junk bonds will be teleopathic even if the project otherwise is not. And regardless of the status of the project, a particular issue of junk bonds will violate distributive justice if the mandate to arrange it has been awarded on the basis of anything but ability to maximise long-term owner value. Equally, ordinary decency will be violated if the terms of the issue have been misrepresented, or if investors have been coerced into buying, or if securities regulations have been violated. But if the junk bond financing is compatible with maximising long-term owner value, and respects distributive justice and ordinary decency, it will be perfectly ethical.

INSIDER TRADING

Like junk bonds and takeovers, insider trading is a subject that has suffered from much public misunderstanding, and many conceptual confusions. A large part of the problem is that the term 'insider trading' is used very loosely, particularly by the media and politicians. Sometimes it is used to encompass all forms of securities-related illegal or immoral activity. Other times it is used to refer to all questionable activities by insiders . . . even when not securities-related. Such promiscuous usage has been encouraged by the term's having no single, generally accepted meaning: ordinarily, insider trading is just whatever it is interpreted to be under local regulation[32]—when such regulation exists. Insider trading is thus a prime example of the need to distinguish between the ethical and the legal: it is important to identify exactly what is wrong, so that appropriate action can be taken and legislation can be properly judged.

The activities referred to as insider trading and the ways in which they are treated vary enormously, even in sophisticated markets. In some major jurisdictions[33], insider trading is no crime[34]. Traditionally, it has been an expected, and perfectly acceptable, perquisite of certain sorts of employment: brokers get inside information, the way that bankers get subsidised mortgages and airline staff get cheap flights. Until quite recently, this was the attitude to insider trading even in the US and the UK. Since the late 1960s, however, insider trading has attracted stern disapproval and strict regulatory control in both America and England. Though meaning very different things in the two jurisdictions, insider trading was criminalised in both during the 1980s, and was blamed for many of the major financial scandals of the 1980s and 1990s. But much of the condemnation has been politically motivated[35], and many of the practices condemned have not been insider trading at all.

So what is insider trading? For the purposes of this discussion, 'insider trading' will be used to mean what it does in the European Community's 1989 Insider Dealing Directive[36]: dealing on the basis of material, unpublished price-sensitive information that is possessed as a result of one's employment, profession or duties. Besides being illegal in some jurisdictions, what is wrong about insider trading understood in this way? In principle it seems only right for the more assiduous, inquiring, analytical investor—or broker—to be able to achieve better investment results than those not bothering to do their prep. And who better, after all, to 'counsel' the purchase or sale of shares than those closest to, and presumably best informed about, a company's plans and prospects? Yet insider trading is now regularly denounced as immoral. Why is this so?

Common criticisms

Equality of Opportunity
The traditional view is that insider trading is unfair, usually
because it is thought somehow to violate equality of opportunity. But this view is mistaken. Equality of opportunity is not
infringed by insiders' having advantages not enjoyed by outsiders: equality of opportunity does not require that all
potential competitors have the same natural abilities or posi-
tional advantages. To suppose that it does, is to confound
equality of opportunity with equality of outcomes . . . with
absurd results. The essence of equality of opportunity is simply that all those seeking a good be allowed to compete for it
equally on their merits. It does *not* require that the candidates
or the outcomes be equal; it does not even require that it be
equally easy for all to satisfy the entry requirements and participate in the competition.

How does this analysis of equality of opportunity apply to
trading in securities? The good in question consists of trading profits, or a reduction of trading losses; the rules for allocating them are the laws of supply and demand operating in
the market.[37] For equality of opportunity to exist, all that is
required is that access to the market be unimpeded, and that
the rules apply equally to all. No prospective trader should be
excluded from dealing on the basis of his identity, or the size
of the mooted transaction, or the source of funds used[38], and
orders should be processed on a strictly 'first come, first
served' basis.[39]

It is thus entirely possible for some traders to be better
informed or more perspicacious, or cleverer or richer or
even more successful, without there being any violation of
equality of opportunity. Equality of opportunity specifically
does not require that all potential traders have equal information or even equal access to information. Lacking insiders' information, outsiders' transactions will probably be less
successful than insiders' are. But outsiders' access to the market is nevertheless unimpeded: the fact of insiders' having
privileged information imposes no legal or coercive or arbitrary barriers to stop the outsiders from trading.

Nor indeed are there any legal or coercive obstacles to prevent outsiders from becoming insiders: equality of opportunity exists both with respect to trading and to acquiring positions that potentially have access to unpublished price-sensitive information. A trader who wants to benefit from insider knowledge can simply do what is necessary to become an insider—a corporate executive or a corporate cleaner, a professional adviser or a financial printer. Achieving such positions may well require considerable time and effort, but so may acquiring the capital with which to trade. So long as there are no coercive barriers to competing, however, the difficulties of achieving success are irrelevant to the existence of equality of opportunity.

Does anything in the securities markets violate equality of opportunity? Certainly. Equality of opportunity is, for example, clearly violated when there is a legal ban preventing an individual from trading simply because of the relationship he bears to a company. But this is exactly what happens when insider trading is officially prohibited. It is therefore regulation *against* insider trading, not insider trading itself, that violates equality of opportunity in trading securities.

Level Playing Fields and Handicapping
Perhaps, then, what is unfair about insider trading is instead that it precludes a 'level playing field' between insiders and outsiders? Once again, however, the suggestion is misguided. The sporting metaphor does not mean what its advocates in finance often seem to believe. A level playing field is no guarantee that the teams will be of equal ability, or have equal resources or stamina, or equal chances of winning. It does not even mean that the field of play will be either smooth or horizontal.

All that provision of a level playing field normally means is that some—not all—of the more obvious physical obstacles facing one side will also be faced by the other. If the field is steeply inclined, the obstacle to scoring that the slope represents will normally be reduced—not by getting out the bulldozer, but by making competitors change sides midway. Even so, however, the sun may still shine unequally into the eyes of the players.

In the field of securities trading, players regularly change roles. Just as sellers in one transaction will be buyers in others and vice versa, traders who are insiders in one transaction will be outsiders in others. Similarly, investors are sometimes existing shareholders and at other times are not. To the extent that the metaphor of the level playing field is relevant, therefore, the conditions implied by it seem to be compatible with insider trading. It is therefore not the absence of a level playing field that makes insider trading unfair or immoral.

It is interesting to note that although providing a level playing field does nothing to reduce participants' inequalities, there is a sporting operation that does: handicapping. Whether the objective is to encourage weaker players, or to create more exciting contests, handicapping serves precisely to prevent those with obvious natural advantages, or a record of greater success, from winning as easily as they might—and it does so specifically by denying them the benefits of their advantages. Thus favoured race-horses carry heavier weights, and skilled golfers start with higher scores.

It is therefore handicapping, not providing a level playing field, that much British securities regulation seems designed to achieve. In order to encourage wider share ownership, the UK government has sought to make investing in equities more attractive to individual investors. One of its main methods has been to try and convince retail investors that they are not irretrievably disadvantaged vis-à-vis professional, institutional investors. Accordingly, regulation has been introduced to limit institutions' ability to benefit from their size and comparative sophistication. Since one of the chief institutional advantages is direct access to company information, many traditional practices by which institutions gained that advantage, such as information meetings with companies, have been attacked by UK insider trading laws. But though the objective of equalising investors' chances may make such handicapping intelligible, it does not address what is really wrong with insider trading.

Teleopathy and misappropriation

And some, though by no means all, forms of insider trading are genuinely unethical. But they are not unethical because everyone is entitled to corporate information, and outsiders are unfairly disadvantaged compared with insiders: no such general entitlement exists. The only people who are morally entitled to possess information about a business are its owners, and even their rights to information are limited when they are shareholders. But it is only when the owners—the current shareholders[40]—are being deprived of their entitlements that insider trading is unfair. The immorality of insider trading is that information which belongs to the corporation (and thus ultimately to the shareholders), and which should in a business corporation be used to promote owner value, is instead misappropriated for the insiders' own interests.

Those who possess inside information directly are ordinarily those who have been entrusted with the information in their capacity as corporate employees, advisers or agents. When, therefore, they use the information for anything that hinders or undermines the corporate purposes, as insider trading often does, they violate their fiduciary responsibilities to the corporation. They violate those responsibilities regardless of whether they themselves deal on that information in ways that harm corporate ends, or whether they transmit the information to third parties who do so. It is equally irrelevant whether the third party is the classic 'tippee' in a dealing ring, or the in-house market maker in an integrated investment bank.

But not all unethical insider trading results from violations of fiduciary responsibility. If instead of being given the information by the corporation or its representatives, the insider dealers have simply taken the information, then what is involved is outright theft. And it is theft even though the information may remain to be used by its proper owners for other purposes after it has been used by the insiders: what is stolen is the chance to use that information first in a securities' transaction. In efficient markets, timing is critical: it matters when information is acted upon. If the benefit of being first goes to the errant insider rather than to the corporation or its shareholders, then they have been robbed of a significant asset.

Ethical insider trading

Understanding that it is misappropriation that makes insider trading unethical has several important implications. First, it makes it clear that not all insider trading is unethical: the manner of acquiring the inside information makes a difference to whether the insider trading is immoral or not. Trading on information obtained by virtue of conscientious observation and analysis, or assiduous investigation, must be distinguished from trading on information acquired through a breach of confidence or theft. The trader's relationship to the source of the information and to the subject of the information are therefore essential to determining the ethical status of any particular case of insider trading. If the information has been acquired incidentally or accidentally, trading on it may not be unethical.

Consider an example. A mathematics professor knows that his best Ph.D. student, who is capable of great things, is about to go to work for a computing company. The professor thus has unpublished, price-sensitive information that he has acquired as the result of his profession. If he then buys shares in the company, he is guilty of insider trading. But there is nothing immoral about his action. He has not misappropriated the information: he has no fiduciary responsibility to the company. And no information has been stolen, from the student or from the university. The professor is simply in a position to learn and appreciate the significance of a piece of information that might give rise to a trading advantage.

Equally, insider trading that is performed with the full knowledge and consent of the shareholders is not unethical. Shareholders who voluntarily surrender the benefits of the information they own, and who choose to allocate it instead to their functionaries, have made a legitimate decision about the disposition of their property. It may be a foolish decision, insofar as it creates a potential conflict of interest: employees who can profitably trade on information concerning their company's misfortunes may have less incentive to prevent them. But authorised insider trading cannot be teleopathic: the corporation's ends are just those determined by its shareholders. By agreeing that corporate insiders may trade for their own account using inside information, the shareholders have redefined their representatives' fiduciary responsibilities concerning their securities' trading activities. Since the insiders have been expressly allowed to employ the information for the purposes of their own trading, they will neither have misused nor misappropriated it in doing so. Consequently, insider trading to which the shareholders consent is not unethical.

Not a 'Victimless Crime'

Nonetheless, unethical insider trading is not a 'victimless crime'. Understanding that it is misappropriation that renders insider trading wrong makes it very clear who the victims of unethical insider trading are: they are the shareholders whose corporate information has been misappropriated.

Shareholders normally suffer when their corporate property is stolen, whether what is purloined is a trade secret, a company car or material price-sensitive trading information. The damage to owners that results from insider trading may be most obvious when the inside information is that of an impending takeover. But it can result as well from less dramatic news, from the company's entering a new market or selling a loss-making subsidiary. Trading by corporate insiders automatically harms owner value when it causes the company's share price to fall. But insider trading can hurt owners even when it causes prices to rise: if insider trading raises a target company's share price, it makes a takeover more expensive.

Although the primary victims of unethical insider trading are the shareholders of the company which is the subject of the inside information, they are not the only ones to suffer. If the insider trader is employed not by the subject company, but by a firm which was providing services to it, then that other firm and its shareholders will suffer as well. Because of the employee's fiduciary irresponsibility or theft, that organisation's reputation as a reliable adviser or agent, and consequently its ability to attract future custom, can be impaired.

Finally, immoral insider trading harms the market itself. It is not just the traders who are on the opposite side of the insiders' transactions[41] who lose; the overall reputation and viability of the securities exchange may well be diminished. When an exchange permits insider traders to rob shareholders of what is rightfully theirs, investors will be disinclined to trade on that exchange, and will be less willing to buy securities issued on it. Not only, therefore, will market liquidity be potentially reduced, but less capital will be available for corporate development.[42] Indirectly, at least, the entire economy is a victim of unethical insider trading.

In summary, then, insider trading is unethical when, but only when, the inside information has been misappropriated, when it has been acquired through violation of fiduciary responsibility or through theft. It is therefore not insider trading as such but misappropriation that should be recognised as the criminal offence. What is unfair about immoral insider trading is that in it, information that is owned by the corporation and that should be employed to promote the interests of its owners, is diverted instead to the private purposes of corporate agents or outright thieves. When, therefore, owners authorise insiders to use corporate information for their private purposes, the consequent inside trading is not unethical. When they do not, however, they are the clearest and most direct victims of unethical insider trading.

III

ETHICAL DIRECTION

8

Corporate Governance

'All corporate constituencies—management, stockholders, employees, customers and communities—win from a sound long-term strategy and fair treatment. Fair treatment of shareholders is the key to maintaining public confidence in the markets, financial institutions and public companies.'

Edward Johnson, Chairman of Fidelity Investments[1]

'The basic responsibility of an owner is to see that his property is properly looked after.'

Sir Adrian Cadbury[2]

'Corporate governance' is a phrase that has become increasingly common in public debate, especially in Britain. Disturbed by prominent examples of corporate wrongdoing, concerned about companies' dividend policies and high executive remuneration, and worried about 'short-termism' and firms' vulnerability to hostile takeovers, commentators have routinely prescribed better corporate governance as the cure.

Unfortunately, corporate governance is often misconstrued, and interpreted as if its task were not governing corporations but making them more like governments.[3] Many of the issues commonly raised in the name of corporate governance are in fact ones of public policy rather than business ethics. The corporate governance challenge is not to bind businesses to advancing macroeconomic aims or industrial policy—they should not, for that is not the purpose of business. Nor is corporate governance about balancing the claims of stakeholders. Properly understood, corporate governance refers simply to the need for, and ways of, ensuring that the corporation is pursuing its proper ends, typically by keeping directors and managers accountable to the shareholders.[4] The specifically ethical task of corporate governance is that of holding stakeholders to their proper corporate purposes.

THE NATURE OF THE CORPORATION: DEFINITION, CONDITIONS AND GOALS[5]

So far this book has concentrated primarily on business, not on the corporation that represents but one form of it. The corporate form is used by so very many businesses, however, that the ethical problems of corporate governance cannot be ignored. In this chapter, therefore, the focus will shift to the corporation.

A corporation is a legal fiction, an artificial person with a defining purpose which is normally but not necessarily that of doing business. Originally chartered only for special purposes, corporations are now routinely created, but are still differentiated by the ends for which they are formed and which they characteristically pursue.

The shareholders of a corporation are, collectively, its owners. In exchange for contributing capital and bearing the residual risk of the corporation, the shareholders ordinarily have a permanent, proportional participation in its profits (via dividends), its prospects (via capital gains) and its control (via voting rights and approval of directors). As the property of its shareholders, the corporation is accountable to them. The responsible shareholder holds the corporation and its agents to the corporate ends, the ones for which equity capital was provided: it is the shareholders who are ultimately responsible for corporate governance.

The corporate form is most characteristically used to achieve long-term ends, and has historically been granted two key privileges—limited liability and notional perpetual life—in order to promote sustained endeavours. Since, however, there are conditions that must be satisfied for long-term objectives to be achieved, part of what is involved in corporate governance and in being a responsible shareholder is ensuring that those underlying conditions are satisfied.

In particular, since operating over the long-term requires maintaining certain minimal conditions of confidence, a responsible shareholder will insist that the corporation's dealings be characterised by the ordinary decency necessary for preserving trust: honesty, fairness, the absence of coercion and violence, and at least the presumption of legality are thus essential. Furthermore, since the corporate objective is most likely to be achieved when it is contributions to that end, and not some other, that are rewarded by the corporation, classical distributive justice must be observed in the corporation's dealings. The responsible shareholder will thus ensure that the corporation and its agents comply with the demands of distributive justice and ordinary decency in pursuing corporate ends. Already identified as essential for business, these conditions apply to other corporate objectives as well.

Subject only to distributive justice, ordinary decency and local law, the ends sought by the ethical corporation can be anything that the shareholders agree they should be; a corporation need not have a business purpose. Many US corporations are explicitly 'not-for-profit', while the corporate form is often used for non-business purposes in less obvious ways: in Japan, for example, gangsters have been encouraged to incorporate[6].

Determining the corporate ends should be recognised as one of the shareholders' most important rights, and one of the fundamental ways in which ethical values can be imparted to what is otherwise a morally neutral form. Although it is wrong for employees or other stakeholders to impose their moral views on the corporation[7], the shareholders who collectively own it have the right to choose its objectives, and consequently can endow a company with an ethical stance. Even long after the corporation's founding, shareholders have the power to alter the corporate purposes: unlike the other stakeholders, who can only vote with their feet, the shareholders can vote at General Meetings.

The primary decision they must make is whether the corporation is to be a business at all. If it is, then the next determination is the *extent* to which it will be. They must decide the degree to which maximising long-term owner value will be qualified by other objectives—political correctness or religious orthodoxy or environmental purity, for example. Although in practice these decisions are typically made on the run, if at all, and are seldom presented to the shareholders for their explicit approval, they are in principle a key shareholder prerogative.

SHAREHOLDER RESPONSIBILITIES

Although in their capacities as moral agents shareholders have moral responsibilities that are many and varied, in their capacities as shareholders their moral responsibilities are very few: they are limited to those that arise from the nature of the corporation.

First, shareholders have responsibilities to their co-owners, the other shareholders. They should respect joint decisions made concerning the conduct of the corporation, and should make those decisions in accordance with the agreed rules, and with due regard for the corporate purpose. Reference to the corporate purpose is crucial: without agreement on a common objective, common ownership founders in even the simplest matters. When one joint-purchaser of a motorcar plans to maintain it as a classic museum piece, but the other wants to use it as a family runabout, the outcome is unlikely to be happy motoring.

Given the impersonal, fragmented nature of share ownership that obtains in the UK and the US, what does this responsibility to co-owners mean in practice? Despite the growing concentration of ownership in institutional hands, shareholders very rarely consult one another before making decisions; typically, shareholders do not even know who the other shareholders are. Moreover, different shareholders legitimately have different objectives, even investment objectives; they have different time scales, levels of sophistication and risk/reward profiles, different interests in and resources for enforcing their own interests.

What the responsibility to co-owners involves is simply that in their capacity as shareholders, and while they are shareholders, each co-owner should make the distinguishing purpose of the corporation the basis for his/its decisions concerning the conduct of the corporation. If all shareholders independently act on that same principle, they will not necessarily agree about what is right, but they will at least understand what is relevant. A responsible shareholder who wants to change the purpose of the corporation, or to use some principle other than the current corporate end as the basis for his decisions concerning the corporation, will make that fact explicit.

Does the shareholder, in his capacity as shareholder, have automatic responsibilities to anyone but the other shareholders? Yes, but only of the same very limited sort. As a public entity with a publicly declared purpose, the corporation creates *prima facie* expectations about the way in which it will behave. Since those expectations influence others' actions, shareholding in a corporation entails obligations to those others, normally the stakeholders, to ensure that those expectations are either corrected or satisfied. The shareholders are therefore responsible for ensuring that the corporation is pursuing its presumed purpose, or for giving notice that its purpose is other than that commonly supposed. This does not mean that the shareholders must undertake market research to determine the public's view of their property. Nor does it mean that the public's expectations are legitimate; frequently they are not. What it does mean is that shareholders should have a care to declare and respect the corporate aims.

Is this really necessary? Yes. Significant examples of teleopathy are all too common, and are responsible for many of the ills that provoke calls for better corporate governance. In its mildest forms, teleopathy wastes substantial time, effort and energy; in its more serious forms, the consequences can be fatal. Amongst the gravest instances of teleopathy are those corporations or associations that look like businesses, but in fact are not[8]: whether their actual ends are imperial, ideological or just personal, such organisations are typically a serious danger to themselves and to others. Failure to be clear about corporate purposes is particularly serious when organisations are seeking long-term commitments by employees. If the real objective of the organisation is not business but satisfying management's ambitions, then however diligently an employee may strive to maximise long-term owner value, his career will depend instead on gratifying management's possibly capricious whims. In such organisations, it is not just invested capital, but lives that are at stake.

'Short-termism'

Nevertheless, the governance charge most commonly laid against business is not teleopathy, but 'short-termism'. Shareholders' short-sighted demands for dividends and for constant improvement in company profits are, it is alleged, responsible for undermining long-term investment and planning. Instead of supporting British industry, shareholders 'disloyally' desert corporations for better returns elsewhere, and 'treacherously' accept takeover bids. Like so many popular criticisms, however, 'short-termism' in fact conceals a great many confused notions. Sometimes it is used as shorthand for the more fundamental complaint that British business is insufficiently productive or competitive or innovative. And sometimes it masks the converse fear, that British business is too innovative, all too ready opportunistically to desert traditional manufacturing for growth in the service sector.

But though commonplace, these criticisms are misguided.[9] To the extent that shareholders are at fault, it is not so much in failing to fulfil their obligations, as in failing to protect their rights: it is in respect of looking after their own interests that shareholders have been notably deficient. Major research studies have shown that it is typically not the shareholders, but the industrial managers, whose perspective is excessively short term.[10] According to these studies, investment analysts tend to judge a company's performance on the basis of long-term sustainable cash flows, whereas industrial managers tend to evaluate projects on the basis of brief pay-back periods and the short-term profits that typically determine their own remuneration.

The flaw that would rightly be criticised as 'short-termism' is using an inappropriately short-term measure for evaluating corporate performance: current period accounting profits are not necessarily a good gauge of long-term owner value. 'Short-termism' can accordingly be understood as another example of teleopathy: it is a misunderstanding of the objective to be sought, and of the appropriate criterion to be used in measuring achievement of that end. If industry and investors—otherwise known as managers and owners—are using different criteria, then it is hardly surprising that they are working at cross purposes. The solution is for both to use the same measure in pursuit of the same end: the proper purpose of the business corporation, maximising long-term owner value.

Shareholder loyalty

Nevertheless, institutions are still frequently exhorted to take a more 'responsible' attitude to their investments, to support the companies they invest in when things go wrong, not sell their shares.[11] But however well-meant this injunction may be, it is nevertheless based on a confused understanding of the role of the shareholder and of the corporation. To say that all shareholders should necessarily be active or long-term holders is to reverse the relationship of owner to property: if any fealty is owed, it is by the corporation to the shareholder, not vice versa.

There is, ordinarily, no moral obligation to become, or to continue to be, a shareholder. Being a shareholder is only one of the myriad roles open to an individual or an institution, and the reasons for choosing to be a shareholder are equally as diverse. Though some objectives encourage long-term holdings, others do not; they can, however, be equally legitimate reasons for owning shares. But it is the shareholder's objectives for owning shares that should determine if a particular holding is to be bought or kept or sold: the long-term goals appropriate for a pension fund may well not be sensible for any particular pensioner.

Insofar as an individual's or institution's objective in owning shares is to maximise financial gain, the buy/hold/sell decision will turn on whether the proceeds obtainable from selling the shares are greater than the value expected from keeping them. If they are, it is *right* to sell.[12] Nevertheless, shareholders are routinely criticised for doing so: their decisions to sell are castigated as somehow wrong, or irresponsible, especially if the sale is to a hostile bidder or a foreigner. What such charges imply, however, is that either the shareholder's calculation is inaccurate, or that the objective of financial maximisation is illegitimate. But if such financial maximisation is illegitimate, then so is business. . . .

Loyalty does not require that shareholders stick with a company when its performance is deficient. It may sometimes be appropriate to allow a company time to recover, or to help it do so, but the relationship of shareholder to corporation is not that of friend or family member, social worker or doctor; shareholders do not have a Hippocratic duty to heal or preserve the corporation. Nor do corporations have any right to life. The notional perpetual life enjoyed by a corporation enables it to survive any particular group of mortal investors, but should the corporation no longer meet the requirements of its shareholders, it can be wound up. And if it cannot meet its debts, then it can be forcibly liquidated.

The right way to ensure loyalty and long-term holdings is not to shackle investors to their investments, as some commentators have suggested. The proper solution is instead to make sure that shareholders' key objectives in owning shares are indeed best achieved by their holding on to them. And that is most likely if business corporations actually do maximise the long-term owner value that is their reason for being.

Why be a responsible shareholder?

So there is a connection between long-term shareholding and being a responsible shareholder after all. What links them, however, is not any responsibility of a shareholder to continue to be a shareholder: no such general responsibility exists, and long-term holdings are not necessarily responsible. The link is not that responsibility prescribes long-term holdings, but that it can and does foster them. If a shareholder acts responsibly as a shareholder, and holds the corporation to its proper ends, then that corporation will be more likely to merit and attract his continued investment. The best practical reason for being a responsible shareholder is simply that responsible shareholding can promote achievement of the very objectives for which shares are owned. In the US, activism has thus widely come to be seen as 'one of the soundest investments of the season'[13].

Some institutional shareholders have started to take a more active role in corporate governance, recognising that if shareholders can't or won't be bothered to protect their most fundamental rights, those rights may cease to function. But investment objectives are not always best served by shareholder activism: the structural and administrative obstacles to being a responsible shareholder are such that it can genuinely make more sense to cut and run. Mechanisms for enforcing accountability to shareholders are few and relatively feeble. And given the internal strictures imposed on many institutional shareholders, the costs to them of intervening, even of voting on board resolutions, may well exceed the benefits that they can reasonably expect to achieve.[14] The way to encourage responsible shareholding is, however, not to make sales of shares more difficult by impeding the market or by hindering takeovers. Nor is it to ape Germany or Japan, where owners have even fewer enforceable rights. The correct response is instead improved corporate governance: devising ways to ease the task of keeping corporations accountable to their shareholders.

Keeping them accountable is becoming all the more important, because the increasing concentration of ownership in institutional hands is making the sale of shares progressively less rewarding. When investment performance is measured against the market overall, selling shares of companies that constitute a large part of market capitalisation can be counterproductive even for funds that are not formally indexed. Moreover, the very size of US and UK institutional holdings can make them hard to sell without depressing prices, and hard to replace with suitable alternative investments. So institutional concentration may itself promote longer term views and greater responsibility: 'if one can't sell, one must care'.[15]

Institutional concentration could further reinforce responsible shareholding if the institutional investors were themselves held more strictly to their own constitutive ends and their associated fiduciary and contractual duties.[16] If the beneficiaries of pension funds, and the owners of insurance companies and of unit and investment trusts, were more demanding in respect of their property's performance, those institutions would in turn have to be more responsible in their capacity as shareholders.

Understanding the nature of the corporation, and the need to keep it accountable to its proper ends and owners, thus clarifies the proper meaning of shareholder responsibility. The same teleological method can illuminate the ethical implications of, *inter alia*, whistle-blowing, executive remuneration and dividend policies.

WHISTLE-BLOWING

Whether the expression comes from the referee blowing the whistle to stop play, or the policeman summoning aid to catch a runaway thief, whistle-blowing in its most general form involves calling (public) attention to wrongdoing, typically in order to avert harm. Although most frequently discussed in terms of an employee disclosing the dangerous or illegal or immoral activities of his employer, it could equally well arise in respect of exposing a friend's secret terrorist activities, or a physician's professionally murderous ones.

Whistle-blowing in business is often denounced as morally unjustifiable, on the presumption that it violates the duties of loyalty and confidentiality owed to the business. Alternatively, whistle-blowing is deemed to involve a fundamental clash of duties: the specific duties of loyalty and confidentiality to the firm are presented as conflicting both with a general duty to the public good, and with the whistle-blower's personal obligations to himself and his family. But both of these approaches are wrong. Whistle-blowing that reveals genuine wrongs[17] can be wholly consistent with personal, public and business duties.

To understand whistle-blowing properly, and to assess whether particular instances of whistle-blowing are ethical, it is necessary to untangle a series of related but conceptually distinct problems. What constitutes loyalty to a business? When, if ever, is whistle-blowing morally justifiable?[18] Under what circumstances, if any, is whistle-blowing morally obligatory? When is whistle-blowing prudent? When is it efficacious? These issues must be separated out and resolved to determine when whistle-blowing is morally justified, and to ensure that whistle-blowing in business is treated ethically.

Loyalty, confidentiality and justifiable whistle-blowing

Does whistle-blowing violate business loyalty? In answering the question, it is essential to recognise that there are many different sorts of loyalty, which give rise to correspondingly different obligations. Team loyalty is not the same as brand loyalty, and family loyalty differs from both allegiance to the flag and fidelity to one's friends. Loyalty to a group—a team, a club, a political party—is normally loyalty to that which defines and distinguishes the group; loyalty of group members typically derives from their shared commitment to the group's distinctive goals. What constitutes loyal behaviour by associates therefore critically depends on the objectives that define them as a group.

Because business has a specific, limited purpose, business loyalty is correspondingly limited. It is not the purpose of business to be a friend or a relative or a source of spiritual comfort. Accordingly, despite much misguided rhetoric to the contrary, it is inappropriate to demand friendly or familial loyalty from, or for, a business[19]: the limits of business relationships are legal and contractual. Supplemental loyalties may, of course, develop within a business: one's colleagues may also be one's friends. But the loyalties owed to them as friends must be recognised as different in kind from the obligations that arise out of the purely business association.[20]

What does business loyalty involve? The standard notion is that having taken the business's shilling, the employee is somehow obliged to promote its interests, and not to give aid and comfort to its competitors or its detractors. But this does not mean cleaving to the business whatever it may do, or whatever the consequences. Nor does it mean that shareholders, directors, managers and employees must unquestioningly support the current format of the enterprise, or its current staff. Still less does it mean adhering to one's immediate colleagues, right or wrong. Real business loyalty is instead being true to the proper purpose of the ethical business: maximising long-term owner value by selling goods or services, while respecting distributive justice and ordinary decency.

So understood, business loyalty does not normally preclude whistle-blowing: ordinarily, owner value is best served when the business avoids wrongdoing. That which harms or alienates stakeholders, or discourages repeat business, or is illegal or immoral, typically undermines long-term owner value. Even secret wrongdoing can do so, by incurring the costs of covering up and creating a liability to blackmail. Accordingly, attempts to identify, avert and remedy organisational wrongdoing will normally benefit the business, even if they temporarily reduce accounting profits. Stakeholders are therefore being loyal, not disloyal, when they criticise or attempt to prevent business abuses. Far from being incompatible with business loyalty, whistle-blowing to protect long-term owner value may indeed be required by it. Whistle-blowing is properly understood not as informing[21], but as relaying essential information to those responsible for getting things right.

Doesn't the duty of confidentiality preclude whistle-blowing? Not ordinarily. An employee, or indeed any stakeholder, might even sign a specific confidentiality agreement without making whistle-blowing unjustifiable. For logically, a business cannot bind its stakeholders to do, or to keep silent about, that which is illegal or contrary to its definitive purpose. Even the law recognises that there is 'no confidence in iniquity' and that 'fraud unravels all'. So confidentiality does not automatically rule out whistle-blowing.

The chief moral constraint on factually justified whistle-blowing is not confidentiality, but fairness: those most closely responsible for the suspected wrong should be given the opportunity to rebut the charges, or to acknowledge and remedy their mistakes. The whistle should thus normally be blown at the lowest hierarchical level that is likely to prove efficacious within the chain of command; whenever possible, established organisational procedures should be used. Typically, blowing the whistle fairly protects long-term owner value: damage and disruption can ordinarily be minimised when they are corrected locally and speedily. Initial whistle-blowing will thus normally be internal.

Can whistle-blowing to authorities external to the business also be justifiable? It depends. If internal channels have been exhausted, or are unavailable or unusable, then whistle-blowing to reveal a genuine wrong will be morally justifiable, regardless of the audience. External whistle-blowing will not be justified[22], of course, when the charge is factually mistaken. But that is because the accusations lack substance, not because the act is disloyal or the audience is wrong.

Whistle-blowing, internal or external, can even be justifiable if it threatens long-term owner value. For ethical business does not consist in maximising long-term owner value come what may, but in doing so subject to distributive justice and ordinary decency. When, therefore, the wrongs are genuine, and constitute violations of those fundamental conditions of ethical business, whistle-blowing will be justifiable even if owner value suffers.

Moral irrelevancies

It is important to note what the moral justification of whistle-blowing does *not* require. Most significantly, morally justifiable whistle-blowing does not presuppose any particular kind of motive. In assessing the act of whistle-blowing, it does not matter whether the whistle is blown out of pure public-spiritedness, or from bitterest spite; whatever the motive, if a real wrongdoing is disclosed, then the whistle-blowing is justifiable. It is true that the whistle-blower whose motives are thought to be pure is more likely to be listened to and believed than one whose motives are questionable[23]. But what the motive affects is the likely *efficacy* of the whistle-blowing, not its moral justification. Though motives are important for the moral purpose of judging the whistle-blower, they are relevant to the business mainly when the whistle-blower's allegation proves to be unfounded, and the firm must differentiate honest mistake from deliberate malice.

Other features often thought essential to the moral justification of whistle-blowing are equally irrelevant. Anonymous whistle-blowing may be more suspect, and thus less likely to be efficacious than the acknowledged, open sort, but it can be perfectly justifiable[24]. Similarly, though greater heed may be paid to a whistle-blower who suffers for his cause, his suffering is unrelated to the moral justification of the whistle-blowing. So are the degree to which the alleged wrongdoing can initially be documented by the whistle-blower, and the means by which he has come by his suspicions.[25] Whistle-blowing that is trivial or unsupported by hard evidence may well be imprudent or counterproductive: directors, shareholders and outside authorities are unlikely to pay much heed to petty or unproven complaints. But so long as the wrongdoing is genuine, the whistle-blowing is morally justifiable.

Moral obligation

Is whistle-blowing ever morally obligatory? To the extent that an individual has a positive obligation to serve the ethical business objective, he has a moral obligation to prevent actions that would undermine the business objective or violate distributive justice or ordinary decency. The degree of an individual's obligation to the business objective is typically a function of the specific contractual and other undertakings that he has assumed. Normally, directors and senior executives have a greater responsibility for what their companies do than casual labourers; they are therefore under a greater obligation to blow the whistle.

But isn't there a moral obligation to prevent things simply because they are wrong? If the wrongdoing is other than a breach of the ethical business objective, that question is equivalent to asking whether there is a moral obligation to put some other value—public health, for instance, or safety or public order—ahead of business. The extent to which non-business values should take priority over business is a fundamental moral question, and one that needs to be addressed. It is, however, a question that necessarily lies outside the scope of business ethics; the way to deal with it will be discussed in The Limits of Business Ethics, in Chapter 10 below.

The point that is significant for business ethics is that more whistle-blowing is likely to be morally justifiable than morally obligatory. Consequently, determining whether the whistle should actually be blown on any given occasion will normally require a careful weighing of prudential considerations. To be justified, whistle-blowing must not only be morally justifiable, but also the appropriate thing to do in the circumstances. Whistle-blowing will be inappropriate if it is useless, or counterproductive, or if the harmful effects of blowing the whistle would outweigh the likely benefits. It is therefore important to make morally justifiable whistle-blowing easier, safer and more efficacious.

Whistle-blowing and corporate governance

It should, accordingly, be a key corporate governance responsibility to facilitate internal whistle-blowing. Properly regarded as a source of critical corporate information, whistle-blowing is essential for good corporate governance: corporate purposes are best achieved when corporate agents are properly informed about corporate performance. Since fear of retaliation is normally a major deterrent to whistle-blowing, it is vital to ensure that justified whistle-blowers[26] are not penalised for their efforts on behalf of the business. Not only does the business that betrays its benefactors typically forfeit the benefits of (merely justifiable) whistle-blowing, but it violates distributive justice. Because distributive justice demands that vigilance be rewarded, and that conscientious staff be assiduously recruited, it is the managers who fail to defend and reward such staff who deserve punishment, not the justified whistle-blowers. In theory, therefore, no conflict should arise between the whistle-blower's duties to himself or his family and his duties to the business.

In practice, of course, whistle-blowers often suffer grievously for their efforts, and in ways ranging from the merely unfortunate to the clearly outrageous. As they normally function, corporate hierarchies are particularly slow to recognise or remedy corporate wrongdoing. Because correcting a problem requires acknowledging its existence, and possibly taking direct or indirect responsibility for its occurrence, managers typically deny that problems exist, even in the face of the most blatant evidence. So concerned are they to avoid even the appearance of error or responsibility, that they expend vast amounts of time, energy and shareholder money in covering up rather than facing up to what is wrong. Accordingly, when run by corrupt managements, 'open door' policies have typically worked against whistle-blowers, serving mainly to identify the trouble-makers to be ejected. It is therefore not surprising that shareholders, even directors, are frequently the last to know about corporate depredations, while those who are in direct contact with corporate wrongs, and typically feel strongly about them, wish vainly for support in setting things right.

The solution is to devise internal mechanisms that will transmit both suspicion and passion about corporate wrongdoing to those who are responsible for correcting it. Two such mechanisms, which will be discussed more fully in Chapter 9, are critical information systems and governance committees. The purpose of critical information systems is to encourage the flow of critical information to those responsible for dealing with its consequences. The purpose of a governance committee is to ensure strict adherence to the corporate purposes, subject to distributive justice and ordinary decency[27].

The governance committee is therefore the natural recipient of that critical information which either cannot or would not be handled properly elsewhere. As a committee of the board, composed exclusively of non-executive directors, it has the power to investigate and to resolve complaints, and has little incentive to victimise whistle-blowers. By receiving (signed) complaints from whistle-blowers, and pursuing those complaints in its own name, the committee can afford whistle-blowers a measure of confidentiality, and immediate protection against retaliation. And since it is responsible for enforcing distributive justice and ordinary decency, it should also prevent subsequent victimisation. Should there be matters that even the governance committee cannot resolve, recourse must be to the owners themselves. Corporate communications might then acquire a new and far more significant meaning.

PAYOUT LEVELS

Two subjects that have suffered from exceptionally poor corporate communications are the high remuneration paid to senior executives, and dividend payouts; both have provoked angry calls for better corporate governance. In both cases, however, the UK debate has typically, and inappropriately, been conducted in terms more relevant to public policy.

Executive remuneration

Far more than in the US or in continental Europe, levels of executive remuneration have provoked a public outcry in Britain; envious or incredulous commentators have regularly doubted the possibility of high remuneration's being justified. Leaders of both major political parties have condemned the sharply increased pay enjoyed by the chief executives of privatised industries, and the media have routinely castigated executive greed, and called for public action. But such critics all miss the point. Although intelligible in the context of political and economic debate, references to the sharpening inequalities between workers and executives, to greed and to the 'going rate', to inflation and to international comparisons, are all irrelevant to the ethics of executive remuneration. So, in principle, are the administrative means used for determining the pay package: it is not the percentage of non-executive directors on a remuneration committee that makes remuneration appropriate, but the criterion of payment employed.

The sole principle that should govern the allocation of rewards within the ethical business or corporation is distributive justice: remuneration and responsibilities and honours should be proportional to contributions made to the business or corporate end. In a business, therefore, the remuneration of top executives and directors, like that of all employees, should directly reflect contributions to long-term owner value. For a shirking worker, £5,000 a year is too much; £5,000,000 may be too little for the creator of a product generating profits many times that amount.

The only way in which pay can legitimately be deemed too high is if there is no commensurate contribution to owner value. And by that criterion, some payments certainly have been too high: the executive whose remuneration increases while the value of the company he manages declines, is indeed being rewarded unfairly. Some of the discrepancies arise from time-lagged remuneration, and the exercise of options awarded in palmier times. But all too often, executive pay is simply based on the wrong sort of performance[28]—typically sales or earnings per share or pre-tax profits—over periods that are too short[29]; as such, executive pay is altogether too 'loser friendly'.

Since executive remuneration is so emotionally charged an issue, it is especially important for it not only to be fair, but to be seen to be. A remuneration committee consisting exclusively of non-executive directors may be of some help, but what is really needed is greater disclosure of all components of remuneration for both management and directors. Moreover, just as executives' pay should be determined by the remuneration committee, directors' pay should require approval by the shareholders.

Dividends

Another subject desperately in need of better corporate communications is dividend policy, which is problematical largely because the role of dividends is so widely misconstrued. Managements and shareholders alike have focused mainly on dividends' signalling function, whereby they are offered and accepted as markers of corporate confidence. In consequence, both groups have tended to overlook dividends' more fundamental significance: dividends are distributions to the corporation's owners of cash that ultimately, though residually, belongs to them. Dividends are neither gifts from the management, nor guaranteed income; the level of dividend payout appropriate in any given company depends crucially on corporate circumstances.

Dividend policy can be substantially clarified by the teleological approach. As in sole proprietorships and partnerships, funds should be retained in corporate businesses only to the extent that they are needed for achieving the owners' business objectives. All too often, however, managers treat corporate cash as though it were their own, available for projects that promote management power rather than long-term owner value.

When retained funds are actually used to maximise long-term owner value, there should be no objection to low or no dividend payouts; investors should be indifferent to receiving their value in dividends or capital gains[30]. And selectively, at least, investors have been indifferent: US high-growth high-technology companies, which ploughed all their profits back into the business, were historically much favoured by UK investment trusts. Perhaps because they are less confident that UK companies will use their funds productively, however, UK investors have been much less tolerant of low dividends from their British investments. While a major investor relations survey confirmed that the UK's largest fund managers do not automatically sell the shares of companies that cut their dividends, it warned that cutting dividends could well jeopardise long-term relationships with shareholders[31]. And on one level, of course, this is wholly appropriate: a company that cannot provide a satisfactory return on investment will naturally be less attractive to investors.

Confusion results, however, when the dividend is regarded as more important than the long-term owner value of which it is at best a partial measure—another example of teleopathy. Dividends have come to be such a mark of corporate virility, that managements have felt under pressure to maintain them even when cash is short . . . even at the expense of cutting productive capital expenditure, or of excessive borrowing, or of costly rights issues. But payouts that undercut the corporation's ability to pursue its purpose are counterproductive . . . unless, of course, the point of the payout is specifically to wind up the corporation. Rational shareholders should therefore oppose such damaging payouts.

Nevertheless, key UK institutional investors have sharply criticised companies for cutting dividends in hard times[32]. Having so often been offered as signals rather than as distributions, dividend payments are now inappropriately considered by some shareholders to be a necessary condition of corporate success. But this is wrong: unlike interest on debt, dividend payments are not fixed obligations of the company. In the interests of consistency and reciprocal long-term relationships it may well be prudent to smooth payments upwards as well as downwards, and to fulfil those expectations that have been allowed or even encouraged to develop. It is also sensible to respect shareholders' wishes in the disposition of the corporate property that is ultimately theirs. Nevertheless, dividends should not be taken for granted: they are simply the distributions of that residual value that remains after all the business's contractual obligations are met[33].

As shareholders' direct compensation for bearing the risk of the company, dividends are by their very nature variable and vulnerable to changing circumstances. The principle for determining dividends is the same for all companies—payouts should be set at that level that maximises long-term owner value. But that principle naturally produces varying results when applied to companies in different circumstances. It is therefore inappropriate to expect the same level of dividends from all investments, whether that level is measured in terms of dividend yield or payout ratios.

IMPLICATIONS FOR TAKEOVERS

Better corporate governance has implications not only for executive remuneration and dividend payouts, but for takeovers. Takeovers are now the main method for enforcing business accountability, at least in the UK and the US. The corporate governance challenge is to devise more precise and flexible mechanisms for censuring and, if necessary, removing managers and directors. If directors were more genuinely accountable to shareholders, and in turn strictly required operational management to achieve shareholder objectives, takeovers would be less necessary: a change of ownership would not be needed to remove bad management or wayward directors. And takeovers would also be less likely: managers' takeover proposals would be subject to more careful and critical scrutiny, and approved only if they clearly promoted long-term owner value.

Takeovers could, in fact, be partially supplanted by a more direct market for corporate control.[34] Companies could compete for shareholders on the basis of the degree of accountability they offered to shareholders, just as US states now compete to be sites of business incorporation on the basis of the protection they offer to managements. The competition for shareholders could be based on the extent to which directors were independent of management, the ease with which they could be elected or replaced or chastised by shareholders, the percentage of shareholder votes required to approve Extraordinary General Meetings and propose and approve specific types of resolutions, the extent to which executive and board remuneration were disclosed and subject to board/shareholder approval, the kinds of takeover provisions permitted, etc., etc.

Given the relative silence of UK law on corporate governance[35], the field provides a fertile opportunity for corporate creativity. Properly designed and implemented, such mechanisms should minimise the obstacles to, and the costs of, shareholder responsibility, thereby eliminating shareholders' excuses for not keeping their corporations accountable. The ethical challenge to investors would then realistically be: 'Put your money where your clout is'.

9

Ethical Accountability

'The directors . . . being the managers rather of other people's money than of their own, it cannot well be expected that they should watch over it with the same anxious vigilance with which the partners in a private copartnery frequently watch over their own . . . Negligence and profusion, therefore, must always prevail, more or less, in the management of the affairs of such a company.'

Adam Smith[1]

'The objective should be to design structures which make it as easy as possible for office-holders to do what is expected of them.'

Sir Adrian Cadbury[2]

Given the fundamental importance of accountability to ethical business conduct and good corporate governance, this chapter will examine the ways in which it can be strengthened through the use of business systems and structures. In particular, it will consider how incentives and critical information systems can promote good corporate governance. It will suggest how directors can be made more independent of management and accountable to shareholders, how governance committees can aid accountability, and how owners can be more like proprietors. And it will investigate who should be held accountable for corporate wrongdoing. Finally, it will explore the contributions that ethical audits, codes of conduct, ethical training and business ethics consultants can make to the indispensable task of keeping business accountable.

ETHICAL SYSTEMS

All businesses have systems, which are simply organised ways of doing things. Like everything else within business, systems are ethical to the extent that they aim at maximising long-term owner value while respecting distributive justice and ordinary decency. Given the complexity and diversity of human responses, no system can be guaranteed to produce ethical outcomes. But when supplemented—and implemented—with good sense, systems can be devised that make it more likely that right will be done. Ethical systems can actively promote ethical business action by encouraging stakeholders both to adhere to the business objective, and to pursue it with distributive justice and ordinary decency. Whereas ordinary business systems often constitute a moral hazard, ethical systems provide moral support.

Ethical systems are possible because the ethical actions that properly concern businesses are simply actual deeds. Since stakeholders' motives and characters are largely irrelevant to business, and since there is no moral merit in doing things the hard way, there is no ethical obstacle to systems that make it both easy and gratifying to do what is right. The best way to encourage stakeholders to behave properly with respect to the business, is to make the right thing to do the simplest and most rewarding thing.

Incentives

One business system that preeminently needs to be ethical is the business's incentive system: it is typically the business's chief means of conveying and reinforcing its values. Pious speeches and codes of conduct may proclaim the business's official goals, but what the business truly prizes is most clearly revealed by its actions, and especially its actions in bestowing rewards. It is therefore vital that the business use its incentive system, and structure performance-related pay, so as to give the right signals and produce the right effects; all too often, incentives are insufficiently related to the business aim.[3] And several of the ways to make performance-related pay reflect distributive justice and the business purpose have already been discussed, in Chapter 6 above.

One feature that has not yet been addressed, however, is the sad fact that organisational high-flyers often progress by outrunning their mistakes. When properly structured to express distributive justice, incentive systems should prevent that injustice, and ensure that executives reap the true consequences of their business actions. In ethical organisations, 'willingness to assume responsibility' means not only eagerness to make decisions, but the determination to acknowledge and deal with the consequences of those decisions. The erring executive whose response is to admit his mistakes, is more likely to maximise long-term owner value than the one who determinedly denies the existence of problems. And the executive who then seeks to set things right, deserves better than one who accepts blame without seeing the need to effect improvements.

One obvious way to make it harder to outrun mistakes is simply to review executives' past performance critically, especially when considering candidates for promotion. It may be too soon to assess the long-term consequences of a manager's current actions, but what about the decisions he took five years ago? Three years ago? In his previous position in the firm? Did the policies he initiated, and the staff he hired, and the contracts he signed, result in the business's being better off? Or did they encumber the business with long-term problems, which transformed short-term gains into continuing burdens?

Even the outcomes of recent decisions can be estimated . . . if the right sorts of questions are asked. What has the manager been doing to improve the fundamentals of the business? What has he been contributing to product or staff or capital development? Have his actions been calculated to leave the business more or less fit to face the future? Definitive answers will not always be available, but even putting the questions makes outrunning mistakes more difficult.

Accountability can be further enhanced by linking payoffs to specific long-term consequences. When properly structured, performance-related pay not only measures the right performances, it makes the rewards contingent on the right outcomes . . . and delays delivery of rewards until the results are known.[4] Temporal lagging already features in those executive option schemes that have a vesting period before the options can be exercised. For such delays to be most effective, however, they should be combined with a long-term performance trigger, which allows the options to be exercised only if owner value actually increases over an extended period.[5]

Critical information

Another key area in which systems can assist ethical business conduct is in eliciting and channelling critical information. Critical information is information that is vital for the business's proper functioning. As such, it can consist of information that is critical of the business's functioning. For the business to improve its performance, it must know in what ways its current activities fall short of maximising long-term owner value, and how they violate distributive justice or ordinary decency.

Much of the unethical conduct of large organisations occurs because people with critical information lack power, while those with power lack essential information. Critical information systems should therefore ensure that managers and directors and owners are routinely confronted with, not shielded from, uncomfortable facts. The ethical business should not respond defensively to critical information, and castigate its provision as whistle-blowing; it should actively seek out critical information, and welcome it as an invaluable management resource.

The importance of critical information has seldom been fully appreciated. Depending on their focus, most businesses recognise the worth of sales leads, or market research or proprietary technology. But though businesses routinely pay substantial sums to consultants and researchers to obtain an informative advantage, they often fail to take advantage of an information source that is both cheap and immediately available: the business's own stakeholders. Even businesses that claim to value customer feedback and employee consultation seldom pursue them systematically. Rather than waste this valuable resource, business should exploit it actively.

Business should regard its stakeholders, and particularly its employees and customers, as a natural early-warning system. Stakeholders can discover opportunities that would otherwise be missed, and highlight problems before they become serious. This is not to say that it is the role of the stakeholders to manage the business: it is not. The information that the stakeholders offer may be incomplete or incorrect or irrelevant. Nevertheless, the business that lacks internal means for dealing with stakeholder concerns is more likely to suffer from them, and from external whistle-blowing. Repercussions and expenses tend to mushroom when the timing and nature of corrections are determined by the media or the law rather than by the business itself: control over the problem is lost. Since few businesses are beyond criticism, the best way to avoid external whistle-blowing is for the business to respond constructively to problems as they arise. Critical information systems make both that and responding to opportunities easier to do.

To achieve these benefits, critical information systems need to perform three functions. First, they should encourage stakeholder vigilance. Everyone dealing with the business should be aware of the business purpose, and of how it affects his particular function. All should recognise what counts as the ethical achievement of the business purpose, should be able to identify what falls short, and should actively seek improvements.

Second, critical information systems should encourage those who have critical information to make it available to the business. Providing critical information—speaking up, alerting—should be made easy. Mechanisms for registering suggestions, complaints and criticisms should be readily accessible to all stakeholders. And crucially, it should be made more rewarding[6] to identify and resolve problems than to ignore them.[7] At all levels of the business, constructive dissent and raising concerns should be fostered and positively valued. Stakeholders who take the trouble to volunteer critical information should be rewarded as trouble-shooters, not dismissed as trouble-makers.

Third, information systems should channel the critical information to those responsible for dealing with its consequences. It is not enough to collect information; to be useful, information must inform action. And for that to happen, it must be conveyed to individuals who are accountable for assessing the information and for using it to maximise long-term owner value ethically.

Properly structured, critical information systems help create a virtuous circle. Because when they perform their three key functions, critical information systems also help develop good stakeholder habits . . . of openness and honesty, of vigilance and constant improvement. A business whose stakeholders are receptive, responsive and keen to do better is one that is more likely to maximise long-term owner value ethically.

ETHICAL STRUCTURES

Business accountability is so important, that it should be built into the very structure of the business. When businesses are corporations, ethical structures can make directors act more like owners, and owners act more like proprietors; they should always make directors more accountable to shareholders, and all other corporate agents more accountable to the directors.

Professional directors

When management is detached from ownership, and especially when ownership is diffused, managers are prone to manage a corporation to suit their own ends rather than the owners'. Given the ease with which damaging conflicts of interest can arise between owners and managers, it is essential that directors be equipped to keep corporations to their proper ends. Four conditions must be met: the distinctive responsibilities of directors must be recognised, directors must be properly qualified to perform their role, directors' structural independence of management must be increased, and directors' accountability to shareholders must be strengthened.

Directors' Responsibilities
A director is not simply a senior sort of manager. The responsibility of a director is to direct the corporation, to ensure that it achieves the shareholders' objectives. The responsibility of the executives, in contrast, is to execute the directors' strategy. Though in practice the directors of firms are often the senior managers of those same firms, the responsibilities they have as operating executives and as directors are conceptually distinct. All directors, however, have the same basic responsibilities in their capacities as directors, whether or not they are executives of the corporation they direct.

The role of the director incorporates elements of representative and steward, trustee and watchdog[8]. As an artificial person, a corporation needs actual people—directors—to represent it. But though the directors represent the corporation, they also represent the shareholders; the corporation is run by the directors, but it is the shareholders' property. Directors have a fiduciary responsibility to use the corporate assets and their corporate powers to achieve the objectives of the shareholders. To ensure that those corporate purposes are achieved, directors must oversee the actions of corporate management. Like watchdogs, directors are responsible for identifying problems and raising the alert. Unlike canine watchdogs, however, directors are also responsible for diagnosing and correcting what is wrong.

Directors' Requirements
For directors to perform their role properly, they need specific abilities and traits of character that are significantly different from those often supposed. Despite what is implied by some commonly used selection procedures, the prime requisite of a director is neither 'clubability' nor having influential contacts. Indeed, since critically scrutinising corporate agents is so

essential a directorial function, the desire to be liked can be a positive handicap. This is not to say that social skills are not valuable: to the extent that they help the director do his proper job, they are clearly an important asset. But they are only part of the kit that an effective director needs.

Equally, the chief qualifications for being a good director are not specific business experience, academic degrees or professional credentials: other things being equal they all are good to have, but they are neither necessary nor sufficient for being a good director. Just as managerial ability is distinct from technical expertise, so the qualities needed for being a director are not the same as managerial skill. One can be a successful line manager and still lack the focus and moral courage needed for being a director; conversely, one can have little or no experience of a given business and still be entirely capable of acting as an effective watchdog. A business director must, of course, understand very clearly what business is about; he must understand the language of business, and know how owner value is maximised. But such understanding requires critical intelligence, not direct experience of all or indeed any specific business function: it is not necessary to be an accountant to understand financial statements.

The essential qualities of a good director are those that enable him to ask the questions necessary for safeguarding the owners' interests, and to get and evaluate and act on the answers. The relevant qualities are those of a good steward: loyalty and sound judgement and moral courage.

First, directors must be committed to achieving the goals of the shareholders. Directors' loyalty must be to the corporate purpose, not to the managers or the employees or customers[9]. Directors should not see themselves as representatives of any (non-shareholder) stakeholding group or corporate function[10]; the role of the director is to pursue corporate objectives, not to promote sectional interests. For a business corporation, directors must fully understand and endorse the business purpose of maximising long-term owner value. And if the business is to be ethical, the directors must be committed to achieving that goal in accordance with distributive justice and ordinary decency.

Second, business directors must have sound business and moral judgement. They must know what counts as achievement of the business goal, and appreciate what is likely to bring it about. They must be able to estimate the long-term consequences of corporate actions, and to determine whether those actions are compatible with distributive justice and ordinary decency. And they must know what information they need to make such assessments and how to get it.

Finally, directors must have moral courage. They must understand when and how to challenge management's actions, and when to bring matters directly to the attention of the shareholders. They must also be ready to act on that understanding. A director who cannot cope with confrontation, who is not prepared to ask hard questions and demand satisfactory answers, is as unqualified for the job as one who cannot understand a profit and loss account. Directors must scrutinise actual and proposed corporate activities, and allow only those projects and policies that conform to the definitive corporate end.

It may be objected that paragons capable of taking on these onerous duties will be difficult to find. And it may well be unrealistic to expect part-time, low-paid, non-executive directors to perform these critical functions, especially when they are nominated by managements. To increase directors' ability to perform their duties effectively, it is therefore appropriate to provide them with financial and structural support: directors need independence, information and additional resources.

Ensuring Independence

The independence that is required for directors to perform their function is above all independence of management. Given the importance of directors' supervisory function, and the need for critical assessment of management, it will normally be prudent for most directors to be non-executives, and for the Chairman of the Board not to be the Chief Executive. Increasing the proportion of independent, non-executive directors decreases the likelihood that the board will suffer from internal conflicts of interest.

This is not to say that executives should be barred from being directors by law. It would be absurd if the original founders/owners of a business, who were also its managers, were not allowed to become directors when their business became corporate in form. Nor would it be sensible to deny a business the talents of those exceptional individuals who are fully capable of fulfilling both roles simultaneously. But it is usually easier for a director to view the acts of the managers critically if he is not one of them himself, if he does not share their vested interest in defending the status quo.

Directorial independence does, however, require more than directors' not being executives of the company. Genuine independence also requires that the directors' appointment and information and access to advice be independent of the company's management. Traditionally, agendas are set and board papers are prepared by corporate executives. For directors to be able to perform their supervisory function effectively, however, all directors, including the non-executives, need to have independent access to company information and the company's staff, and to have the expenses they incur in investigating company matters met by the corporation.

Independence does not, however, require excluding directors from company performance-related pay, profit-sharing or pension schemes:[11] the independence that directors require is independence of management, not independence of results. If management remuneration schemes are determined and approved by directors, then directors' remuneration should, of course, be governed by separate schemes, requiring explicit approval by the shareholders. Like all remuneration, however, that of directors must be linked to maximising long-term owner value if it is to be in accord with distributive justice. It is when directors are insulated from corporate performance, and do not directly suffer the consequences of their acts, that they are most likely to act irresponsibly.

Nevertheless, it is frequently asserted that non-executive directors' remuneration should not represent a significant part of their total income.[12] The fear is, presumably, that if a director is financially dependent on his director's fees, he will be less likely to exercise independent judgement, and less inclined to do the right thing on behalf of the shareholders. This fear may be justified if the director's appointment is dependent on the management he must oversee, and if the director lacks the requisite moral character for performing his duties. The right solution, however, is not to decrease non-executives' financial dependence on company performance, but to increase directors' structural independence of the management. Then directors' rewards can be directly linked to achieving the shareholders' objectives, and doing what is right for the shareholders can also be right and financially rewarding for the directors.

Ensuring Accountability

But even ensuring directors' independence of management is not enough; it is also vital to ensure directors' accountability to the shareholders. That accountability, which has traditionally been loose at best, can be significantly increased with the use of ethical structures. Directors should be selected as well as appointed by the shareholders; directors should be engaged on short, fixed-term contracts of service; and directors should be delegated fewer general powers.

Since directors are the shareholders' stewards, and must be wholly independent of management, it is essential that their appointment not be controlled by management. Shareholders should therefore not only approve the directors, but also be able to nominate them.[13] Having prospective directors selected by a nomination committee of non-executive directors is preferable to having them proposed by managers. But even wholly non-executive nomination and remuneration committees can be insufficient when the non-executives of one firm are the executives of another, and cross-directorships are commonplace.

In their own interest, shareholders should therefore ensure that there are alternate routes on to the ballot: shareholders should be able to nominate and consider whatever candidates they like. Even if would-be nominees were permitted to propose themselves, frivolous candidates could be excluded by requiring nominations to be supported by a minimum number of shareholders, by requiring candidates to have a minimum shareholding in the company, or by having them forfeit a deposit if they failed to secure a stipulated number of shareholder votes.[14] To assure that no able candidate is excluded from consideration, the basic expenses of electing directors should be for the account of the company: it is in the shareholders' interest to get the best directors possible.

Electing directors can best protect shareholder interests when two further conditions are met. First, the competition for board membership should be based on the candidates' perceived abilities to promote and protect shareholder interests. Prospective directors should therefore compete on the basis of their strategic and tactical plans for the corporation, their professional and moral judgement, and their independence of and ability to direct management. Second, elections should be held frequently, so that errant directors can be readily chastised and removed: long-term owner value is most likely to be maximised when immunity is minimised. Directors should therefore be engaged only for short, fixed terms of office[15]. To reinforce directors' accountability, all elements of their remuneration should require explicit approval by the shareholders.[16]

Finally, increasing accountability requires limiting the powers delegated to directors by the Memorandum & Articles of Association of the corporation. Traditionally, directors have been empowered to do whatever is necessary to achieve corporate purposes. To improve accountability, however, those purposes should be made more precise and should be strictly limited.[17] In business corporations, for example, directors should only be empowered to maximise long-term owner value, and should be restricted to means that are compatible with distributive justice and ordinary decency. And directors should not be indemnified against penalties or legal fees for actions that are contrary either to the corporate purposes or to regulation; indeed, they should be liable to reimburse the corporation for at least some[18] of the financial damage that they cause.

If paragons able to be directors are relatively rare, those willing to accept the full burdens of accountability may well prove even rarer. One solution might be for shareholders to pay more for the services of 'professional directors'[19], directors who are not the executives of any firm, but who are chosen specifically for their ability to safeguard shareholder interests. Even if such directors acted in a non-executive capacity for more than one firm, they would be less prone to the teleopathic conflicts of interest that typically arise between executive directors and owners.

Such 'professional directors' would not constitute a German-style, second-tier supervisory board. The requirement that directors exercise a watchdog function is perfectly compatible with the Anglo-Saxon unitary structure, in which all directors have the same duties and sit on a single board. There is, however, no legal or logical need for managers to be on that board; the company can enjoy all the benefits of executives' expertise and experience without executives' being directors. Nor should requiring approval by a non-executive board reduce the efficiency of the company. Unlike members of a German supervisory board, 'professional directors' would not be representatives of factional interests. And since they would be charged with, and remunerated on the basis of, maximising long-term owner value, such directors would have every incentive to refrain from non-constructive interference.

Ultimately, however, the best way to ensure that directors serve shareholders' interests is for directors to be substantial shareholders. If company directors hold sizeable equity stakes in their corporations, or the shareholders of a corporation are members of its board, it is more likely that their interests will coincide, and that the corporation will indeed be run in the interests of its owners.

Professional owners

But even increasing the overlap between directors and shareholders is not enough to ensure adherence to the corporate goals. To do that, shareholders must be vigilant and vigorous in exercising their rights of ownership: accountability requires efforts from both sides.

Shareholders must first make the corporate objectives clear. Those who want their corporations to be ethical businesses should be sure that the corporate purpose is nothing but maximising long-term owner value in accordance with distributive justice and ordinary decency. Equally, if shareholders want their corporation to pursue some purpose other than business, they should make that other objective plain, to prevent stakeholders from interacting with their corporation on false pretences.

Once the corporate purpose has been set, shareholders should insist that all deviations from it require their explicit approval. If the management or the directors of a business corporation want to use shareholders' funds for non-business purposes—be they contributions to political parties or to charities—getting explicit authorisation from the shareholders should be required. Shareholder approval should also be required for all expansion and changes of direction sufficiently large to alter the nature of a business. A shift from being a retailer to a manufacturer should need explicit shareholder consent; so should a change from producing tools to producing tanks. Equally, the powers most prone to abuse should be curbed. Specific shareholder approval should therefore be required not only for acquisitions and for capital raising, but for greenmail payments and for 'shark repellents'. Shareholders should insist on being notified of all merger and takeover approaches—given or received[20]—and on having pre-emptive rights to all primary offerings of equity[21].

Having determined the corporate purpose, shareholders must also enforce its achievement. Care should be exercised in the appointment of qualified, critical directors, who must be held to account for their stewardship. Shareholders must therefore insist on sufficient disclosure to make assessment of the board possible, must retain full power to dismiss errant directors, and must actually use their powers to remove directors who fail in their duties.

Given the relatively diffuse nature of most corporate share-holdings, however, performing even these basic tasks has frequently proved difficult.[22] Regulation introduced to protect shareholders as investors has actually made it harder for shareholders to exercise their rights as proprietors. EU/UK insider trading regulation prevents shareholders from trading when they are 'contaminated' with insider information; it therefore gives investors an incentive not to investigate their corporate holdings too closely. SEC rules make it complicated for shareholders to communicate with other shareholders. And stakes large enough to make active management worthwhile may trigger the need to bid for the whole company under the UK Takeover Code. Moreover, few shareholders have the time, energy or expertise necessary for keeping a corporation or even its directors accountable. Even major institutional investors are not normally well-equipped to exercise their ownership rights: their skills are typically in picking stocks, not monitoring directors.

There are, however, a few notable exceptions. Some public companies[23] specialise in investing in other companies, and take an active interest in the ways those companies are run. A similar function is often performed by private buyout specialists[24] in respect of the businesses they finance. In their different ways, such 'professional owners' all act more like traditional proprietors than typical shareholders do. They have the resources and expertise to do more than just understand and monitor a securities portfolio; they can actively contribute to the direction and even the management of the businesses in which they invest. By commanding top performance from those companies, such professional owners serve their own interests. And they also render a significant service to those who invest along with them.[25]

But employing another layer of intermediaries as 'professional owners' is just one possible way of achieving the benefits of vigilant ownership; it is not the only way. Exercising the rights of ownership requires holding directors to account, not doing the job of a director; just as direction is conceptually distinct from management, ownership is conceptually distinct from them both. Ultimately, shareholders simply need to know what they want from the companies that they own, and need to exert the effort necessary to keep directors accountable for achieving those goals.

Governance committees

One simple mechanism that can aid them in that endeavour is the introduction of a governance committee; consisting exclusively of non-executive directors, the governance committee would be charged with ensuring strict adherence to the corporate purpose.[26] Theoretically, of course, this is the job of the board overall. And if the board were composed only of non-executive directors, a special governance committee would be unnecessary except as a way of dividing up the tasks. But to the extent that a board has executive members, the potential conflict of interest between managers and owners that makes non-executive auditing of financial compliance prudent, makes non-executive oversight of corporate purposes essential.

A central function of the governance committee is to safeguard the tools of ethical management. One of its key responsibilities is therefore to ensure that the business's management accounts provide the information necessary for accurately measuring and maximising long-term owner value; equally, it should ensure that reports to shareholders provide the information they need for assessing business performance. A second major role of the governance committee is to oversee the operation of the Ethical Decision Model, to ensure that it is used for all key decisions and that it is used properly. A third function is to monitor the structure and operation of the business's critical information systems, and to act as a conduit for critical information provided by internal whistle-blowers. Finally, the governance committee should be in charge of appointing ethical auditors, both internal and external; it should receive their reports, and be responsible for implementing any consequential changes.

CORPORATE WRONGDOING

Ethical structures are particularly important for ensuring accountability when a business transgresses. The difficulty of making abstract business organisations accountable for their wrongdoing has evoked two common but equally misguided responses. Eager to make businesses pay for the wrongs they have done, some commentators have posited the existence of a business entity that can have intentions separate and distinct from those of any human agent. Others, recognising that even corporate businesses are not people, have denied that businesses can be held accountable for the evils that they do. But both these notions are wrong. It is possible to attribute actions to businesses, and to judge those actions, without positing a self-willed business entity capable of acting on its own.

There is, of course, a sense in which a business can legitimately be considered to be an independent entity. Corporations are legal persons and have an official existence separate from their owners. Furthermore, even non-corporate businesses can have distinctive personalities. Like individual characters, businesses typically have customary and habitual ways of doing things; some businesses are characteristically scrupulous, others are characteristically sloppy.

Having characters, businesses are often deemed to be characters, for two significant reasons. First, it is sometimes the case that outcomes that were clearly brought about by a business—environmental disasters, for example, and defective products—were nevertheless not wanted or intended by anyone in the business. In the absence of an identifiable human intender, it can be tempting to assume that it must have been the business itself that intended the outcome. But that conclusion would be incorrect.

When the people intending a business event cannot be identified, the most probable reason is that the event was in fact not intended: not all outcomes are deliberately brought about. Even carefully considered decisions can have genuinely unexpected consequences; given the degree of unconsidered action taken by large organisations, and the gaps in

lines of responsibility that allow problems to develop unde-
tected or uncorrected, it is not surprising that unforseen,
unwanted results sometimes ensue. But that events may occur
without being specifically intended does not mean that no one
is responsible for them. No intention need be established for
negligence to be culpable, and acts of omission can be as
blameworthy as acts of commission. Assigning responsibility
for unintended outcomes does not require positing a mythical
intender; it requires establishing exactly how the outcomes
came about and determining who did what in allowing them
to happen.

It is when serious harm results that the second reason for
holding business entities responsible typically comes into
play: because businesses tend to be richer than individuals,
victims often look to businesses for compensation. To take
advantage of a business's deep pockets, however, it is normally necessary to show that it was the business as such that
was responsible for the wrongdoing. But holding a business
responsible does not require that there be a business entity
that can have intentions independent of any individuals'
intentions. The way to ascribe responsibility to a business is to
understand what is properly meant by business action, and to
have mechanisms that make the individuals who are actually
responsible for it fully accountable.

'Business actions' or 'the actions of the business' are those
actions that are taken in the name of a business by its authorised representatives. Like all actions, business actions are
actually performed by individuals; even though it is businesses, not individuals, that merge, mergers only occur when
individuals sign and implement merger agreements. To
count as business actions, the actions of individuals must satisfy two conditions. The actions themselves must be the right
sorts of actions, ones that a business can perform: though
businesses can merge, they cannot marry. And the actions
must be performed by the right individuals, those who have
been authorised to represent the business;[27] even the chief
executive of business X cannot act on behalf of unrelated
business Y.[28]

Accordingly, as common sense and the law generally
recognise, the way to deal with business wrongdoing is to

identify those individuals who, acting in their business capacities, were actually responsible for what happened. Individuals are as responsible for the actions they take in their business capacities as they are for the actions they take in their private capacities[29]. It may well be that the business action would never have been undertaken by the individual acting privately. But that does not eliminate the individual's responsibility for taking the action. Nor does the fact that he may have been instructed[30] to perform the action by his boss ... though in that case, the boss will, of course, share responsibility for it. It is always the individual's responsibility to decide what he will do: each individual must determine what objectives he will pursue, what employment he will accept, what orders he will obey.[31]

Responsibility for a business's actions rests ultimately with those who are in charge of the business. In the case of sole proprietorships and partnerships, which are typically run by their owners, it is normally the owners who are responsible. For corporate businesses, however, the situation is more complex. Shareholders do, of course, automatically suffer whenever their corporations are suspected of wrongdoing; investigation and litigation divert resources from the corporate objectives, and even accusations can hurt a business's prospects.[32] Until and unless shareholders actually control their corporations, however, it would be unfair to hold them directly responsible for corporate wrongdoing. Primary corporate responsibility falls instead on the directors, who are directly or indirectly responsible for all the actions of the corporation.

Directors normally have three sorts of responsibility for corporate actions. First, they are responsible for their own actions and decisions with respect to the firm: if a director smashes his company car, he has a personal responsibility for having done so. Second, as members of the board of directors, directors have collective, 'cabinet' responsibility for all the board's actions; unless they resign, even directors who have opposed board decisions are deemed to have assented to them, and share responsibility for their consequences. Third, directors have 'ministerial' responsibility for the actions of their subordinates: it is up to the directors to know what the corporation's managers and employees are doing, and to make sure that it is directed to achieving corporate purposes.

Corporate accountability starts with the directors, but it does not end there: all corporate employees and managers are accountable to the directors. The extent to which responsibility spreads will depend on who has actually done what, and with what authority. If the transgressors have acted in violation of company policy, then those 'rogues' are to blame, and should be disciplined.[33] Even then, however, the directors cannot escape responsibility: they may have expressly forbidden the particular misdeed, but in employing the rogues, and in not knowing, and adequately controlling, how the business was run, they made it possible for the misconduct to happen.

When the wrongdoing has been undertaken with clear shareholder approval, the shareholders also share moral responsibility. It would hardly be right if those who knowingly funded a contract killing business could escape responsibility, simply because the murderous enterprise was corporate in form[34]. It may be protested that small shareholders have little influence over corporate purposes, and should therefore not be held even morally responsible for corporate wrongdoing. But if shareholders are in a position to reap the benefits of wrongdoing, they should also be liable to suffer the moral costs. If they consider that responsibility to be disproportionate to their degree of corporate control, shareholders have two choices. They can abstain from being shareholders, and avoid the responsibility. Or they can insist on greater control, and demand the structural improvements that would enable them properly to supervise their corporate property and hold their directors and agents strictly to account.

THE ETHICAL AUDIT

One of the key tools available to help owners keep their businesses accountable is the ethical audit. Just as a financial audit confirms whether a business's financial statements have been generated according to Generally Accepted Accounting Principles, an ethical audit determines whether its operations are being conducted in accordance with generically applicable apodeictic[35] principles. For a business, the applicable principles are those that define its purpose and key values: an ethical audit checks the extent to which a firm's actions are directed at maximising long-term owner value, and the extent to which they accord with distributive justice and ordinary decency.

Contrary to popular belief, ethical audits are neither impossible nor impractical. The existence of divergent ethical views is no obstacle to conducting an ethical audit: an ethical audit does not evaluate business conduct against the varied moral or religious standards of the community. Nor is it a problem that character and motives are often difficult to assess: a properly formulated ethical audit does not attempt to measure how friendly or how kind or how altruistic an organisation is; it does not delve into motives at all. An ethical audit does not measure pious intentions or good works or even the cost of ethical choices. What an ethical audit does assess is a business's structures and its procedures, its systems and its policies. And it measures them against principles—of maximising owner value, distributive justice and ordinary decency—that are at least as clear as the standards enjoined by accounting standards boards. In both financial and ethical audits, what is measured is the extent to which actual activities comply with publicly defined criteria.

When properly conducted, the ethical audit serves as a key management tool. Through a combination of inspection and interviews, the ethical audit determines the extent to which company decisions at all levels are actually directed at maximising long-term owner value, and the extent to which they are compatible with distributive justice and ordinary decency. By systematically evaluating business practice, the ethical audit provides a critical assessment of how the business is actually run. It carefully scrutinises the basis on which management accounts are drawn up, and so ensures that management have reliable information to use in running the business. And by identifying ethical problems early, it protects the business from the 'boiled frog phenomenon'[36], in which an otherwise correctable problem becomes fatal for not being detected and tackled in time. Ethical audits are particularly important when businesses undergo major alterations, whether through rapid growth, restructuring or rationalisation; they should routinely form part of the due diligence investigation of all potential acquisitions.

Since ethical audits indicate where the objectives and standards of the business are either misunderstood or not properly implemented, audits indicate where training is necessary and what sorts of training are required. Ethical audits also measure the effectiveness of such training and are, furthermore, normally educational in themselves. To answer the questions posed by the ethical auditor, stakeholders are forced to consider how what they do is meant to maximise long-term owner value, and whether it complies with distributive justice and ordinary decency.

When performed by an external auditor, the ethical audit provides an objective measure of ethical performance, and enables a business to document and to benefit from its ethical conduct. Given the increasing attention paid to the character of firms, the ethical audit can be a valuable tool for attracting investment and quality stakeholders. Even if the firm's ethical rating shows room for improvement, the act of conducting an ethical audit can provide evidence of the business's commitment to ethical performance. And it does so for an outlay that is typically small compared with public relations and advertising budgets.

An ethical audit actually provides what BS EN ISO 9000 (BS 5750) is often—but erroneously—presumed to offer: a standard of quality. BS 9000 cannot measure quality, because all it checks is whether a company has applied its procedures systematically; it does not examine the content of those procedures. Unless a procedure is directed at the right end, however, its consistent application simply guarantees consistent wrongness; by actively inhibiting change, BS 9000 can actually prevent improvement. Unlike BS 9000, a properly conducted ethical audit assesses the contents of rules as well as their systematic application. In addition, since it assesses them against the ethical business objective, the audit both measures and promotes the quality that actually enhances business performance.

Finally, the ethical audit is a key instrument for improving corporate governance. It ensures that the financial information that is necessary for evaluating business performance is both available and reliable. Moreover, by explicitly evaluating the ways in which stakeholders fulfil their responsibilities, the ethical audit provides the information needed to keep the corporation true to its proper purpose. The ethical audit enables shareholders to evaluate the performance of directors, and enables directors to assess the conduct of the other stakeholders.

CODES OF CONDUCT

Another tool that can be used to promote accountability is the code of conduct. The value of codes is often overstated: on their own, and unaccompanied by the appropriate habits, expectations and sanctions, codes of conduct are of little value[37]. Equally, the appropriate basis for codes of conduct is often misunderstood: what legitimises codes is not stakeholder consent but ethical content. Nevertheless, codes of conduct can be extremely useful. By communicating corporate purposes explicitly, by expressly identifying corporate policy about controversial matters, and by clarifying which stakeholder expectations are legitimate, codes of conduct can do much to eliminate ignorance as an excuse. Accordingly, they can be an effective tool for sharpening business accountability and improving corporate governance.

To perform those roles, however, codes must be properly structured. Codes need not, and indeed often should not, reflect the prevailing values or culture of the firm. When the existing culture is less than perfect, enshrining it in a code merely reinforces bad practice; for a code of conduct to improve organisational conduct, what it prescribes must be better than the existing norm. When it does, however, it is important to announce that a change is being made, and to explain why. Unless the code is recognised to be a reflection of new ownership, or new management, or of turning over a new leaf, the higher standards of the code are likely to be dismissed—probably correctly—as mere hypocrisy.

Contrary to popular belief, employee consultation is not necessary for legitimising a moral code: a code of conduct is not a survey of employees' ethical attitudes. If a code of conduct is meant to express a company's fundamental aims and values, then it is for the company's owners, not for its employees, to stipulate what those aims and values are. And if the code is meant to be normative, and set out what constitutes ethical conduct for the business, then its validity depends solely on the correctness of the values and principles it expresses, not on employee agreement. Ideally, of course, stakeholders will share the values embodied in the code. But if they do not, it is the stakeholders, not the code, that should be changed.

Employee involvement can, nevertheless, be valuable. A code will be most effective if it addresses matters that actually cause concern. It can therefore be sensible to consult stakeholders, and especially employees, to determine what situations are genuinely problematical. Consultation can also provide useful information about the stringency (or laxity) of employees' ethical standards, and the degree of ethical diversity prevailing in a heterogeneous workforce; such knowledge may be helpful in determining the language and style of the code. Finally, making employees part of the code-making process may improve compliance with the code: if employees feel they have had a role in forming it, they are more likely to understand the code and observe its strictures.

The most important element in ensuring a code's effectiveness, however, is the active support of the business's directors and senior executives. By both proclamation and example they must explicitly endorse the values that it proclaims; they must make it clear that it will be enforced; and they must show that they consider themselves to be bound by it. To be worthy of respect, a code must apply, and be seen to apply, to every person in the firm.

And to be taken seriously, a code of conduct must be realistic. A code that purports to guarantee righteousness, or to eliminate risk, is likely to call into question both its own soundness and that of the business adopting it. An ethical code for business should confine itself to that which is within the power of business: maximising long-term owner value ethically. The code should set out the implications of the business purpose and the principles of distributive justice and ordinary decency for the conduct of the particular business. The code should make it abundantly clear that deviations from those principles will not be acceptable, and that abuses of power will not be tolerated. It should also stress the positive importance of disclosure concerning potential conflicts of interest and product or process risk.

Effective codes of conduct can be written or unwritten. The chief benefit of a written code is that it allows less room for ambiguity and uncertainty. By indicating that certain types of behaviour are unacceptable, it offers stakeholders additional ammunition in refusing invitations to transgress. And by helping to define legitimate expectations, it makes it less likely that inappropriate demands will be made of the business. Publishing a formal code can also serve as an explicit signal of an organisation's commitment to ethical conduct; the act of writing the code can reinforce and clarify that commitment. It is important, however, to beware of an excessively legalistic approach. Specifying conduct in detail runs the risk of undermining the development of sensitivity and ethical judgement. And defining the bounds too precisely can be positively counterproductive: when what once was a grey area is declared to be acceptable, borderline behaviour may well increase.

ETHICAL TRAINING

Codes are most likely to be efficacious if they are accompanied by explicit ethical training. Unfortunately, ethical training is subject to the same sorts of misunderstanding and scepticism that afflict ethical audits. If 'ethical' is associated

246 Just Business: Ethical Direction

with woolly sentiments or pious works, then the business advantage of ethical training is indeed questionable. Properly understood, however, ethical training is as practical as instruction in the use of the firm's new software. Ethical training explains how to maximise owner value ethically: it is realistic and analytical, not remedial or mystical.

The central lesson of ethical training is that business's proper objective is maximising long-term owner value, and that being ethical in business means pursuing that end with distributive justice and ordinary decency. Training teaches employees to identify those activities that are properly business, and helps to correct those unreflective responses that undermine business effectiveness; it therefore helps staff to focus their efforts more productively. By explaining key concepts, ethical training equips employees to cope with ethical problems in whatever forms they may arise. Finally, ethical training can save the business substantial sums, by providing a legal defence when employees transgress: in many jurisdictions, firms with ethical training programmes can face significantly lower legal penalties.

Ethical training is best achieved through a combination of classroom instruction and on-the-job coaching. Classroom instruction is most appropriate for introducing principles that apply throughout the business: for elucidating the business's code of conduct and explaining the use of the Ethical Decision Model. Specialised instruction is also helpful when established patterns of behaviour need to be changed: to stop the unjustified victimisation of whistle-blowers, for example, or teleopathic prejudice. Explicit ethical training is particularly valuable when new standards or policies are being adopted, or when new employees are being indoctrinated; it is essential for those being promoted to management or to the board.

The most important ethical training, however, is provided on the job. A large part of ethical training consists of simply reinforcing ethical conduct by example . . . everywhere, every time, by everyone in the business. Apprentices should be shown not only where supplies are kept, but how tools are cared for. Sales instruction should include not just how to book an order, but what kind of sales talk is acceptable, and what sort of customer service is to be provided automatically. Management trainees should be shown not just how to fill out expense forms, but how to treat their staff fairly. Whenever the 'way things are done around here' is explained, it should be by reference to maximising long-term owner value with distributive justice and ordinary decency.

THE ROLE OF THE BUSINESS ETHICS CONSULTANT

The best source of ethical training programmes is often a business ethics consultant: a consultant can assess a firm's ethical training needs, and devise and deliver suitable training materials and classroom instruction. But professional business ethics consultants can do much more. When skilled in the use of the Ethical Decision Model, they can provide valuable problem-solving advice and crisis management. They can also provide key corporate governance tools, in the form of ethical audits and codes of conduct.

Business ethics consultants can therefore help most firms, not just those faced with fraud or sexual harassment or other headline-grabbing charges. The services of a business ethics consultant can, of course, be valuable in a crisis, when his experience of managing acute ethical problems can help the business minimise the damaging effects of mass redundancies, sabotage and environmental and other disasters. But a business ethics consultant skilled in the use of the Ethical Decision Model can actually help clarify what is at stake in all business decisions. He can help identify what the alternatives are, what their costs and consequences are likely to be, and who should be held accountable. Many standard business difficulties, including low productivity, high staff turnover and inadequate profitability, are the result of underlying ethical problems. Experienced in the causes and consequences of ethical misconduct, a professional business ethics consultant can identify what is wrong. By translating general principles into policies and procedures that are specifically designed to resolve those problems, a professional business ethics consultant can improve a firm's profitability, as well as its chances of attracting and keeping the best stakeholders.

Can't businessmen perform these functions themselves? Sometimes. But although the Ethical Decision Model is fundamentally simple, applying it properly calls for experience and judgement and a clear understanding of the principles involved. When such business ethics expertise is lacking, employing a professional business ethics consultant can be the best and most cost-effective way of remedying the deficiency.

Even when businesses have a firm grasp of the Ethical Decision Model, there are four important ways in which they can benefit from employing an independent business ethics consultant. First, an independent consultant can ordinarily provide a more detached and objective view of a business's ethical performance than any insider can. Only an external business ethics consultant can evaluate a firm's ethical condition unfettered by the functional, personal and political loyalties that typically constrain insiders. Because he is free of such partisan interests, and able to guarantee anonymity, the external consultant can often gain access to information that would be denied to a colleague. Moreover, he can analyse that information with the independence necessary for achieving an unbiased, impartial view.

Second, an independent consultant is in a better position to recognise and proclaim hard truths when they are necessary. Unpopular decisions may be more palatable and easier to implement if they are seen to come from an external source, particularly one characterised as 'expert'. Ethical judgements are also more likely to be applied impartially to all staff, even the most senior, when they are applied by an outsider.

Third, a positive ethical assessment is likely to carry more weight, and thus be of greater value to the business, if it is provided by an independent consultant. Just as achieving BS 5750 can help a business to attract customers and suppliers, staff and funds, so too can external business ethics certification help a firm to gain recognition for, and thus additional advantage from, its good ethical conduct. Ethical audits are thus more productively performed by independent business ethics consultants than by a business's own staff.

Finally, an independent consultant can bring the benefit of his experience to the firm. Given his professional immersion in business ethics, he can suggest proven methods of dealing with common problems and can alert firms to changing public concerns.

But who is qualified to be a business ethics consultant? To help a business, a business ethics consultant must combine solid business realism with analytical rigour. Communications or public relations skills are not enough; it is necessary to have something significant to say. Nor is business experience sufficient: the extension of unreflective practice from one business to another may simply lead to the spread of bad habits. Nor are academic degrees enough: applying confused philosophical theories to misunderstood business practice does business more harm than good.

To be effective at making business better, a business ethics consultant must have both a thorough understanding of what is involved in doing business, and the analytical ability to identify and actually resolve business ethics issues: he must be well-versed in both the theoretical basis and the application of the Ethical Decision Model. Only then will he be equipped with an approach to business ethics that is coherent, that can be justified and communicated, and that can be applied systematically to real business situations in all their variety and complexity.

To sum up, then, accountability is essential for keeping businesses ethical. Accountability can be improved through the introduction of systems that minimise moral hazards and make the right thing also the easy and rewarding thing to do. Critical information systems that provide feedback, and incentive schemes that penalise wrongdoing, can make corporate governance more effective; so can governance committees charged with maintaining adherence to the business purpose. A corporation is more likely to adhere to its shareholders' objectives if directors are independent of management but fully accountable to shareholders. And shareholders can also help, by actually exercising their ownership rights.

Properly structured ethical audits, codes of conduct and ethical training can enhance accountability. Ethical audits measure the extent to which businesses are conducted so as to maximise long-term owner value, subject to distributive justice and ordinary decency; codes of conduct and ethical training make ignorance of business purposes and policies no excuse. A professional business ethics consultant, expert in applying the Ethical Decision Model, can supply not only audits, codes and training, but also valuable problem-solving and crisis management support.

10

Morals and Markets

'. . . it is by doing just acts that the just man is produced. . . . But most people do not do these, but take refuge in theory . . . behaving somewhat like patients who listen attentively to their doctors, but do none of the things they are ordered to do. As the latter will not be made well in body by such a course of treatment, the former will not be made well in the soul by such a course of philosophy.'

Aristotle[1]

Throughout this book, business has been defined in terms of its objective: maximising long-term owner value by selling goods or services. That objective, it has been argued, largely determines what counts as proper conduct for a business; 'social responsibility', for example, has been rejected as teleopathic. The time has now come to put the business objective in a larger context, by confronting three fundamental issues.

First, how does the business objective relate to other human objectives? This chapter will argue that if members of society have views about the proper conduct of business, or about the extent to which the business objective should be subordinated to other goals, then those views should be expressed in their personal interactions with business. When individuals in their private capacities act conscientiously in deciding whether and when to engage with business, their moral values both influence business's actual activities and determine business's importance relative to other objectives. Properly understood as such conscientious individual action, 'social responsibility' is the responsibility of each member of society.

The second major issue that must be addressed is the comparative value of the business objective, which is greater than is normally supposed.

The third fundamental issue that remains is the extent to which business methods can be extended to other sectors. Healthcare, education, government and other non-business institutions are increasingly being enjoined to be more 'businesslike'. But unless the objective of business is clearly differentiated from the notions of efficiency, accountability and competition, attempts to apply either market mechanisms or business methods more widely will be seriously counterproductive.

THE LIMITS OF BUSINESS ETHICS

The subject of this book so far has been what constitutes ethical conduct for businesses and for people acting in their business capacities. Ethical conduct for both has been defined in terms of the purpose of business, and of the associated values of distributive justice and ordinary decency. And the Ethical Decision Model has been successfully employed in resolving central questions of personnel and finance and corporate governance.

But there have been some notable occasions in the argument when, though an issue has been raised, no resolution has been offered. When, for example, the question arose as to whether selling pornography or armaments might be immoral, or whether whistle-blowing might be obligatory to prevent threats to public safety, the Ethical Decision Model was not applied. And in the discussion of corporate wrongdoing, nothing was said about how individuals should determine which business orders they should obey. Such questions cannot be resolved in the same way as ordinary business ethics issues because, strictly speaking, they are not questions of business ethics.

Many significant questions are not questions of business ethics, just because so much of life lies outside of business; business ethics does not encompass most, far less the whole, of the moral life. Business ethics relates only to those ethical problems that arise within the activity of business, to the ethical issues that face business as business; how much a business should pay its employees, for example, is an archetypal business ethics issue. But the question of whether an individual should work for or buy from or invest in a firm that sells arms to tyrants typically is not. It is an ethical issue as important as many business ethics issues, and may be logically prior to them. But just as questions of microwave engineering are not a part of cookery, and questions of how to fund hospitals are not medical questions, questions of whether and when an individual ought to deal with a business normally are not part either of business or of business ethics.[2]

It is vital to establish which questions are not questions of business ethics because, as has already been shown, being able to answer questions depends crucially on identifying exactly what is being asked. Throughout this book, questions have been elucidated and answered teleologically, by referring to ends or purposes. What counts as the proper conduct of an activity is determined by reference to that activity's purpose; what counts as a good lunch depends on whether the aim is to eat well or to conclude a deal. But which of those aims an individual in his private capacity should pursue cannot be determined by cookery or business: logically, a purpose cannot establish either its own value, or its relationship to other purposes. Questions about the comparative values of purposes, about how purposes are to be ranked, and about which purposes should be pursued, can only be answered by reference to something outside the purposes in question.

Accordingly, questions that investigate the relationship of the business purpose to other purposes require going beyond the bounds of business and business ethics. To what extent should business objectives be subordinated to non-business goals? When is it right to engage in business? Is the business purpose one that should be pursued? What is the value of business compared with other human activities? Logically, it is only by reference to some broader, more comprehensive end that the business purpose can properly be assessed against the alternatives. Ultimately, indeed, the end against which human goals must be judged is nothing less than the purpose of human life itself.

Once it is clear how basic the issues are, and what is really at stake, it becomes understandable why questions about the role and value of business often seem so perplexing: it is because they raise questions about the most fundamental human values. When that is appreciated, however, so should the need to address the questions seriously. All too often, such questions are treated casually or emotively and are relegated to the level of ideological debate. But fundamental questions call for fundamental answers. Disputes about basic values need to be considered on their merits as vital moral questions.

Profoundly important though such questions are, however, this book will not attempt to answer them[3]: the subject of *Just Business* is business ethics, not the meaning of life. But it is also not necessary to answer such fundamental questions to explain how moral values influence business. The key mechanism for transmitting moral values to business is largely independent of the content of those values. In a liberal, pluralistic, free-market society, individuals' actions critically affect the conduct of business and the role that business actually plays, regardless of how their moral priorities have been derived, and whether or not their views are correct[4].

WORKING VALUES

How are those moral views transmitted to business? Consider a question that often agitates commentators on business: what is the ethical status of businesses that sell questionable goods—tobacco, pornography or armaments, for example? The first thing to be noted is that the question can be interpreted on two quite different levels. On one, it asks a straightforward business ethics question: whether particular businesses that sell such goods are ethical. And on that level, the answer is equally clear. Like all other businesses, businesses that sell such products operate ethically as businesses if they seek to maximise long-term owner value while respecting distributive justice and ordinary decency; they are unethical if they violate those conditions.

It is on what might be called the meta[5]-business level that the question becomes problematical: is it right to maximise owner value by selling products that may be dangerous or harmful? There are some activities—contract killing, protection rackets and white slavery, for example—that are intrinsically incompatible with ordinary decency and can be ruled out directly. But when the activities are not necessarily dishonest or unfair, coercive or illegal, the answer will depend on many factors. Some of the considerations are primarily scientific and economic: the degree that the product actually will harm health or damage the environment, the likelihood that it will do so, the degree to which such harm may be accompanied by economic benefits.

But other considerations are explicitly moral, and require making judgements about the comparative importance of fundamental human vales. Avoiding physical harm is important, but it is not the only human value. The value of avoiding physical harm must be weighed against the value of economic well-being and the value of human creativity, the value of moral responsibility and the value of free choice. The comparative importance that individuals attach to such values depends on their personal views of human life and worth. Disputes about potentially harmful kinds of business are usually disagreements about just such fundamental moral issues.

Whatever a person's views may be, however, moral integrity demands consistency between those views and his actions; when an individual's actions do not accord with his moral beliefs, then normally either they are weak[6] or he is. Accordingly if—for whatever reason—an individual believes that selling a particular product is morally wrong, then other things being equal, it will also be wrong[7] for him to support businesses that sell it. If someone is opposed to the sale of tobacco, then if he is acting on his principles he should not buy tobacco. And to be consistent, he also ought not to work for or lend to or invest in tobacco firms, or even other businesses, such as public relations agencies, that provide important services to tobacco firms.

An individual's anti-tobacco convictions may, of course, conflict with his other values. Given the complexity of life, it is often the case that not all values can be pursued simultaneously; hard choices may sometimes be required. The need to earn a living, for example, may be difficult to reconcile with principled objections to dealing with certain sorts of firms. But even when jobs are scarce, individuals must decide which values they will sacrifice and which they will make sacrifices for. Individuals' moral characters are defined by just such choices: by the priorities that they attach to different values, by the ways that they determine those priorities, and by the degree to which their actions conscientiously accord with them.

What they choose has important consequences for business, because the definitive business end makes it essential for businesses to heed stakeholder preferences[8]. To maximise long-term owner value by selling goods or services, a business must actually sell goods or services. To do so, however, it has to attract the voluntary participation of customers and suppliers, employees and finance. The business is therefore obliged to take into account the preferences of the potential stakeholders for which it is competing. If UK consumers want their television cabinets to look like wood or their crisps to be flavoured with salt and vinegar, then businesses competing for their custom must ordinarily reflect those wishes.

If potential stakeholders act on their moral views—if they selectively support firms that are kind or courageous or charitable—then those moral views will equally have to be taken into account. For the 'invisible hand' conveys not just economic but moral information; it automatically transforms the personal choices of individuals into commercial data for business. If enough individuals refuse to support firms that sell tobacco or kill dolphins, then it will not be economically rewarding to continue those activities; the businesses pursuing them will have to change their ways or go out of business. Because of the nature of the definitive business end, the same moral considerations that are teleopathic when heeded independent of maximising long-term owner value, must be respected when they affect it[9].

Accordingly, though only owners have the right to determine the firm's objectives, everyone can influence business conduct. By choosing whether or not, and to what extent, to support particular businesses with their investment or custom or labour, everyone can contribute to the economic conditions that critically affect business decisions. If, therefore, individuals have views as to how business should be conducted, they should ensure that their individual choices accurately reflect those views. If they find the product or the manufacturing process objectionable, or consider the service or the advertising offensive, or judge the declared values of the board or the management to be misguided, then it is up to them not to support the firm. When each potential stakeholder—otherwise known as every member of society[10]—acts conscientiously in his personal capacity, and strategically bestows or withholds his economic support on the basis of his moral values, then the operation of market forces will automatically lead businesses to reflect those values.

SOCIAL RESPONSIBILITY REVISITED

It is as such conscientious individual action that social responsibility is properly understood. Using the term more loosely, to suggest some unspecified organisational responsibility to society, is subject to two fundamental flaws.

First, consider what might be meant by a responsibility to society. Most actions have consequences that extend beyond the individuals making them. Insofar as those consequences affect other members of society, individuals might well be said to have a responsibility to take those consequences into account. But the need to do so cannot be what defines 'social responsibility', because it is a condition of all responsibility: being responsible means considering the consequences of one's actions, and being accountable for them.

Equally, the distinguishing feature of social responsibility cannot be that it is exercised by social institutions. For the distinctive responsibility of organisations, or of individuals in their organisational capacities, is to achieve the definitive aims of those organisations. Society might perhaps be better off if institutional goals were sometimes subordinated to wider social or moral goals. But it cannot be a part of ordinary organisational responsibility to make such judgements or to pursue those wider ends: within an organisation, organisational purposes are binding.

If, therefore, social responsibility in respect of business consists of subordinating business ends to wider social or moral ones, it cannot be chosen by businesses. When individuals act in a business capacity, their choices are necessarily constrained: they are bound by legal and contractual limitations and by the definitive business purpose that they have already accepted. Within a business, decisions as to which candidate to hire, which supplier to appoint, which project to undertake, are properly made not by reference to the decider's personal values, but by the definitive business purpose and the principle of ethical selection. It is only when individuals act in their private capacities that their choices can freely[11] reflect the values they attach to different ends, and they can pursue social welfare or environmental protection or artistic expression in preference to maximising owner value.

It may be protested that decisions about fundamental goals are too important to be left to individuals, and that the proper way of subordinating business to other objectives is through regulation or legislation. And on one level, this is right. If individuals' assets are to be appropriated forcibly for 'socially responsible' purposes, then decisions to do so are properly public policy decisions; as such, they should be taken by elected legislators, not private individuals[12].

It should be noted, however, that at best[13], regulation can normally bring about only the performance of 'socially responsible' acts, not social responsibility. For social responsibility necessarily operates in the realm of voluntary action: being responsible and acting conscientiously both require a freedom to choose that is undermined by the coercive force of law. This accords with our ordinary understanding of 'social responsibility'. It is precisely in respect of those matters that are not legally required, and are matters of choice, that businesses and other institutions are typically enjoined to be 'socially responsible'.

Social responsibility is exercised when individuals express their own values in their own acts, acting separately or in concert; it is not exercised when they force their views on others. A socially responsible individual objects to low wages by refusing to work for them. If he feels strongly about the evils of low wages, he can attempt to dissuade other workers from accepting them, and he can boycott products and producers who benefit from them. He can even try to persuade the owners of businesses to transform their firms into social welfare organisations. But if he acts to prevent other workers from accepting, or businesses from offering, wage levels that are acceptable to them both, he is obstructing social responsibility, not exercising it. Individuals have no more right to force other adults to adopt their moral priorities than they have to dictate their religious beliefs.[14]

It is because it is up to individuals to make their own choices, and to decide which businesses they will support, that individual employees properly share responsibility for corporate wrongdoing, and may have a responsibility to blow the whistle. Within a business, of course, it is no more legitimate for employees to defy business orders than it is for them to alter the business's objectives; employees are legally and morally bound to respect their contractual commitments[15]. It is, however, always an individual's responsibility to decide what commitments he will accept, what policies he will endorse, what purposes and organisations he will support; individuals are responsible for aligning their activities with their moral principles. An employee who considers that his employer is acting illegally or immorally, and who does not want to share responsibility for that wrongdoing, should either act to correct it or resign.[16]

The responsible time to express one's moral views, however, is normally before making a binding commitment. Though changes of organisational character and individuals' minds may sometimes make subsequent protests necessary, accepting a job ordinarily means agreeing to do that job. Potential job opportunities should therefore be screened not only for their pay and perks, but for their ethical suitability. A responsible animal rights enthusiast will recognise that work on a factory farm normally involves confining and killing animals, and will therefore be wary of such employment: in accepting a factory farm job, he would either be committing himself to violate his principles, or would be lying about his willingness to do the necessary. The responsible way not to obey unacceptable orders, is to steer clear of the jobs that produce them; if enough people do so, those jobs will not be done.

Understood as the strategic expression of moral values in individuals' own commercial and other choices, social responsibility can be a significant force. As dramatically illustrated by social investing, the green consumer movement[17] and the growth of 'vigilante consumerism', acting conscientiously in deciding to be a stakeholder—what might be called 'conscientious stakeholding'—can sharply affect the way business is conducted.[18] It can affect the products that businesses produce, influencing whether they are useful or decorative or good value for money. It can affect the conduct of business in producing them, influencing whether procedures are environmentally friendly or efficient or paternalistic. And it can affect the strategic direction and structure of businesses, influencing what sorts of activities they pursue, and what sorts of powers and protection that corporate businesses afford their shareholders.

But socially responsible, strategic stakeholding can do even more: it can also influence the extent to which business, as opposed to other human activities, is pursued at all. And this accords with what is normally expected of social responsibility. For though calls for social responsibility are frequently disguised as proclamations of business ethics, they are actually assertions about the comparative value of different human objectives. Saying that it is more socially responsible for a firm to provide basic nutrition for the starving, rather than to develop yet another profitable snack food, is normally to recommend that it substitute social welfare ends for business ones, at least in part.

By strategically bestowing their capital, their labour and their custom, individuals can influence which objectives will be pursued. They can, of course, also do so by strategically bestowing their votes in governmental elections: how public resources are allocated, and in what way activities should be subject to regulation, are key matters of public policy. But even without invoking the force of the law, individuals can affect the role of business. Instead of committing their resources to businesses of various sorts, people can simply dedicate them to other ends—to charity or to healthcare, to education or to religion, to art or sport or gardening. Individuals who want to champion political, educational or artistic causes can devote their money, energy and working lives to those objectives rather than to business. They can contribute to charity instead of buying goods or shares; they can buy things from charity shops instead of ordinary retailers; they can devote their time to charity rather than to advancing their business careers. If enough people devote their services and donate their funds to non-business ends, then non-business ends will prevail.

THE VALUE OF BUSINESS

In making that decision, however, the value of business should not be underestimated. Business is often regarded as an unworthy objective, because of the widespread belief that it has little to do with the 'higher' values. Business, it is dismissively suggested, is only about money, not about truth or honour or creativity. But that suggestion is fundamentally mistaken.

First, truth and justice and fairness are not alien to business but intimately related to it. They are essential conditions for the existence of business as an activity, and are central components of the distributive justice and ordinary decency that define ethical conduct for business. If honour means steadfast adherence to moral principles, then ethical business is automatically honourable.

Second, business plays a vital role in financing 'higher' values. Non-business activities tend to be users rather than sources of finance: social welfare and medical research and religion do not normally create[19] the wealth needed for their functioning. That wealth ordinarily comes from business[20].

By enriching its stakeholders, who can use their increased wealth to support the objectives of their choice, business makes the achievement of other values possible.

Business can provide such wealth because it is intrinsically creative. In order for long-term owner (financial) value to be maximised, (non-financial) value must first be created: goods and services must be produced and value must be added. But adding value is creating value. Business is also creative in the sense of being innovative and imaginative. The best businesses do not just respond to customers' needs, they anticipate them; they create new kinds of goods and new ways of serving customers effectively.

And significantly, the value that business creates is just the value that society actually wants. When markets are free, business can only thrive by satisfying consumer preferences, by, that is, supplying what consumers genuinely value. It may be protested that the junk food and disposable goods provided by business cannot be what a civilised society really values. But the true values of a society are expressed in what it does, not what it says . . . not in what people are eager to do with other peoples' money[21], but in what they actually do with their own. A community that claims to prize charity, but whose members will not use their own time or money or labour to achieve eleemosynary ends, is not charitable but hypocritical. Those institutions, those values, for which no one in a free society is willing voluntarily to pay, are those that it considers literally not worth having.

BEING BUSINESSLIKE

Nevertheless, people still want business to do what they cannot or will not do themselves: they want business to house the homeless and save the whale and make life meaningful. Willy Sutton robbed banks because that was where the money was; similarly, individuals and governments often turn to business because it is such a locus of wealth and power and effectiveness. To seek help from business is, however, both mistaken—since it is teleopathic for business to pursue non-business ends—and quite unnecessary. Business is not the only effective component of the private sector. The resources in question—both the funds and the skills—are ultimately the property of, and are at the disposal of, individuals.

The way to improve the achievement of non-business goals is not to divert business from its proper end, but to improve the ways of accomplishing non-business objectives. Many British public institutions—the health service, education, the police, the civil service—have nevertheless been officially enjoined to be more businesslike. What might this mean?

The one thing it cannot mean is that non-business institutions should take maximising long-term owner value as their objective. And that is simply because if they did, they would not be more businesslike, they would actually be businesses. Though so obvious that it should scarcely need making, this point has been overlooked too often both by advocates and critics of making non-business activities more businesslike. Although healthcare organisations can be profitable, it is not the purpose of healthcare to maximise owner value, or even to make money. If it were, then if a hospital could earn more by selling beds than by curing patients, it would be right to do so. But that would be absurd.

Just as business has a definitive objective that it must pursue, so have other activities. The purpose of healthcare is not to maximise long-term owner value by selling goods or services, but (crudely) to maximise well-being by preventing and curing disease. And as simplistically, the definitive aim of education (as distinct from training) is not to make money or even to provide skilled workers, but to extend and transmit human knowledge, in part by increasing people's ability to think critically. These definitions may not capture all that is essential to their respective activities; as Chapter 2 above should demonstrate, properly defining an activity is a complicated exercise. But they are sufficient to indicate that these activities do have purposes that are distinctively different from that of business, and that must be respected. It is no more right for non-business institutions to take maximising long-term owner value as their purpose in order to be effective, than it is for business to sacrifice that end in order to be ethical.

Keeping objectives clear is even more essential when non-business institutions are required to be self-funding. The need to raise money may often lead them to take on ancillary business activities; it is, after all, normally business that generates wealth. But it must always be clear which activity is under consideration at any given time, and which is paramount; great care must be taken that neither activity consumes the other, and that each is properly conducted according to its own essential standards.

What 'being businesslike' does properly mean, is pursuing non-business objectives with the benefit of those qualities that account for business's superior effectiveness: efficiency, accountability and competition, preferably in the framework of a free market. Although traditionally associated with business, these attributes are altogether distinct from the business purpose; when the distinction is understood, they can be productively applied to improve the effectiveness of a wide range of non-business activities.

Efficiency is a supremely businesslike characteristic, that is naturally supported by distributive justice: efficiency requires eliminating waste and making the best possible use of available resources. What counts as the best use, however, depends critically on the end being sought. Whereas saving documents indefinitely is normally inefficient and wasteful for a business, it is neither for a university archive. Efficiency is always relative to a particular objective; efficiency means maximising the extent to which a stated goal is achieved with a given level of resources.

Confusion often arises, however, because of money's use as a counter for measuring efficiency. When the resources employed in achieving an objective are numerous and diverse, the easiest way to compare different ways of combining them is normally to consider their aggregate monetary costs. Even then, however, money is the measure, not the objective; efficiency is not the same as making or saving money. A hospital that saves money by not providing healthcare is not being efficient but teleopathic. The efficient hospital is instead one that deploys its staff, space and equipment most effectively, to maximise the healthcare it can provide for a given level of expenditure. The objective of efficiency is achievement.

The second major source of business effectiveness is accountability. Accountability means that individuals and institutions are answerable for what they do: they must account to others for their conduct and for their use of resources. Organisations should be held accountable for achieving their objectives. Unless they are held accountable for the right objectives, however, increasing accountability will not promote effectiveness. Holding an institution accountable for achieving the impossible does not make achievement of that impossible goal any more likely; it simply diverts resources from what actually could be done. Holding an orphanage accountable for creating wealth makes no more sense than holding an archive accountable for creating health.

The extent to which accountability improves effectiveness depends on how carefully the objectives are framed, on what mechanisms exist for holding individuals to account for achieving them, and on what penalties apply for unsatisfactory performance. Unlike business, non-business institutions have typically fallen short in all three categories. Historically they have lacked clear objectives, they have had few if any mechanisms for reviewing performance, and they have seldom imposed penalties for failure. By remedying those deficiencies, non-business organisations could do much to foster business-level effectiveness. If organisations are concerned to improve their efficiency, they can make efficiency one of the qualities for which their members are explicitly held accountable. They can introduce mechanisms for measuring efficiency; they can make sure that inefficiency is identified, penalised and corrected.

A third major source of business productivity is competition. Contrary to popular belief, competition does not preclude co-operation or necessitate dirty tricks; competing successfully requires the focused pursuit of stipulated objectives, not incivility. And as a means of increasing effectiveness, what is significant about competition is not aggressive conflict, but the existence of real alternatives. When products or services can be obtained from more than one source, their quality and performance can more easily be compared. More demanding standards can be set, and the best performers can be selected; competition thereby promotes efficiency. Equally, sanctions can operate freely: when alternatives are available, individuals whose performance is deficient can readily be replaced and organisations safely supplanted. Having competitors therefore enhances accountability, as does the very need to compete. Conversely, accountability enhances competition: when institutions and their members are held firmly to their objectives, they are likely to be more formidable competitors.

To be effective, however, competition requires not just the existence of alternatives, but information about them and the freedom to act on that information. The mere existence of other schools does little to raise educational standards if the schools' relative performance is not measured or is concealed, or if pupils' entry to them is officially impeded. By restricting access, the non-business sector has often lost the benefits of competition even when alternatives have been available.

The final buttress of business effectiveness is a powerful mechanism that is only occasionally available to other institutions: the operation of a (relatively) free market. The market is an extraordinarily efficient information system, which automatically translates the individual choices of myriad consumers into simple monetary prices. By transparently reflecting supply and demand, market pricing provides comprehensive information on which things are valued. It is thus an invaluable aid to the efficient allocation of resources.

Like any information system, however, a market is only as good as the information it processes. If the purchasers of the goods and services are not the users of them, then the prices of those goods will not necessarily reflect user preferences. And when individual choices or access to alternatives are artificially constrained by regulation, the pricing information provided by the operation of the market will be correspondingly flawed. If workers are not allowed to work for low wages, or scarce goods are provided free, or are supplied by a single source, then prices will not accurately reflect consumer values. For market mechanisms to be effective, they must be accompanied by the freedom that is necessary for them to work.

Even at their best, however, markets do not and cannot set objectives. Despite popular fears, employing market mechanisms in no way lessens the need for, or the importance of, setting priorities; markets only indicate what choices cost, not which choices should be made. All markets can do is provide information about the costs and availability of the resources that are necessary for achieving stipulated ends; they cannot decide what those ends should be. The market cannot determine whether it is more important to allocate resources for medicine or for education, or within medicine whether resources should be devoted to geriatrics or paediatrics. Those are hard decisions that cannot be avoided. They can be taken by individuals acting in their private capacities, or as elected representatives, or as officials with delegated powers; to the extent that education and healthcare are publicly funded, choices about them represent key public policy decisions. But in all cases, they are choices that must actually be made.

And it is the specific contents of those choices that will determine the best means of achieving them. Some objectives may be deemed too important ever to be subordinated to maximising long-term owner value. When that is so, then whatever the goal—be it healthcare or education, producing the best newspaper or even the very best widgets ever—it is not appropriately pursued as a business. But even—perhaps especially—when such highly valued objectives are at stake, it is important that they be pursued with the full benefits of efficiency, accountability, competition and the free market.

In summary then, efficiency, accountability, competition and the free market are conceptually independent of the business purpose. Efficiency measures the extent to which resources are used effectively in achieving an objective; accountability makes individuals and institutions answerable for achieving a stipulated goal. Competition provides real alternatives that enhance efficiency and accountability. Market pricing supplies information about which things are valued and what resources are available. It is perfectly possible for non-business institutions to achieve businesslike effectiveness without sacrificing their distinctive purposes or adopting business ends.

To do so, however, institutions must be subject to real sanctions, real accountability and real competition. Individuals must know what they want from their institutions, they must insist on their institutions' being accountable, and they must actually hold them to account. If that sounds like hard work, it is because achieving any objective with businesslike effectiveness requires businesslike effort. It is not just liberty, but all substantial values that require eternal vigilance; ultimately, a society gets not just the government, but also the business and the non-business institutions it deserves.

Notes and References

Preface

1 *Just Business: Business Ethics in Action*, Little, Brown & Co. UK 1994, Warner paperback 1995 (*'JB1'*), p. 5.
2 *JB1*, p. 5.
3 Henceforth, *'CGAIM'*.

Introduction: What Makes This Book Distinctive

1 *Nicomachean Ethics*, Book X Chapter 1, 1172b4–7. All references are to the W.D. Ross translation in McKeon, Richard, ed., *The Basic Works of Aristotle*, Random House, 1941.
2 Address to 586 electors at Tamworth, 1834: quoted in *The Economist*, 24 November 1990, Bagehot column, p. 40.
3 Typically some variation of utilitarianism or Kantian deontology.
4 For an analysis of the metaphysical shortcomings of modern ethical theories, see MacIntyre, Alasdair, *After Virtue: a study in moral theory*, Gerald Duckworth & Co. Ltd., 1981. For an investigation of how Aristotelian naturalism avoids those fundamental problems, see Sternberg, Elaine, *The Logical Conditions of Public Experience*, Ph.D. Thesis, London School of Economics, University of London, 1976.
5 For the source of that framework, see the collected works of Aristotle, especially the *Nicomachean Ethics, Metaphysics, Politics, De Anima*, and the *Posterior Analytics*. For a sympathetic introduction to the works of Aristotle, see Randall, John Herman Jr., *Aristotle*, Columbia University Press, 1960.
6 Note that Kenneth Goodpaster's use of the term in "Ethical Imperatives and Corporate Leadership" (1988 Ruffin Lecture; reprinted in Andrews, K.R. ed., *Ethics in Practice: Managing the Moral Corporation*, Harvard Business School Press, 1989, pp. 212–228) is much narrower than mine.
7 For a fuller discussion of, and argument against, ethical relativism, see Chapter 3 below.
8 The principles involved are everywhere and always true, and their rightness is independent of their specific consequences.
9 It can be a fact that something is of value. It is, for example, a fact that cement is better than chocolate as a building material for company headquarters, and that honesty is better than lying for sustaining human trust.
10 Throughout, 'virtue' is used in the Greek sense of 'excellence', and has no sexual connotation.

Chapter 1: The Importance of Business Ethics

1 *Nicomachean Ethics*, Book I Chapter 2, 1094a23–24.

2 *The Company Chairman*, Director Books, Fitzwilliam Publishing Ltd., 1990, p. 187.

3 *A Passion for Excellence: The Leadership Difference*, Fontana/Collins, 1985, p. 333.

4 Though, of course, it may be. And on some occasions in this book, 'ethical' does mean 'ethically correct'; the context should make it clear which sense is intended.

5 See Chapter 3 below.

6 For an extended argument in support of this point, see Chapters 2 and 5 below.

7 E.g., those of the Bank of Credit and Commerce International (BCCI), Drexel Burnham Lambert and the Robert Maxwell and Polly Peck groups.

8 For example, the 'oxymoronic' approach described in the Preface.

9 The term originated in Bird, Frederick B. & Waters, James A., "The Moral Muteness of Managers", *California Management Review*, Vol. 32, No. 1, 1989, p. 73.

10 It is instructive to remember that Einstein defined common sense as 'the collection of prejudices people have accrued by the age of 18'. . . . Reported in Furnham, Adrian, "How do you rate on the common sense scale?", *Financial Times*, 5 May 1993, p. 14.

11 For a detailed discussion of the purpose of business, see Chapter 2 below.

12 As will be argued below in Chapter 3, the discrepancy results not because different ethical principles apply to individuals and businesses, but simply because business's defining purpose is very narrow. It would be as perverse and immoral for a person to limit his activities exclusively to those that are legitimate for a business, as it would be for a business to pursue non-business ends.

13 Except insofar as they influence what will maximise long-term owner value.

14 See Relativism Rejected in Chapter 3 below.

15 See Chapter 5 below.

16 Though it can introduce simplifying order into the handling of complex situations.

17 All too often whingeing, impinging. . . .

18 '*Mens sana in corpore sano*'.

19 To sexual roles, for example, and physical disability.

20 E.g., Barlow Clowes, Guinness, Blue Arrow, Maxwell.

21 In accordance with the US Sentencing Commission Guidelines adopted November 1991.

22 A Mori poll of 1,092 UK workers showed that 62% rated having an 'interesting/enjoyable job', and 46% rated 'accomplishing something worthwhile' as their most important consideration, vs. 38% who thought that basic pay was most important. Reported in Young, Robin, "Job interest rated higher than pay", *The Times*, 9 May 1991, p. 3. A study of more than 10,000 people in Britain and 10 other Western European countries conducted by the European Values Group confirmed that employees 'are becoming more demanding in what they see as acceptable treatment from their bosses'. Reported in Dixon, Michael, "The importance of being expert", *Financial Times*, 23 October 1991, p. 14.

Chapter 2: The Nature of Business

1 *Metaphysics*, Book XI Chapter 5, 1062a12–16, translated by W.D. Ross, in McKeon, R. ed., *The Basic Works of Aristotle*, Random House, 1941.
2 *Capitalism and Freedom*, The University of Chicago Press, 1962, p. 133.
3 Selling here includes leasing, renting, etc.
4 Or both. . . .
5 'By selling goods or services' should be assumed . . . the defining purpose of business is always the same, though the shorter form of words will often be employed for convenience.
6 Though it might equally be a necessary condition for doing so. . . .
7 For a fuller discussion of these and related points, see Aristotle, *Metaphysics*, especially Books IV and XI.
8 See also the Preface above.
9 Consider the General Motors Class E shares issued to reflect the performance of the once-independent Electronic Data Services, and the split of the Racal Group into Vodaphone, Racal Electronics and Chubb Security.
10 The famous slogan 'The public good be damned' can be seen as a pithy reminder of this crucial fact.
11 For a comprehensive discussion of corporate governance, and a defence of the Anglo-Saxon model of corporate governance, see Sternberg, Elaine, *CGAIM, op.cit.*
12 Like actual commercial organisations, actual governments do much more in practice, and arrogate to themselves many diverse functions and objectives. That they do so, however, in no way undermines the correctness of the definition. For a fuller exposition of this notion of the role of government, see, for example, Hayek, Frederich A., *The Road To Serfdom*, University of Chicago Press, 1944, especially Chapter VI, and Friedman, Milton, *Capitalism and Freedom*, *op. cit.*, especially

Chapter II. For its philosophical underpinnings, see Hobbes, Thomas, *Leviathan*, and the works of Michael J. Oakeshott, especially *On Human Conduct*, Oxford University Press, 1975, Section II.

13 Except for self-defence.

14 By conscription into the armed forces, and in some jurisdictions through capital punishment.

15 Subject, of course, to fulfilling any contractual or other commitments they might have undertaken.

16 The choice to live outside the jurisdiction of government is no longer available.

17 Except for those who are underage, convicted felons or mentally defective.

18 Not to be confused with corporate governance.

19 When they do . . . it is arguable that unlike American citizens, whose Bill of Rights is set out as a series of amendments to the (written) Constitution, British subjects had only the right of *habeas corpus* prior to the incorporation of the European Convention on Human Rights into UK law. Even if such rights are considered to be 'natural rights' (see Chapter 6 below), however, they operate chiefly as a limit on coercive force.

20 *New York Times Magazine*, 13 September 1970, pp. 32–3, 122–6.

21 Though such motives may sometimes make criminals less blameworthy; for a fuller discussion of motives and actions see the Preface above and Chapter 4 below.

22 Most contracts of employment commit employees, at least implicitly, to pursue the business purpose.

23 See also the Preface above, and Acts vs. Motives in Chapter 4 below.

24 In some sense, of course, all measures are influenced by management: if management had no effect, it would not be worth having. But as discussed in Chapter 7 below, accounting measures are exceptionally susceptible to management control; even auditing presents few limits on their being used to promote the ends of managers rather than owners.

25 Davis, Evan, Flanders, Stephanie and Star, Jonathan, "Who are the world's most successful companies?", London Business School *Business Strategy Review*, Summer 1991, reported in "The Best Companies", *The Economist*, 7 September 1991, pp. 19–24. Similar arguments apply to the Economic Value Added model advanced by Stern Stewart.

26 When a share is sold, the price received reflects the further dividends forgone; that price will crystallise a capital gain if it is greater than the price paid for the shares.

27 Reportedly in a 1963 internal memo at the Stanford Research

Institute; Freeman, R. Edward, *Strategic Management: a stakeholder approach*, Pitman Publishing Inc., 1984, p. 31.

28 Freeman, *op. cit.*, p.vi.

29 *Ibid*, p. 52.

30 The UK Co-operative Bank explicitly includes both 'past and future generations' in its list of stakeholders; Kellaway, Lucy, 'Stakeholders step up for the generation shuffle', *Financial Times*, 17 March 1997, p. 16. Consider as well the future generations, of whatever species, in whose name ecologists protest against various perceived depredations, and the nameless sea creatures allegedly threatened by, e.g., the disposal of the Brent Spar oil rig at the bottom of the ocean.

31 For a comprehensive analysis of the defects of the stakeholder doctrine, see Sternberg, Elaine, *The Stakeholder Concept: A Mistaken Doctrine*, Foundation for Business Responsibilities, Issue Paper No.4, November 1999, and *CGAIM, op.cit.*, Chapter 6.

32 By, for example, Pennsylvania's notorious anti-takeover Act 36 of 1990.

33 It is noteworthy that stakeholders are commonly described as representing 'constituencies', which in turn are identified with interest groups. The notion that an elected representative's function is to represent the special interests of his particular electors rather than the nation as a whole is itself a debatable, though increasingly common, view of political representation.

34 The fact that business can be held to account by government is a function of the coercive power of government, not its notional role as stakeholder. The extent to which government has any *right* to control business in this way is a quite separate matter, and is a key issue of political philosophy.

35 See, for example, The Business Roundtable, *Corporate Governance and American Competitiveness*, March 1990, p. 13. The Roundtable did, however, repudiate the stakeholder doctrine in 1997.

36 I am grateful to Daniel Moylan for this observation.

37 That is not to say that families are, or should be, content to receive less than the best price available. The point is simply that selling a house in order to obtain a different location or space is different from selling the house simply to maximise financial gain, as a property dealer might do.

38 Or 'optimising' to the extent that it means the same thing.

39 Being obliged to maximise owner value is also what makes the business sensitive to stakeholder preferences; it is thus an important element in the operation of social responsibility. See Social Responsibility Revisited in Chapter 10 below.

40 For a further discussion of the way in which decision criteria rather

than actual outcomes determine the correctness of actions, see the discussion of Fiduciary Responsibility in Chapter 4 below.

41 In their capacity as owners; the same effect should be achieved when there are adequate mechanisms for ensuring that managers (and directors) identify with the business purpose.

42 Which is nonetheless contingent: 'good ethics is good business' is a useful slogan, not a guarantee. See Chapter 3 below.

43 The positive value of business is discussed in The Value of Business in Chapter 10 below.

44 As it does in legally constituted monopolies, for example.

45 Though they can, of course, buy their silence.

Chapter 3: The Business of Ethics

1 *Nicomachean Ethics*, Book I Chapter 7, 1098b3–6.

2 *Making It Happen: Reflections on Leadership*, William Collins Sons & Co., 1988, p. 120.

3 Though they will interpret the question differently, because of the different objectives of business and medicine.

4 Or it might be appropriate (typically when acting outside of business) to try to create such a jurisdiction. See Sternberg, Elaine, 'The Universal Principles of Business Ethics' in Machan, Tibor, ed., *Business Ethics in the Global Market*, Hoover Institution Press, Stanford University, 1999, pp. 1–36.

5 Indeed, it is the mark of the good man to *desire* the good: '... a good man *qua* good delights in virtuous actions and is vexed at vicious ones, as a musical man enjoys beautiful tunes but is pained at bad ones.' Aristotle, *Nicomachean Ethics*, Book IX Chapter 9, 1170a8–10.

6 Glossing suffering merely as god's (unfathomable) will being done has historically raised, rather than resolved, the problem of evil.

7 Though prudence has sometimes been designated a (natural, cardinal) moral virtue.

8 A version of this section was first presented at the Ninth National Conference on Business Ethics, Bentley College, March 1992, and appears as "Relativism Rejected: The Possibility of Transnational Business Ethics" in Hoffman, W. Michael, *et. al.*, eds., *Emerging Global Business Ethics*, Quorum Books, 1994, pp. 143–50.

9 United Kingdom, European Union, Confederation of British Industry or Trades Union Congress.

10 For the basis of the philosophical framework drawn upon here, see the collected works of Aristotle, *op. cit.*

11 Though not with moral impunity.

12 Strictly speaking there are only principles of ethics. The 'principles of business ethics' are simply those general principles most rele-

vant to the objective of business.

13 See Aristotle, *op. cit.*

14 The controlling of a voluntary agent or action by force, usually by threatening physical violence.

15 Because life in the state of nature is the 'war of every man against every man'. Thomas Hobbes, *Leviathan*, 1651, Part I Chapter 13; the quotations are from p. 82 of the Michael Oakeshott edition published by Basil Blackwell. Hobbes' analysis was offered as a justification of civil society; within civil society, key arguments apply equally in support of ordinary decency.

16 Aristotle, *Nicomachean Ethics*, Book V Chapter 3, 1131a25–32.

17 Those who contribute most to the business deserve most from the business.

18 Fourth, what owners receive is only an indirect function of distributive justice, because (at least in theory) the whole business and all that it generates belong to the owners. They should get to keep what is left over after the other contributors to the business receive amounts necessary to maximise long-term owner value in accordance with distributive justice and ordinary decency.

19 It is not necessary separately to exclude lying, cheating and stealing because the other conditions preclude them.

20 I.e., the participants in the business in their business capacities.

21 This includes, for example, giving all who contribute to the business objective their due.

22 Austin, J.L., *How to Do Things with Words*, edited by J.O. Urmson, Oxford University Press, 1962.

23 For example, pharmaceutical companies should disclose both known contra-indications and suspected dangers, and workers should be warned of the actual and potential dangers of radiation and dioxins.

24 And may be teleopathic: the duty of confidentiality arises from the fact that excessive disclosure can damage long-term owner value.

25 But not, sadly, by UK legislators; consider the Property Misdescriptions Act of 1991.

26 Which might be considered 'honesty in action': reliable people are those who can be counted on to do what they say they will.

27 Partly because being ethical does not require any sort of unproductive 'do-gooding'.

28 In their business capacities.

29 So is a kettle that catches fire, because it lacks the essential thermostat. Marsh, Peter and Kynge, James, 'China pulls plug on counterfeit kettles, *Financial Times*, 15 December 1999 (electronic version; no page number given).

30 Consider the 1977 (US) Foreign Corrupt Practices Act ('FCPA'),

which makes it a criminal offence for American persons to offer or provide payments to officials of foreign governments in order to obtain or retain business, even if doing so is not unlawful in the foreign countries concerned.

Chapter 4: Ethical Implications

1 *Nicomachean Ethics*, Book VII Chapter 14, 1154a22–25.
2 Because motives can apply to any purpose, they cannot serve to differentiate activities. Recall the argument of the Preface above. When motive and intention appear to overlap, it is usually when intentions are derived from conventional understandings of motives. For a fuller discussion of motives, intentions and objectives, see Sternberg, Elaine, "A Teleological Approach to Business Ethics", Gasparski, W.W. and Ryan, L.V. eds., *Human Action in Business*, Praxiology Volume 5, Transaction Publishers (Rutgers University), 1996, pp. 51–64.
3 And legal: consider malice aforethought as a condition of murder.
4 Throughout, 'agent' refers to 'moral agent' which, unlike a financial agent, is a principal. . . .
5 Towards the child, the fish or even the body of water: he may wish to save the environment from disturbance.
6 'The agent must also be in a certain condition when he does them; in the first place he must have knowledge, secondly he must choose the acts, and choose them for their own sakes; and thirdly his action must proceed from a firm and unchangeable character.' Aristotle, *op. cit.*, Book II Chapter 3, 1105a32–35.
7 Those that maximise long-term owner value while respecting distributive justice and ordinary decency.
8 In UK law, directors' fiduciary responsibility to shareholders is limited to the common law duty of care.
9 In virtue of offering themselves as experts: advisers are normally employed because they are presumed to be more capable of achieving their clients' objectives than the clients can themselves.
10 Note that although it is typically a corporation's managers who hire the firm's accountants, their duty as auditors is not to them, but to the company's shareholders as a whole.
11 Those terms might stipulate the degree of risk acceptable to the client, the period over which returns were to be maximised, the types of investments to be made, the instruments to be avoided, etc.
12 Defined in terms of the client's objective.
13 Beyond the fees earned for being a fiduciary.
14 Incidentally or otherwise: a business that consists of fulfilling the

fiduciary role will normally thrive only if its clients' interests do.

15 A similar analysis explains why some ways of being teleopathic are unethical for a business, while others preclude the organisation from being a business.

16 In an academic study of 112 newly qualified accountants, 30% were tempted to take short cuts in audits because they found the work boring, and 41% because they thought it unimportant. Jack, Andrew, "'Bored' junior auditors take short cuts", *Financial Times*, 8 April 1993, p. 8.

17 Note, though, that in English common law, a fiduciary has an obligation not to put himself in a position where his interests may conflict with those of his principal.

18 I am grateful to Robert Laird for this observation.

19 Which client the bank should support will depend on the circumstances. The ordinary decency requirement that businesses honour their commitments means that the bank should support the client to which it made the earliest, strongest commitment, e.g., the long-term client for which it is lead banker rather than the new client for which it has just done a single deal. In the unlikely event that commitments are of equal weight and age, then the business should award its advice on the basis of distributive justice, and help the one from which it expects to derive the best business in future.

20 In some situations, when undertaken to avert an even greater wrong, bribery may be the right thing to do. But bribery as such remains wrong nonetheless.

21 If the size of the payment were universally recognised to be the sole criterion for allocating the rewards, then it would be the relevant 'merit': what would be operating then would not be bribery, but an auction.

22 Though as already observed, circumstances may make bribery the least of alternative wrongs, and thus the appropriate thing to do.

23 For a full argument in support of this assertion, see the section on Consultation in Chapter 6 below.

24 Such policies should therefore always be qualified by the need to respect the ethical business objective of maximising long-term owner value while observing distributive justice and ordinary decency.

Chapter 5: The Ethical Enterprise

1 *Nicomachean Ethics*, Book VII Chapter 3, 1146b7.

2 Occasional errors may not be unethical; systematic mismanagement is unethical.

3 Though clear thinking should and educating the public about

business may do so.

4 For a discussion of how business should deal with expectations that are not legitimate, see Breach of Trust in Chapter 7 below.

5 Surviving on those terms may, of course, not be worthwhile; as will be discussed in some detail in Chapter 10 below, the decision to engage in or with business is a key ethical choice.

6 See, for example, Cairncross, Frances, "Cleaning Up: a survey of industry and the environment", *The Economist*, 8 September 1990, p. 4. For the notion of a 'viridity symbol', see p. 5.

7 Under, e.g., US Superfund legislation, for which liability is strict, joint and several, and retroactive.

8 It is only in the unlikely case that all the alternatives both satisfy distributive justice and ordinary decency, and are projected to have equal effects on maximising long-term owner value, that degrees of distributive justice or ordinary decency might be taken into account.

9 It is commonly imagined to be one because utilitarians require cost/benefit analyses both for identifying and for justifying ethical action.

Chapter 6: Personnel

1 *Making It Happen, op. cit.*, pp. 69–70.

2 *Ibid.*, p. 250.

3 US labour leader; quoted by K.E. Goodpaster in "Note on the Corporation as a Moral Environment", in Andrews, K.R., ed., *Ethics in Practice, op. cit.*, p. 111.

4 Used throughout as a generic synonym for 'workforce', and including line as well as support personnel. Similarly, unless otherwise specified, 'employees' will be used to designate any (internal) paid agent of the business, including board members.

5 Except to the extent that they are also its shareholders.

6 According to Ivan Robertson, Professor of Occupational Therapy at the University of Manchester Institute of Science and Technology, the key de-motivators are: links between achievement and effort that are perverse or random; vague, or worse, contradictory work goals that are imposed from above without explanation or consultation; and arbitrary controls. Quoted in Dixon, Michael, "We have ways of turning you off", *Financial Times*, 13 January 1993, p. 11. Similarly, according to Professor Adrian Furnham of University College, London, when workers feel they are treated unfairly, 'The most common reaction . . . is the alienated, uncommitted, unhelpful worker . . .'. Quoted in his "Moving tale of a fair day's work", *Financial Times*, 24 March 1993, p. 14.

7 Though the need to comply with law, and thus EU regulation, may render them necessary.

8 Though normally relevant only to economic justification, productivity is ethically relevant here because of its relation to maximising long-term owner value.

9 The 1930s Hawthorne study of the effects of lighting in Western Electric's bank wiring rooms revealed that productivity rose significantly when lighting was improved. Surprisingly, however, productivity increased still further when the lighting was then lowered, suggesting that it was the attention and not the lighting that was the operative factor. See, e.g., Peters, T. and Austin, N., *A Passion for Excellence, op. cit.,* p. 242.

10 In a study of 1,000 US metal-working plants, productivity (as measured by total production time per unit of output) in the larger firms that had employee participation committees was 46% less than in firms with no 'employee involvement' schemes. Kelley, M., Harrison, B. and Xue, L., *Technology Review,* Massachusetts Institute of Technology, January 1991, p. 74. Quoted in Dixon, Michael, "Lessons on winning the workers' trust", *Financial Times,* 20 February 1991, p. 15.

11 It may be that consultation was resorted to when the firm was doing badly.

12 See also the discussions on whistle-blowing (Chapter 8) and critical information (Chapter 9) below.

13 For example, life, liberty and property.

14 Federal.

15 Or a business. . . .

16 According to research conducted in the late 1980s by the UK Institute of Manpower Research, 'the prime concern of most recruiters is not to seek out the right person for a job, but to *avoid* hiring the *wrong* one.' Quoted in Dixon, Michael, "How to get round the secretary barrier", *Financial Times,* 3 June 1992, p. 13, italics in original.

17 The person responsible for making the choice, who may well not be a member of the personnel department.

18 In the pre-Big Bang City of London, the threat of being excluded from lunch was the main, and extremely effective, deterrent against misconduct.

19 Almost a third of the more than 4,000 UK job advertisements analysed by Industrial Relations Services, including those for self-described 'equal opportunity' employers, included an age bar; of those, four out of five specified that candidates be under 45. *Age Discrimination: no change,* Equal Opportunities Review No.48, March/April 1993, IRS. See also Summers, Diane, "Jobseekers

over the hill at 45, says survey of advertisements", *Financial Times*, 15 March 1993, p. 14.

20 Defined in the banking, retail, hospitality and information technology and many other sectors as 'someone past the age of 40— or sometimes 35 for women' according to a study by the Institute For Employment Studies, Sussex University. *The Fifties Revival*, reported in Welch, Jilly, "Bosses miss out on age of reason", *Financial Times*, 17 August 1999, p. 8.

21 According to a UK Department of Employment study, more than 40% of employers consider older workers to be harder to train. "43% consider age in recruitment", *Financial Times*, 5 August 1993, p. 5.

22 Indeed, a study by Price Waterhouse of 177 finance executives showed that those over 40 years of age scored higher for persuasiveness, friendliness, decisiveness and astuteness, scored the same for reasoning, and scored only marginally less on numerical ability than those who were under 40. Dixon, Michael, "Fresh light on the age-barrier paradox", *Financial Times*, 24 April 1991, p. 15. See also *Fifties Revival, op. cit.*

23 "Let old folk work", Leader, *The Economist*, 4 September 1999, p. 20.

24 It is noteworthy that a study of British businesses by David Storey of Warwick University found that 70% of those started by people over 55 survived, compared with 19% on average. "Ageing Workers", *The Economist*, 4 September 1999, p. 91.

25 As confirmed by the Price Waterhouse study, which showed that the older finance executives were 'more critical and controlling than the younger set . . . it seems that, at the same time as being better equipped to work as managers, over-40s are more difficult to manage.' *Op cit.*

26 Except in those jurisdictions, e.g., in the United States, in which they are illegal.

27 The business's ability to maximise long-term owner value may be threatened even when the candidate's or employee's personal performance is not ordinarily harmed, if use of the drugs in question is illegal in jurisdictions where the business operates. Depending on the drugs involved, and the severity of the relevant drug regulation, the business may, for example, risk losing his services if he is found to have been guilty of an offence.

28 All of which have been used by UK firms. . . . Cane, Alan, "Business advice is all in the mind", *Financial Times*, 16 July 1991, p. 11. "Crystal Balls", *The Economist*, 26 October 1991, p. 106.

29 *Ibid.* See also Blinkhorn, Steve and Johnson, Charles, directors of Psychometric Research and Development, *Nature*, '. . . we see precious little evidence that even the best personality tests predict job

performance'; quoted in Holberton, Simon, "Researchers question value of personality testing", *Financial Times*, 20 December 1990.

30 Furnham, Adrian, "Moving tale of a fair day's work", *Financial Times*, 24 March 1993, p. 14.

31 *Who's Managing the Managers?*, IM Books, Burston Distribution Services, 2A Newbridge Trading Estate, Whitby Road, Bristol BS4 4AX. Reported in Goodhart, David, "Managers report career worries", *Financial Times*, 14 December 1992, p. 7.

32 *Ibid.*

33 Subject to whatever regulatory restrictions might apply in the jurisdiction.

34 Which may of course be awarded confidentially.

35 The extremely high going rate for equity salesmen resulted partly from their being in relatively short supply. When the Big Bang regulatory changes allowed many new firms to enter the equity business, demand for equity salesmen, and consequently their remuneration, skyrocketed. Securities houses were eager to pay, however, because the salesmen were expected to generate many times their salaries in revenues: compared with their expected contributions, the costs, though high, seemed reasonable. Management capabilities, in contrast, were traditionally undervalued in the UK financial services industry, and received correspondingly lower remuneration.

36 Note that standard remuneration negotiations that trade off, e.g., flexible hours against pay, do not involve entitlements and thus do not give rise to proprietary interests. Employees also have no automatic entitlement to continued employment.

37 Note that unlike the economic decision to employ the marginal worker, which turns on his marginal cost and marginal contribution, the ethical decision depends instead on the worker's (long-term) contribution to long-term owner value.

38 It is also noteworthy that attempts artificially to limit the differentials between remuneration levels have typically come to grief; consider, for example, the experience of Ben & Jerry's Ice Cream in the US and *Time Out* in the UK.

39 Subject, as usual, to complying with relevant regulation. It may be that some aspects of remuneration—holiday entitlements, pensions or health care, for example—must be granted to all staff members. Insofar as variations are permitted, however, they should be made on the basis of distributive justice, and thus on the basis of performance.

40 Even when the acquisitions are of assets rather than businesses. When banks linked the rewards of loan officers to the size and number of the loans that they booked, the result was increased

total footings and monstrous loan losses (and sometimes the destruction of the bank: consider the history of Continental Illinois).

41 *Pay and Performance: The Employer Experience*, IMS Report 218, Institute of Manpower Studies, Mantell Buildings, University of Sussex, Falmer, Brighton BN1 9RF; *Performance Management in the UK: An Analysis of the Issues*, Institute of Personnel Management, 1992, p. 6; *The Disappearing Relationship between Directors' Pay and Corporate Performance*, LSE Centre for Economic Performance, 1992.

42 The link between sales and performance-related pay has, for example, been found to be very strong. *The Disappearing Relationship between Directors' Pay and Corporate Performance, ibid.*

43 Which for quoted public companies can be estimated by dividends paid plus share price rises adjusted for general market trends.

44 Within the constraints imposed by the need to maximise long-term owner value while respecting distributive justice and ordinary decency.

45 The same problem arises with guaranteed bonuses of any kind. Arkady, Ostrovsky and Silverman, Gary, "Bonuses: banks' pledges spark concern", 22 December 1999, http://www.ft.com/nbearchive/email-bfq30d842.htm.

46 A not uncommon City practice in the late 1980s.

47 Consider the valued City employee whose reason for leaving a firm was the fact that it employed the personnel officer conducting the exit interview. . . .

48 In practice, this requirement is subject to all sorts of regulatory constraints, and to the fixed-term contracts of employment that may sometimes be justified.

49 A Right Associates study of 1,024 American firms revealed that of the 75% which had cut substantial numbers of jobs during the previous five years, 'most companies [had] little idea of why they were' eliminating jobs; not surprisingly, 75% of the firms saw no improvements in financial results and 66% saw no increases in productivity. Reported in *The Economist*, 28 March 1992, p. 105.

50 That evidence themselves in repeated actions or inactions.

51 Both of which constitute violations of distributive justice and fairness.

52 The principle is thus a modified LIFO: least in, first out.

53 Consider the City joke reported in the *Financial Times* Observer column on 14 February 1991: 'Bankers brooding over their dismissal notices are asking what's the difference between a P45 and a Scud missile. With the missile, you get four minutes warning.'

Chapter 7: Finance

1 *The Company Chairman, op.cit.*, pp. 130–31.

2 Quoted in the *Financial Times* Observer column, 23 November 1992, p. 15.

3 E.g., BCCI and ISC/Ferranti.

4 A survey by Bob Sweeting of the School of Management at the University of Manchester Institute of Science and Technology, and Roy Davies of Price Waterhouse, of how managers in 700 manufacturing companies account for costs showed that 'Many British manufacturers are running their factories in ignorance and confusion because they are not using their accounting systems properly.' Reported in Fazey, Ian Hamilton, "Confused?—they certainly are", *Financial Times*, 8 March 1991.

5 For a description of the operational effects of inaccurate cost accounting, see Fazey, *ibid.*

6 UK auditors are advised to state explicitly that they are not expressing an opinion on the ability of London Stock Exchange listed companies to continue as going concerns (Auditing Practices Board Bulletin 1996/3 *Disclosures Relating to Corporate Governance (Supplement)*, para 19). And the US *Statement on Auditing Standards* No. 59 para 04 states: 'The auditor is not responsible for predicting future conditions or events'. I am grateful to William Arthurs ACA for his advice on these sources.

7 See Chapter 9 below.

8 And particularly of the governance committee, which is charged with ensuring strict adherence to the business purposes; for a description of the role and composition of governance committees, see Chapter 9 below.

9 'Takeovers' is being used here as the generic term to cover all sorts of mergers and acquisitions and buyouts, both friendly and hostile. Since most takeovers and defences involve corporations, the emphasis in this section will be on corporate business and shareholders; for a discussion of the relationship between the corporation and the business, see Chapter 8 below and Sternberg, Elaine, *CGAIM, op. cit.*, especially Chapter 2.

10 Shliefer, Andrei and Summers, Lawrence, "Breach of Trust in Hostile Takeovers" in Auerbach, Alan, ed., *Corporate Takeovers: Causes and Consequences*, University of Chicago Press, 1988.

11 A question may arise if the entity that made the promises, usually the corporation through its agents, fails to survive the takeover. Insofar, however, as the succeeding organisation takes over its assets and obligations, or is believed to do so, it will suffer the prudential consequences of not keeping the promises or undertakings even if it is

284   *Chapter 7: Finance*

not technically bound to do so.

12 Though, as discussed below, there may well be prudential reasons for doing so, and legal obligations to.

13 Or to new management, however achieved.

14 See, e.g., Burrough, Bryan & Helyar, John, *Barbarians at the Gate: The Fall of RJR Nabisco*, Harper & Row, 1990, p. 28 *inter alia.*

15 Which some US states, e.g., Delaware, are not. Consider the decision of the Delaware courts to uphold poison pills adopted without shareholder approval (Moran vs. Household Intl, 1985) and to overrule the wishes of Time's shareholders re the company's acquisition by Warner. See Monks, Robert A.G., and Minnow, Nell, *Power and Accountability*, HarperCollins, 1991, p. 49, pp. 93–4.

16 According to a study by World Markets, the typical shareholding period of large UK institutional investors is 18 years. Riley, Barry, "Short-termism revisited and recalculated", *Financial Times*, 16 April 1997, p. 29. See also Davies, Stephen, "Short-termism and the State We're In", Institute of Directors Economic Research Paper, 1996.

17 Marsh, Paul, *Short-termism on Trial*, Institutional Fund Managers Association, 1990 and Stainer, Gareth, *Shareholder Value Analysis Survey*, Coopers & Lybrand Deloitte, 1991. See also Chapter 8 below and *CGAIM, op.cit.*

18 Since non-executive directors are themselves typically the managers of other firms, US boards also tend to be management-dominated.

19 Though once X takes over Y, maximising the long-term owner value of Y as part of the combined enterprise is, of course, the legitimate business of X.

20 Which, like much other takeover activity, is precluded by the UK Takeover Code.

21 Monks, *op. cit.*, p. 48.

22 Equally, one might consider that the shares are not all the same, insofar as in the context of a takeover, part of a share's identity relates to its being available to the bidder early enough to help him win.

23 Though of course it can be, when, e.g., the purchase is made by the agents of a business but in ways that violate the purpose of the business, or distributive justice or ordinary decency. And in many jurisdictions (including the UK) it has been illegal for a company to buy its own shares.

24 Unless, of course, the greenmailer is a business, and those actions would undermine maximising long-term owner value or violate distributive justice or ordinary decency.

25 Used here as the generic term for all sorts of buyouts, including

MBOs (the generic UK term), LBOs (the generic US term), EBOs (employee buyouts), MBIs and BIMBOs.

26 In honour of the then First Lady's proposed solution to the burgeoning US drugs' problem. . . .

27 The shareholders themselves.

28 Including the information shown to prospective sources of finance for the buyout: in revealing it, the bidding management may well be violating confidentiality and their fiduciary responsibilities.

29 Pre-emptive rights might even be extended to giving existing owners right of first refusal on equity participations in all successor businesses formed through buyouts. . . .

30 I.e., less than BBB/Baa from the major US bond rating agencies, Standard and Poor's and Moody's. It should always be remembered that what is rated by these agencies is not the creditworthiness of the issuers, but the likelihood that the particular issue of debt securities will be repaid in full and on time.

31 Consider the criminal convictions of M. Milken and the semi-extortive practices mentioned in Bruck, Connie, *The Predators' Ball*, The American Lawyer/Simon and Schuster, 1988.

32 In many jurisdictions, for example, insider trading restrictions apply only to equities and not to corporate debt securities.

33 In Germany, for example, insider dealing only became a criminal offence on 1 August 1994, when the second Financial Markets Promotions Act became law, implementing the EU Directive. Waller, David, "Insider dealing law approved by Bundestag", *Financial Times*, 20 June 1994, p. 13.

34 Even if it is a violation of securities or other regulation.

35 Starting with the move to protect widows and orphans in the wake of the stock market Crash of 1929, populist attacks on big business have combined with the political ambitions of prosecutors to make insider trading a favoured US target. In the UK, an ideological commitment to wider share ownership led to the need to make the securities markets seem attractive to retail investors; legislation to create a 'level playing field' (about which more later in this chapter) thus became important.

36 Which is reflected in the treatment of insider dealing in the (UK) Criminal Justice Act which came into effect on 1 March 1994.

37 Which in practice are subject to the regulations governing financial exchanges in their various jurisdictions.

38 Conditions which are, in fact, violated in many jurisdictions; consider, e.g., UK takeover regulations.

39 Sequence is important because, at least according to efficient market theory, all information in the market, including information about the price of the most recent trade, is normally a factor in

determining a security's price.

40 In aggregate. . . . The owners can be presumed to be shareholders because insofar as insider trading relates to dealing in shares, it relates to business in its corporate form.

41 I.e., all those who are selling when insiders are buying, and vice versa; it is not necessary to be the direct counterparty of the insider to suffer.

42 According to a study of monthly data for 103 stockmarkets taken from 1969–98 for developed countries and 1988–98 for developing ones, those countries that had and enforced insider trading laws lowered their cost of equity by an average of 5%. Bjattacharya, Utpal and Daouk, Hazem, "The World Price of Insider Trading", Kelley School of Business, Indiana University working paper, January 2000, reported in "Insider trading: The cost of equity", *The Economist*, 22 January 2000, p. 97.

Chapter 8: Corporate Governance

1 The largest mutual fund (unit trust) company in the US; quoted in Kochan, Nicholas and Syrett, Michel, *New Directions in Corporate Governance*, Business International Limited, 1991, p. 75.

2 *The Company Chairman, op. cit.*, p. 208.

3 See, for example, *New Directions in Corporate Governance, op. cit.*, p. v.; The Business Roundtable, *Corporate Governance and American Competitiveness*, 1990, p. 16.

4 More generally, corporate governance refers to 'ways of ensuring that corporate actions, assets and agents are directed at achieving the corporate objectives established by the corporation's shareholders'. Sternberg, Elaine, *CGAIM, op. cit.*, p. 20.

5 A version of this section and the next section first appeared as "The Responsible Shareholder" in Volume 1, Number 3 of *Business Ethics: a European Review* (Blackwell), July 1992, pp. 192–8. For a fuller discussion of corporate governance, see Sternberg, Elaine, *CGAIM, op. cit.*

6 "Tycoons of crime", *The Economist*, 29 February 1992, p. 62.

7 Though see Social Responsibility Revisited, in Chapter 10 below.

8 E.g., the City of London's response to Big Bang. It is difficult to reconcile the enormities and enormous losses of the UK integrated investment banks with an even marginally competent attempt to maximise long-term owner value. The investment banks' performance does become intelligible, however, when seen instead as the outcome of managers' pursuing very different ends—their own power or prestige, or some ideological or fashionable vision—quite unrelated to any consideration of owner value.

9 See Davies, Stephen, 'Short-termism and the State We're In', *op.cit.*; Congdon, Tim, 'How Britain Benefits from Short-termism' in *Stakeholding and its Critics*, Institute of Economic Affairs Health and Welfare Unit, 1997, pp. 19–36; Marsh, Paul, 'Myths surrounding short-termism', *Financial Times Mastering Finance Supplement 6*, 16 June 1997.

10 Marsh, Paul, "Short-termism on Trial", and Stainer, Gareth, "Shareholder Value Analysis Survey", *op. cit.*

11 To be, in the US term, 'relationship investors'.

12 Morally as well as economically. If the investment activities are pursued as a business, then they need only be directed at maximising long-term owner value, while observing distributive justice and ordinary decency.

13 Monks, Robert A.G., and Minnow, Nell, *Power and Accountability, op. cit.*, p. 234; see also p. 253.

14 For a detailed description of the problems facing US institutional shareholders, and particularly the 'collective cost' prisoners' dilemma, see Monks, *op. cit.*, especially Chapter 6. For a graphic description of the obstacles facing UK institutional investors, see Blair, Alistair, "A coalition versus a dictator", *Financial Times*, 27 May 1992, p. 13.

15 As Georg Siemens, the founder of Deutsche Bank, pointed out more than 100 years ago; quoted in *Financial Times*, 13 March 1991.

16 See Sternberg, Elaine, *CGAIM, op.cit.*, pp. 67–72, 129–30.

17 As distinct from that which someone simply dislikes or wishes to stop; much 'ideological' whistle-blowing by, e.g., safety zealots and environmentalists, fails this test.

18 As distinct from factually justified, which it is whenever the wrong-doing turns out to be as alleged, and morally obligatory, when it not only may be performed, but must be. For the purposes of this analysis, business whistle-blowing will be deemed morally justifiable (though not necessarily *justified*), if it is compatible with business loyalty and confidentiality while not violating distributive justice or ordinary decency.

19 That is so simply because business's distinctive purpose is different from that of the family or friendship, not because its purpose is profit-related.

20 Loyalty between friends normally implies a very broad range of automatic mutual support and *prima facie* preference. That presumption is, however, routinely modified by the friends' other commitments, e.g., to their families. Business obligations can similarly alter what friends may legitimately expect from one another.

21 Aversion to informing is perhaps a carryover from the school room, where commitment to a common purpose is weak, and

pupils are bound mainly by their opposition to authority.

22 Though the whistle-blower might have been, if his concerns were well-grounded. See the discussion on ethical acts vs. acting ethically in Chapter 4 above.

23 Equitable relief in law normally requires that those who voluntarily breach trust in order to volunteer information should 'come with clean hands'.

24 Though fairness demands that an accused be able to confront his accuser, the use of modern technology makes it easier for an accuser to be cross-examined without his identity necessarily being disclosed.

25 Though these factors may well be relevant in determining whether the whistle-blowing will be justified. Like motives, however, they are relevant to the business mainly for judging the whistle-blower when the allegation proves false.

26 As distinct from malicious or ignorant trouble-makers.

27 Assuming that the corporation is meant to be ethical.

28 According to a study of 288 of Britain's top 500 companies from 1983 to 1991, the salary-plus-bonus level for the highest paid director was in fact most closely correlated to increases in sales. *The Disappearing Relationship Between Directors' Pay and Corporate Performance*, LSE Centre for Economic Performance; reported in Goodhart, David, "Pay and performance 'unrelated'", *Financial Times*, 28 November 1992, p. 5.

29 Typically one year. See Korn/Ferry International, *Boards of Directors Study UK*, reported by Holberton, Simon, "Time for directors to think long-term", *Financial Times*, 10 July 1991, p. 15.

30 Subject, again, to tax and legal complications; see Brealy, Richard A. and Myers, Stewart C., *Principles of Corporate Finance*, McGraw-Hill, 1988, pp. 362–5.

31 Cohen, Norma, "Study shows tolerance of dividend cuts", *Financial Times*, 14 February 1992, p. 16.

32 Consider a much-publicised letter from the chairman of M&G Investment Management to the editor of the *Financial Times*, 12 December 1990. M&G then reinforced the point in private letters to the chairmen of nearly 300 companies in which M&G had a 'significant' investment. See Owen, David, "M&G urges companies to maintain dividends", *Financial Times*, 5 January 1991.

33 There may therefore be times when funds are better used for investment than for dividends. That there may be nothing left to distribute to the investors by way of dividends is not a violation of distributive justice. In principle they should be indifferent to whether their rewards come via dividends or capital gains. And while rewards are normally expected for assuming risk, and

rewards are certainly due to those whose capital was essential for the very existence of the business, the meaning of risk is precisely that the returns may not be forthcoming.

34 See Sternberg, Elaine, *CGAIM, op.cit.*, Chapter 7.

35 Pending the outcome of the Company Law Review started by the Department of Trade and Industry in 1999 . . . .

Chapter 9: Ethical Accountability

1 *The Wealth of Nations*, 1776, Vol. II, Book V, Chapter I; Everyman's Library, J.M. Dent & Sons Ltd., 1975, p. 229.

2 *The Company Chairman, op.cit.*, p. 160.

3 See the informal survey reported by Tom Peters and Nancy Austin: 100% of the company presidents interviewed claimed that total customer satisfaction was their chief business priority, but not a single one 'measured it for the purposes of compensation and evaluation'. *A Passion for Excellence, op. cit.*, p. 87. More recently, a survey of Britain's largest 500 companies by a marketing consultancy, Abram, Hawkes, confirmed that less than half had any mechanism for rewarding the achievement of their Total Quality Management targets; not surprisingly, their TQM programmes were producing disappointing results. Reported in Kellaway, Lucy, "Success tool or passing fad?", *Financial Times*, 25 August 1993, p. 9.

4 By, for example, paying bonuses into a notional remuneration account, from which withdrawals can be made only when and if the right outcomes actually occur.

5 E.g., the requirement imposed by the Association of British Insurers and the National Association of (UK) Pension Funds that option schemes reflect 'significant and sustained improvement in underlying financial performance'. Reported in Kellaway, Lucy, "Taking stock of windfalls", *Financial Times*, 16 August 1993, p. 8.

6 A traditional obstacle to employees' suggesting improvements has been the lack of identification between the interests of employees and those of the owners: if productivity gains mean staff cuts, employees have a clear incentive not to recommend them. The answer lies in a strict observance of distributive justice, which rewards vigilance in service of the business goal, and in properly structured performance-related remuneration, which gives everyone an interest in maximising long-term owner value ethically.

7 Though it should be recognised that it is better still for problems not to arise.

8 This is a conceptual analysis of the role of the director; directors' actual legal status depends on the laws of particular jurisdictions.

9 Or to any other personal or ideological objective.

10 UK titles, e.g., 'finance director', 'marketing director', are mis-
leading: although there may well be some division of labour within
a board, and that division may reflect the individuals' executive
roles, the directorial responsibilities of all directors are the same.

11 Contrary to the recommendations of such organisations as the
(UK) Institutional Shareholders Committee (*The Role and Duties of
Directors—A Statement of Best Practice*, April 1991; also August 1993)
and PRO NED (*Remuneration Committees*, p. 11).

12 See, for example, PRO NED, *op.cit.*

13 Where the laws allow . . . . Many US states make it illegal for any but
company directors to nominate candidates for the board. For a
fuller analysis of why traditional procedures are inadequate to
safeguard independence, see Monks, *op.cit.*, especially Chapter 3.

14 These barriers could be made substantial, to ensure the candidate's commitment to the corporate purposes.

15 The campaign by Alastair Ross Goobey, the Chief Executive of
Hermes (formerly Postel, Britain's largest pension fund), against
three-year rolling contracts for directors is a step in the right direction, but does not go far enough. Cohen, Norma and Urry,
Maggie, "Directors cool to plea on contracts", *Financial Times*, 14
June 1993, p. 8. Cf. the campaign by Martin Lipton to guarantee
directors' tenure for a minimum of five years, the better to protect
entrenched managements against takeovers: Lipton, Martin, "An
end to hostile takeovers and short-termism", *Financial Times*, 27
June 1990, p. 21.

16 It is noteworthy that this basic shareholder right is curtailed by
many US state laws, which make it the exclusive prerogative of the
directors themselves. See Monks, *op. cit.*, p. 169. So keen are executives to avoid even the disclosure required in the UK for year-long
contracts, that senior UK executives have been known to shorten
their contracts on elevation to the main board.

17 Doubt is therefore cast on the commitment to accountability of the
(UK) Company Law Review initiated by the UK Labour govern-
ment in 1999. In its consultation documents, the Steering
Committee strongly recommends not only totally eliminating *ultra
vires* (The Company Law Review Steering Group, *Modern
Company Law for a Competitive Economy, The Strategic Framework*,
Department of Trade and Industry, February 1999, para. 5.3.18),
but also dispensing with company objects when new companies are
formed (*ibid* paras. 5.3.18,19; also *Company Formation and Capital
Maintenance*, October 1999, Volume 3, para. 2.17).

18 Perhaps up to a stipulated multiple of their directorial fees.

19 "Redirecting directors", leader, *The Economist*, 17 November 1990,
pp. 19–20.

20 Although speed and secrecy are usually necessary to mount a successful takeover, advance shareholder approval might nonetheless be obtained for transactions of a stipulated size and nature, for example, takeovers of domestic firms in a particular sector with returns on equity exceeding a target level.

21 Although standard in the UK, pre-emptive rights are seldom seen in the US. Respecting pre-emptive rights does *not* necessarily entail doing subsequent offerings of equity by way of a traditional UK-style 'rights issue': conceptually, pre-emptive rights are compatible with many methods of issuing equity.

22 For an excellent analysis of the problem, see "Punters or Proprietors? A Survey of Capitalism", *The Economist*, 5 May 1990, following p. 88.

23 E.g., Hanson Industries in the UK, Berkshire Hathaway in the US, Dynaction in France.

24 Such as the US Kohlberg Kravis Roberts (the famous 'KKR' which after its successful bid for RJR Nabisco became the fifth largest corporate entity in the US; Kaletsky, Anatole, "Reshaping America's corporate skyline", *Financial Times*, 26 October 1988) and Forstmann, Little (Emmott, Bill, "The Ebb Tide: A Survey of International Finance", *The Economist*, 27 April 1991 (following p. 72), p. 50).

25 Even their performance must be monitored, however: consider the successful shareholder battle with Hanson to retain full rights to nominate directors and amend corporate resolutions. Cohen, Norma, "Hanson backs down over proposed rule changes", *Financial Times*, 18 June 1993, p. 17.

26 A similar function can be performed by a subset of the partners in respect of a large partnership.

27 The basic rules governing who may authorise what, and how authorisations are to be effected, are normally set out in the business's constitution.

28 The actions of imposters, who use the business name without being authorised to do so, are not actions of the business.

29 As in all cases, the extent of blame attaching to the individual will depend on the exact circumstances of the case.

30 As distinct from physically forced or coerced.

31 Subject, normally, to legal restraints and contractual commitments. For a fuller discussion of the moral constraints on such decisions, see Chapter 10 below.

32 A business may be able to increase its prices to cover some of the resulting costs, but its ability to do so is limited by market resistance to higher prices.

33 Whether the actions so committed count as 'business actions'

depends on the facts of the case.

34 A business whose proposed ends were clearly illegal would not be allowed to incorporate; in the UK, for example, the persons forming a company must be associated for a 'lawful purpose' (Companies Act 1985 section 1(1)). It is possible, however, that a corporation could be formed with ends that were vague enough to seem legal ('providing troubleshooting services', perhaps) while accommodating the illegal objectives of its shareholders.

35 In this case, largely Aristotelian. . . .

36 So called because a frog that is perfectly capable of jumping out of the pot may be so lulled by the gently heating water, that it does not jump and ends up being cooked to death.

37 Consider the old Soviet constitution . . . though it notionally enshrined all sorts of civil liberties, few were actually enjoyed by the Soviet people.

Chapter 10: Morals and Markets

1 *Nicomachean Ethics*, Book II Chapter 4, 1105b12–18.

2 Though the question of whether a business ought to take up a particular business opportunity normally is.

3 Though Aristotle, of course, has done so; see the *Nicomachean Ethics*.

4 Just so long as they are legal. . . .

5 From the Greek 'after', as in '*Metaphysics*', the book which came after the *Physics* in the Aristotelian corpus.

6 Either incoherent and incapable of directing action, or weakly held.

7 That other, even greater, wrongs might perhaps make supporting such a business the lesser evil, and thus the right thing to do in particular circumstances, does not remove its wrongness.

8 Contrary to popular belief, stakeholder preferences are mainly effective not in spite of the business purpose, but precisely because the definitive business end of maximising long-term owner value requires that they be taken into account. Taking them into account is, of course, not the same as accepting them uncritically.

9 Subject, of course, to those considerations respecting distributive justice and ordinary decency.

10 Even infants and the infirm are consumers. . . .

11 Subject, of course, to the law and any prior commitments they may have made.

12 Even when the individuals are operating through quasi-autonomous non-governmental organisations: 'qangos'.

13 For a discussion of some of the dangers and limitations of regula-

tion and legislation, see Sternberg, Elaine, *CGAIM, op.cit.,* pp. 108–116.

14 Insofar as they are not yet full moral agents, children may be subjected to the views of their parents and guardians.

15 Though on rare occasions, the wrong of breaking a contract may be necessary to avert an even greater wrong.

16 Taking into account, of course, his contractual commitments.

17 See Cairncross, Frances, "Cleaning Up", *op. cit.,* p. 4.

18 Consider as well the effect of 'animal rights' protests in reducing the amount of pharmaceutical and cosmetic testing done on animals.

19 Though their effects may free wealth to be used for more productive purposes, e.g., by eradicating illnesses that require costly treatment, medical research can free wealth to be used for improving nutrition.

20 Even when funds are proximately supplied by the state, they are indirectly provided by business since it generates the income and value added that is taxed to provide state funds.

21 Including, notably, taxes.

Selected Bibliography
Works Cited in More Than One Chapter

Andrews, K.R., ed., *Ethics in Practice: Managing the Moral Corporation,* Harvard Business School Press, 1989

Aristotle, *Metaphysics*

——, *Nicomachean Ethics*

Business Roundtable, *Corporate Governance and American Competitiveness,* March 1990

Cadbury, Sir Adrian, *The Company Chairman,* Director Books, Fitzwilliam Publishing Ltd., 1990

Cairncross, Frances, "Cleaning Up: a survey of industry and the environment", *The Economist,* 8 September 1990

Davies, Stephen, "Short-termism and the State We're In", Institute of Directors Economic Research Paper, 1996

Harvey-Jones, Sir John, *Making It Happen: Reflections on Leadership,* Collins, 1988

Kochan, Nicholas and Syrett, Michel, *New Directions in Corporate Governance,* Business International Limited, 1991

LSE Centre for Economic Performance, *The Disappearing Relationship between Directors' Pay and Corporate Performance,* 1992

McKeon, Richard, ed., *The Basic Works of Aristotle,* Random House, 1941

Marsh, Paul, "Short-termism on Trial", Institutional Fund Managers Association, 1990

Monks, Robert A.G. and Minnow, Nell, *Power and Accountability,* HarperCollins, 1991

Peters, Tom and Austin, Nancy, *A Passion for Excellence: The Leadership Difference,* Fontana/Collins, 1985

Stainer, Gareth, "Shareholder Value Analysis Survey", Coopers & Lybrand Deloitte, 1991

Sternberg, Elaine, *Corporate Governance: Accountability in the Marketplace,* Hobart Paper 137, The Institute of Economic Affairs, 1998

Index